TABLE OF CONTENTS

Top 20 Test Taking Tips

1. Carefully follow all the test registration procedures
2. Know the test directions, duration, topics, question types, how many questions
3. Setup a flexible study schedule at least 3-4 weeks before test day
4. Study during the time of day you are most alert, relaxed, and stress free
5. Maximize your learning style; visual learner use visual study aids, auditory learner use auditory study aids
6. Focus on your weakest knowledge base
7. Find a study partner to review with and help clarify questions
8. Practice, practice, practice
9. Get a good night's sleep; don't try to cram the night before the test
10. Eat a well balanced meal
11. Know the exact physical location of the testing site; drive the route to the site prior to test day
12. Bring a set of ear plugs; the testing center could be noisy
13. Wear comfortable, loose fitting, layered clothing to the testing center; prepare for it to be either cold or hot during the test
14. Bring at least 2 current forms of ID to the testing center
15. Arrive to the test early; be prepared to wait and be patient
16. Eliminate the obviously wrong answer choices, then guess the first remaining choice
17. Pace yourself; don't rush, but keep working and move on if you get stuck
18. Maintain a positive attitude even if the test is going poorly
19. Keep your first answer unless you are positive it is wrong
20. Check your work, don't make a careless mistake

English Language Arts

Prose and poetry

Prose is language as it is ordinarily spoken as opposed to verse or language with metric patterns. Prose is used for everyday communication, and is found in textbooks, memos, reports, articles, short stories, and novels. Distinguishing characteristics of prose include:
- It may have some sort of rhythm, but there is no formal arrangement.
- The common unit of organization is the sentence.
- It may include literary devices of repetition and balance.
- It must have more coherent relationships among sentences than a list would.

Poetry, or verse, is the manipulation of language with respect to meaning, meter, sound, and rhythm. A line of poetry can be any length and may or may not rhyme. Related groups of lines are called stanzas, and may also be any length. Some poems are as short as a few lines, and some are as long as a book. Poetry is a more ancient form of literature than prose.

Fiction and nonfiction

Fiction is a literary work usually presented in prose form that is not true. It is the product of the writer's imagination. Examples of fiction are novels, short stories, television scripts, and screenplays.

Nonfiction is a literary work that is based on facts. In other words, the material is true. The purposeful inclusion of false information is considered dishonest, but the expression of opinions or suppositions is acceptable. Libraries divide their collections into works of fiction and nonfiction. Examples of nonfiction include historical materials, scientific reports, memoirs, biographies, most essays, journals, textbooks, documentaries, user manuals, and news reports.

Style, tone, and point of view

Style is the manner in which a writer uses language in prose or poetry. Style is affected by:
- Diction or word choices
- Sentence structure and syntax
- Types and extent of use of figurative language
- Patterns of rhythm or sound
- Conventional or creative use of punctuation

Tone is the attitude of the writer or narrator towards the theme of, subject of, or characters in a work. Sometimes the attitude is stated, but it is most often implied through word choices. Examples of tone are serious, humorous, satiric, stoic, cynical, flippant, and surprised.

Point of view is the angle from which a story is told. It is the perspective of the narrator, which is established by the author. Common points of view are:
- Third person – Third person points of view include omniscient (knows everything) and limited (confined to what is known by a single character or a limited number of

characters). When the third person is used, characters are referred to as he, she, or they.

- First person – When this point of view is used, the narrator refers to himself or herself as "I."

Alliteration, assonance, and onomatopoeia

Alliteration is the repetition of the first sounds or stressed syllables (usually consonants) in words in close proximity. An example is: "Chirp, chirp," said the chickadee.

Assonance is the repetition of identical or similar vowel sounds, particularly in stressed syllables, in words in close proximity. Assonance is considered to be a form of near rhyme. An example is: the quiet bride cried.

Onomatopoeia refers to words that imitate sounds. It is sometimes called echoism. Examples are hiss, buzz, burp, rattle, and pop. It may also refer to words that correspond symbolically to what they describe, with high tones suggesting light and low tones suggesting darkness. An example is the *gloom* of night versus the *gleam* of the stars.

Meter

A recurring pattern of stressed and unstressed syllables in language creates a rhythm when spoken. When the pattern is regular, it is called meter. When meter is used in a composition, it is called verse. The most common types of meter are:

- Iambic – An unstressed syllable followed by a stressed syllable
- Anapestic – Two unstressed syllables followed by a stressed syllable
- Trochaic – One stressed syllable followed by an unstressed syllable
- Dactylic – A stressed syllable followed by two unstressed syllables
- Spondaic – Two consecutive syllables that are stressed almost equally
- Pyrrhic – Two consecutive syllables that are equally unstressed

Blank and free verse

Blank verse is unrhymed verse that consists of lines of iambic pentameter, which is five feet (sets) of unstressed and stressed syllables. The rhythm that results is the closest to natural human speech. It is the most commonly used type of verse because of its versatility. Well-known examples of blank verse are Shakespearean plays, Milton's epic poems, and T. S. Eliot's *The Waste Land*.

Free verse lacks regular patterns of poetic feet, but has more controlled rhythm than prose in terms of pace and pauses. Free verse has no rhyme and is usually written in short lines of irregular length. Well-known examples of free verse are the King James translation of the Psalms, Walt Whitman's *Leaves of Grass*, and the poetry of Ezra Pound and William Carlos Williams.

Short story

A short story is prose fiction that has the same elements as a novel, such as plot, characters, and point of view. Edgar Allan Poe defined the short story as a narrative that can be read in one sitting (one-half to two hours), and is limited to a single effect. In a short story, there is no time for extensive character development, large numbers of characters, in-depth analysis, complicated plot lines, or detailed backgrounds. Historically, the short story is related to the fable, the exemplum, and the folktale. Short stories have become mainly an American art form. Famous short story writers include William Faulkner, Katherine Anne Porter, Eudora Welty, Flannery O'Connor, O. Henry, and J. D. Salinger.

Primary and secondary research information

Primary research material is material that comes from the "horse's mouth." It is a document or object that was created by the person under study or during the time period under study. Examples of primary sources are original documents such as manuscripts, diaries, interviews, autobiographies, government records, letters, news videos, and artifacts (such as Native American pottery or wall writings in Egyptian tombs).

Secondary research material is anything that is not primary. Secondary sources are those things that are written or otherwise recorded about the main subject. Examples include a critical analysis of a literary work (a poem by William Blake is primary, but the analysis of the poem by T. S. Eliot is secondary), a magazine article about a person (a direct quote would be primary, but the report is secondary), histories, commentaries, and encyclopedias.

Emotions

Poetry is designed to appeal to the physical and emotional senses. Using appeals to the physical senses through words that evoke sight, sound, taste, smell, and touch also causes the imagination to respond emotionally. Poetry appeals to the soul and memories with language that can be intriguingly novel and profoundly emotional in connotation. Poetry can focus on any topic, but the feelings associated with the topic are magnified by the ordered presentation found in poetry. Verse, however, is merely a matter of structure. The thing that turns words into poetry is the feeling packed into those words. People write poetry to express their feelings and people read poetry to try to experience those same feelings. Poetry interprets the human condition with understanding and insight. Children respond well to poetry because it has an inviting, entertaining sound that they are eager to mimic.

Line structure

A line of poetry can be any length and can have any metrical pattern. A line is determined by the physical position of words on a page. A line is simply a group of words on a single line. Consider the following example:

> "When I consider how my light is spent,
> E're half my days, in this dark world and wide,"

These are two lines of poetry written by John Milton. Lines may or may not have punctuation at the end, depending, of course, on the need for punctuation. If these two lines were written out in a paragraph, they would be written with a slash line and a space in between the lines: "When I consider how my light is spent, / E're half my days, in this dark world and wide."

Stanza

A stanza is a group of lines. The grouping denotes a relationship among the lines. A stanza can be any length, but the separation of lines into different stanzas indicates an intentional pattern created by the poet. The breaks between stanzas indicate a change of subject or thought. As a group of lines, the stanza is a melodic unit that can be analyzed for metrical and rhyme patterns. Various common rhyme patterns have been named. The Spenserian stanza, which has a rhyme pattern of a b a b b c b c c, is an example. Stanzas of a certain length also have names. Examples include the couplet, which has two lines; the tercet, which has three lines; and the quatrain, which has four lines.

Literacy

Literacy is commonly understood to refer to the ability to read and write. UNESCO has further defined literacy as the "ability to identify, understand, interpret, create, communicate, compute, and use printed and written materials associated with varying contexts." Under the UNESCO definition, understanding cultural, political, and historical contexts of communities falls under the definition of literacy.

While reading literacy may be gauged simply by the ability to read a newspaper, writing literacy includes spelling, grammar, and sentence structure. To be literate in a foreign language, one would also need to have the ability to understand a language by listening and to speak the language. Some argue that visual representation and numeracy should be included in the requirements one must meet to be considered literate. Computer literacy refers to one's ability to utilize the basic functions of computers and other technologies.

Subsets of reading literacy include phonological awareness, decoding, comprehension, and vocabulary.

Phonological awareness

A subskill of literacy, phonological awareness is the ability to perceive sound structures in a spoken word, such as syllables and the individual phonemes within syllables. Phonemes are the sounds represented by the letters in the alphabet. The ability to separate, blend, and manipulate sounds is critical to developing reading and spelling skills.

Phonological awareness is concerned with not only syllables, but also onset sounds (the sounds at the beginning of words) and rime (the same thing as rhyme, but spelled differently to distinguish syllable rime from poetic rhyme). Phonological awareness is an auditory skill that does not necessarily involve print. It should be developed before the student has learned letter to sound correspondences. A student's phonological awareness is an indicator of future reading success.

Teaching phonological awareness

Classroom activities that teach phonological awareness include language play and exposure to a variety of sounds and contexts of sounds. Activities that teach phonological awareness include:
- Clapping to the sounds of individual words, names, or all words in a sentence
- Practicing saying blended phonemes

- Singing songs that involve phoneme replacement (e.g., The Name Game)
- Reading poems, songs, and nursery rhymes out loud
- Reading patterned and predictable texts out loud
- Listening to environmental sounds or following verbal directions
- Playing games with rhyming chants or fingerplays
- Reading alliterative texts out loud
- Grouping objects by beginning sounds
- Reordering words in a well-known sentence or making silly phrases by deleting words from a well-known sentence (perhaps from a favorite storybook)

Alphabetic principle

The alphabetic principle refers to the use of letters and combinations of letters to represent speech sounds. The way letters are combined and pronounced is guided by a system of rules that establishes relationships between written and spoken words and their letter symbols. Alphabet writing systems are common around the world. Some are phonological in that each letter stands for an individual sound and words are spelled just as they sound. However, there are other writing systems as well, such as the Chinese logographic system and the Japanese syllabic system.

Language skill development

Children learn language through interacting with others, by experiencing language in daily and relevant context, and through understanding that speaking and listening are necessary for effective communication. Teachers can promote language development by intensifying the opportunities a child has to experience and understand language.
Teachers can assist language development by:
- Modeling enriched vocabulary and teaching new words
- Using questions and examples to extend a child's descriptive language skills
- Providing ample response time to encourage children to practice speech
- Asking for clarification to provide students with the opportunity to develop communication skills
- Promoting conversations among children
- Providing feedback to let children know they have been heard and understood, and providing further explanation when needed

Oral and written language development

Oral and written language develops simultaneously. The acquisition of skills in one area supports the acquisition of skills in the other. However, oral language is not a prerequisite to written language. An immature form of oral language development is babbling, and an immature form of written language development is scribbling.

Oral language development does not occur naturally, but does occur in a social context. This means it is best to include children in conversations rather than simply talk at them. Written language development can occur without direct instruction. In fact, reading and writing do not necessarily need to be taught through formal lessons if the child is exposed to a print-rich environment. A teacher can assist a child's language development by building on what the child already knows, discussing relevant and meaningful events and experiences, teaching vocabulary and literacy skills, and providing opportunities to acquire more complex language.

Print-rich classroom environment

A teacher can provide a print-rich environment in the classroom in a number of ways. These include:

A. Displaying the following in the classroom:
- Children's names in print or cursive
- Children's written work
- Newspapers and magazines
- Instructional charts
- Written schedules
- Signs and labels
- Printed songs, poems, and rhymes

B. Using graphic organizers such as KWL charts or story road maps to:
- Remind students about what was read and discussed
- Expand on the lesson topic or theme
- Show the relationships among books, ideas, and words

C. Using big books to:
- Point out features of print, such as specific letters and punctuation
- Track print from right to left
- Emphasize the concept of words and the fact that they are used to communicate

Print and book awareness

Print and book awareness helps a child understand:
- That there is a connection between print and messages contained on signs, labels, and other print forms in the child's environment
- That reading and writing are ways to obtain information and communicate ideas
- That print runs from left to right and from top to bottom
- That a book has parts, such as a title, a cover, a title page, and a table of contents
- That a book has an author and contains a story
- That illustrations can carry meaning
- That letters and words are different
- That words and sentences are separated by spaces and punctuation
- That different text forms are used for different functions
- That print represents spoken language

Letters

To be appropriately prepared to learn to read and write, a child should learn:
- That each letter is distinct in appearance
- What direction and shape must be used to make each letter
- That each letter has a name, which can be associated with the shape of a letter

- That there are 26 letters in the English alphabet, and letters are grouped in a certain order
- That letters represent sounds of speech
- That words are composed of letters and have meaning
- That one must be able to correspond letters and sounds to read

Decoding

Decoding is the method or strategy used to make sense of printed words and figure out how to correctly pronounce them. In order to decode, a student needs to know the relationships between letters and sounds, including letter patterns; that words are constructed from phonemes and phoneme blends; and that a printed word represents a word that can be spoken. This knowledge will help the student recognize familiar words and make informed guesses about the pronunciation of unfamiliar words. Decoding is not the same as comprehension. It does not require an understanding of the meaning of a word, only a knowledge of how to recognize and pronounce it. Decoding can also refer to the skills a student uses to determine the meaning of a sentence. These skills include applying knowledge of vocabulary, sentence structure, and context.

Reading through phonics

Phonics is the process of learning to read by learning how spoken language is represented by letters. Students learn to read phonetically by sounding out the phonemes in words and then blending them together to produce the correct sounds in words. In other words, the student connects speech sounds with letters or groups of letters and blends the sounds together to determine the pronunciation of an unknown word.

Phonics is a commonly used method to teach decoding and reading, but has been challenged by other methods, such as the whole language approach. Despite the complexity of pronunciation and combined sounds in the English language, research shows that phonics is a highly effective way to teach reading. Being able to read or pronounce a word does not mean the student comprehends the meaning of the word, but context aids comprehension. When phonics is used as a foundation for decoding, children eventually learn to recognize words automatically and advance to decoding multisyllable words with practice.

Fluency

Fluency is the goal of literacy development. It is the ability to read accurately and quickly. Evidence of fluency includes the ability to recognize words automatically and group words for comprehension. At this point, the student no longer needs to decode words except for complex, unfamiliar ones. He or she is able to move to the next level and understand the meaning of a text. The student should be able to self-check for comprehension and should feel comfortable expressing ideas in writing.

Teachers can help students build fluency by continuing to provide: reading experiences and discussions about text, gradually increasing the level of difficulty; reading practice, both silently and out loud; word analysis practice; instruction on reading comprehension strategies; and opportunities to express responses to readings through writing.

Vocabulary

When students do not know the meaning of words in a text, their comprehension is limited. As a result, the text becomes boring or confusing. The larger a student's vocabulary is, the better their reading comprehension will be. A larger vocabulary is also associated with an enhanced ability to communicate in speech and writing. It is the teacher's role to help students develop a good working vocabulary. Students learn most of the words they use and understand from listening to the world around them (adults, other students, media, etc.) They also learn from their reading experiences, which include being read to and reading independently.

Carefully designed activities can also stimulate vocabulary growth, and should emphasize useful words that students see frequently, important words necessary for understanding text, and difficult words such as idioms or words with more than one meaning.

Promoting vocabulary development

A student's vocabulary can be developed by:
- Calling upon a student's prior knowledge and making comparisons to that knowledge
- Defining a word and providing multiple examples of the use of the word in context
- Showing a student how to use context clues to discover the meaning of a word
- Providing instruction on prefixes, roots, and suffixes to help students break a word into its parts and decipher its meaning
- Showing students how to use a dictionary and a thesaurus
- Asking students to practice new vocabulary by using the words in their own writing
- Providing a print-rich environment with a word wall
- Studying a group of words related to a single subject, such as farm words, transportation words, etc. so that concept development is enhanced.

Affixes, prefixes, and root words

Affixes are syllables attached to the beginning or end of a word to make a derivative or inflectional form of a word. Both prefixes and suffixes are affixes.

A prefix is a syllable that appears at the beginning of a word that, in combination with the root or base word, creates a specific meaning. For example, the prefix "mis" means "wrong." When combined with the root word "spelling," the word "misspelling" is created, which means the "wrong spelling."

A root word is the base of a word to which affixes can be added. For example, the prefix "in" or "pre" can be added to the root word "vent" to create "invent" or "prevent," respectively. The suffix "er" can be added to the root word "work" to create "worker," which means "one who works." The suffix "able," meaning "capable of," can be added to "work" to create "workable," which means "capable of working."

- 12 -

Suffix

A suffix is a syllable that appears at the end of a word that, in combination with the root or base word, creates a specific meaning. There are three types of suffixes:

- Noun suffixes – There are two types of noun suffixes. One denotes the act of, state of, or quality of. For example, "ment" added to "argue" becomes "argument," which is defined as "the act of arguing." The other denotes the doer, or one who acts. For example "eer" added to "auction" becomes "auctioneer," meaning "one who auctions." Other examples include "hood," "ness," "tion," "ship," and "ism."
- Verb suffixes – These denote "to make" or "to perform the act of." For example, "en" added to "soft" makes "soften," which means "to make soft." Other verb suffixes are "ate" (perpetuate), "fy" (dignify), and "ize" (sterilize).
- Adjectival suffixes – These include suffixes such as "ful," which means "full of." When added to "care," the word "careful" is formed, which means "full of care." Other examples are "ish," "less," and "able."

Context clues

Context clues are words or phrases that help the reader figure out the meaning of an unknown word. They are built into a sentence or paragraph by the writer to help the reader develop a clear understanding of the writer's message. Context clues can be used to make intelligent guesses about the meaning of a word instead of relying on a dictionary. Context clues are the reason most vocabulary is learned through reading.
There are four types of commonly used context clues:

- Synonyms – A word with the same meaning as the unknown word is placed close by for comparison.
- Antonyms – A word with the opposite meaning as the unknown word is placed close by for contrast.
- Explanations – An obvious explanation is given close to the unknown word.
- Examples – Examples of what the word means are given to help the reader define the term.

Comprehension

The whole point of reading is to comprehend what someone else is trying to say through writing. Without comprehension, a student is just reading the words without understanding them or increasing knowledge of a topic. Comprehension results when the student has the vocabulary and reading skills necessary to make sense of the whole picture, not just individual words. Students can self-monitor because they know when they are comprehending the material and when they are not. Teachers can help students solve problems with comprehension by teaching them strategies such as pre-reading titles, sidebars, and follow-up questions; looking at illustrations; predicting what's going to happen in the story; asking questions to check understanding while reading; connecting to background knowledge; and relating to the experiences or feelings of the characters.

Improving comprehension

Teachers can model in a read-aloud the strategies students can use on their own to better comprehend a text. First, the teacher should do a walk-through of the story illustrations and ask, "What's happening here?" Based on what they have seen, the teacher should then ask students to predict what the story will be about. As the book is read, the teacher should ask open-ended questions such as, "Why do you think the character did this?" and "How do you think the character feels?" The teacher should also ask students if they can relate to the story or have background knowledge of something similar. After the reading, the teacher should ask the students to retell the story in their own words to check for comprehension. This retelling can take the form of a puppet show or summarizing the story to a partner.

Prior knowledge

Even preschool children have some literacy skills, and the extent and type of these skills have implications for instructional approaches. Comprehension results from relating two or more pieces of information. One piece comes from the text, and another piece might come from prior knowledge (something from a student's long-term memory). For a child, that prior knowledge comes from being read to at home; taking part in other literacy experiences, such as playing computer or word games; being exposed to a print-rich environment at home; and observing examples of parents' reading habits. Children who have had extensive literacy experience are better prepared to further develop their literacy skills in school than children who have not been read to, have few books or magazines in their homes, are seldom exposed to high-level oral or written language activities, and seldom witness adults engaged in reading and writing. Children with a scant literacy background are at a disadvantage. The teacher must not make any assumptions about their prior knowledge, and should use intense, targeted instruction. Otherwise, reading comprehension will be limited.

Literal vs. critical comprehension

Literal comprehension refers to the skills a reader uses to deal with the actual words in a text. It involves skills such as identifying the topic sentence, main idea, important facts, and supporting details; using context clues to determine the meaning of a word; and sequencing events.

Critical comprehension involves prior knowledge and an understanding that written material, especially in nonfiction, is the author's version of the subject and not necessarily anybody else's. Critical comprehension involves analysis of meaning, evaluation, validation, questioning, and the reasoning skills a reader uses to recognize:
- Inferences and conclusions
- Purpose, tone, point of view, and themes
- The organizational pattern of a work
- Explicit and implicit relationships among words, phrases, and sentences
- Biased language, persuasive tactics, valid arguments, and the difference between fact and opinion

Metacognition

Metacognition is thinking about thinking. For the student, this involves taking control of their own learning process, self-monitoring progress, evaluating the effectiveness of strategies, and making adjustments to strategies and learning behaviors as needed.

Students who develop good metacognitive skills become more independent and confident about learning. They develop a sense of ownership about their education and realize that information is readily available to them.

Metacognitive skills can be grouped into three categories:
- Awareness – This involves identifying prior knowledge; defining learning goals; inventorying resources such as textbooks, libraries, computers, and study time; identifying task requirements and evaluation standards; and recognizing motivation and anxiety levels.
- Planning – This involves doing time estimates for tasks, prioritizing, scheduling study time, making checklists of tasks, gathering needed materials, and choosing strategies for problem solving or task comprehension.
- Self-monitoring and reflection – This involves identifying which strategies or techniques work best, questioning throughout the process, considering feedback, and maintaining focus and motivation.

Metacognitive skills

In terms of literacy development, metacognitive skills include taking an active role in reading, recognizing reading behaviors and changing them to employ the behaviors that are most effective, relating information to prior knowledge, and being aware of text structures.

For example, if there is a problem with comprehension, the student can try to form a mental image of what is described, read the text again, adjust the rate of reading, or employ other reading strategies such as identifying unknown vocabulary and predicting meaning.

Being aware of text structures is critical to being able to follow the author's ideas and relationships among ideas. Being aware of difficulties with text structure allows the student to employ strategies such as hierarchical summaries, thematic organizers, or concept maps to remedy the problem.

Puppetry

Using puppets in the classroom puts students at ease and allows them to enjoy a learning experience as if it were play. The purpose of using puppetry is to generate ideas, encourage imagination, and foster language development. Using a puppet helps a child "become" the character and therefore experience a different outlook.

Language development is enhanced through the student interpreting a story that has been read in class and practicing new words from that story in the puppet show. Children will also have the opportunity to practice using descriptive adjectives for the characters and the scene, which will help them learn the function of adjectives.

Descriptive adjectives and verbs can also be learned by practicing facial expressions and movements with puppets. The teacher can model happy, sad, eating, sleeping, and similar words with a puppet, and then ask students to do the same with their puppets. This is an especially effective vocabulary activity for ESL children.

Drama activities

Drama activities are fun learning experiences that capture a child's attention, engage the imagination, and motivate vocabulary expansion.

For example, after reading a story, the teacher could ask children to act it out as the teacher repeats the story. This activity, which works best with very young learners, will help children work on listening skills and their ability to pretend. The best stories to use for this passive improvisation are ones that have lots of simple actions that children will be able to understand and perform easily. Older children can create their own improvisational skits and possibly write scripts.

Visualization also calls upon the imagination and encourages concentration and bodily awareness. Children can be given a prompt for the visualization and then asked to draw what they see in their mind's eye.

Charades is another way to act out words and improve vocabulary skills. This activity can be especially helpful to encourage ESL students to express thoughts and ideas in English. These students should be given easier words to act out to promote confidence.

Types of figurative language

A simile is a comparison between two unlike things using the words "like" or "as." Examples are Robert Burn's sentence "O my love's like a red, red, rose" or the common expression "as pretty as a picture."

A metaphor is a direct comparison between two unlike things without the use of "like" or "as." One thing is identified as the other instead of simply compared to it. An example is D. H. Lawrence's sentence "My soul is a dark forest."

Personification is the giving of human characteristics to a non-human thing or idea. An example is "The hurricane howled its frightful rage."

Synecdoche is the use of a part of something to signify the whole. For example, "boots on the ground" could be used to describe soldiers in a field.

Metonymy is the use of one term that is closely associated with another to mean the other. An example is referring to the "crown" to refer to the monarchy.

Graphic organizers

The purpose of graphic organizers is to help students classify ideas and communicate more efficiently and effectively. Graphic organizers are visual outlines or templates that help students grasp key concepts and master subject matter by simplifying them down to basic points. They also help guide students through processes related to any subject area or task. Examples of processes include brainstorming, problem solving, decision making, research and project planning, and studying.

Examples of graphic organizers include:
- Reading – These can include beginning, middle, and end graphs or event maps.
- Science – These can include charts that show what animals need or how to classify living things.
- Math – These can include horizontal bar graphs or time lines.
- Language arts – These can include alphabet organizers or charts showing the components of the five-paragraph essay.
- General – These can include KWL charts or weekly planners.

Second language acquisition

Since some students may have limited understanding of English, a teacher should employ the following practices to promote second language acquisition:
- Make all instruction as understandable as possible and use simple and repeated terms.
- Relate instruction to the cultures of ESL children.
- Increase interactive activities and use gestures or non-verbal actions when modeling.
- Provide language and literacy development instruction in all curriculum areas.
- Establish consistent routines that help children connect words and events.
- Use a schedule so children know what will happen next and will not feel lost.
- Integrate ESL children into group activities with non-ESL children.
- Appoint bilingual students to act as student translators.
- Explain actions as activities happen so that a word to action relationship is established.
- Initiate opportunities for ESL children to experiment with and practice new language.
- Employ multisensory learning.

Summarization, question generation, and textual marking

It is important to teach students to use critical thinking skills when reading. Three of the critical thinking tools that engage the reader are:
- Summarization – The student reviews the main point(s) of the reading selection and identifies important details. For nonfiction, a good summary will briefly describe the main arguments and the examples that support those arguments. For fiction, a good summary will identify the main characters and events of the story.
- Question generation – A good reader will constantly ask questions while reading about comprehension, vocabulary, connections to personal knowledge or experience, predictions, etc.

- Textual marking – This skill engages the reader by having him or her interact with the text. The student should mark the text with questions or comments that are generated by the text using underlining, highlighting, or shorthand marks such as "?," "!," and "*" that indicate lack of understanding, importance, or key points, for example.

Theories of language development

Four theories of language development are:
- Learning approach – This theory assumes that language is first learned by imitating the speech of adults. It is then solidified in school through drills about the rules of language structures.
- Linguistic approach – Championed by Noam Chomsky in the 1950s, this theory proposes that the ability to use a language is innate. This is a biological approach rather than one based on cognition or social patterning.
- Cognitive approach – Developed in the 1970s and based on the work of Piaget, this theory states that children must develop appropriate cognitive skills before they can acquire language.
- Sociocognitive approach – In the 1970s, some researchers proposed that language development is a complex interaction of linguistic, social, and cognitive influences

This theory best explains the lack of language skills among children who are neglected, have uneducated parents, or lives in poverty.

Fairy tales, fables, and tall tales

A fairy tale is a fictional story involving humans, magical events, and usually animals. Characters such as fairies, elves, giants, and talking animals are taken from folklore. The plot often involves impossible events (as in "Jack and the Beanstalk") and/or an enchantment (as in "Sleeping Beauty"). Other examples of fairy tales include "Cinderella," "Little Red Riding Hood," and "Rumpelstiltskin."

A fable is a tale in which animals, plants, and forces of nature act like humans. A fable also teaches a moral lesson. Examples are "The Tortoise and the Hare," *The Lion King*, and *Animal Farm*.

A tall tale exaggerates human abilities or describes unbelievable events as if the story were true. Often, the narrator seems to have witnessed the event described. Examples are fish stories, Paul Bunyan and Pecos Bill stories, and hyperboles about real people such as Davy Crockett, Mike Fink, and Calamity Jane.

Preadolescent and adolescent literature

Preadolescent literature is mostly concerned with the "tween" issues of changing lives, relationships, and bodies. Adolescents seeking escape from their sometimes difficult lives enjoy fantasy and science fiction. For both groups, books about modern, real people are more interesting than those about historical figures or legends. Boys especially enjoy nonfiction. Reading interests as well as reading levels for this group vary. Reading levels will usually range from 6.0 to 8.9. Examples of popular literature for this age group and reading level include:

- Series – Sweet Valley High, Bluford High, Nancy Drew, Hardy Boys, and Little House on the Prairie
- Juvenile fiction authors – Judy Blume and S. E. Hinton
- Fantasy and horror authors – Ursula LeGuin and Stephen King
- Science fiction authors – Isaac Asimov, Ray Bradbury, and H. G. Wells
- Classic books: *Lilies of the Field, Charlie and the Chocolate Factory, Pippi Longstocking, National Velvet, Call of the Wild, Anne of Green Gables, The Hobbit, The Member of the Wedding,* and *Tom Sawyer*

Topic sentence

The topic sentence of a paragraph states the paragraph's subject. It presents the main idea. The rest of the paragraph should be related to the topic sentence, which should be explained and supported with facts, details, proofs, and examples.

The topic sentence is more general than the body sentences, and should cover all the ideas in the body of the paragraph. It may contain words such as "many," "most," or "several." The topic sentence is usually the first sentence in a paragraph, but it can appear after an introductory or background sentence, can be the last sentence in a paragraph, or may simply be implied, meaning a topic sentence is not present.

Supporting sentences can often be identified by their use of transition terms such as "for example" or "that is." Supporting sentences may also be presented in numbered sequence.

The topic sentence provides unity to a paragraph because it ties together the supporting details into a coherent whole.

Cause and effect

Causes are reasons for actions or events. Effects are the results of a cause or causes. There may be multiple causes for one effect (evolutionary extinction, climate changes, and a massive comet caused the demise of the dinosaurs, for example) or multiple effects from one cause (the break-up of the Soviet Union has had multiple effects on the world stage, for instance). Sometimes, one thing leads to another and the effect of one action becomes the cause for another (breaking an arm leads to not driving, which leads to reading more while staying home, for example).

The ability to identify causes and effects is part of critical thinking, and enables the reader to follow the course of events, make connections among events, and identify the instigators and receivers of actions. This ability improves comprehension.

Facts and opinions

Facts are statements that can be verified through research. Facts answer the questions of who, what, when, and where, and evidence can be provided to prove factual statements. For example, it is a fact that water turns into ice when the temperature drops below 32 degrees Fahrenheit. This fact has been proven repeatedly. Water never becomes ice at a higher temperature.

Opinions are personal views, but facts may be used to support opinions. For example, it may be one person's opinion that Jack is a great athlete, but the fact that he has made many achievements related to sports supports that opinion.

It is important for a reader to be able to distinguish between fact and opinion to determine the validity of an argument. Readers need to understand that some unethical writers will try to pass off an opinion as a fact. Readers with good critical thinking skills will not be deceived by this tactic.

Invalid arguments

There are a number of invalid or false arguments that are used unethically to gain an advantage, such as:
- The "ad hominem" or "against the person" argument – This type attacks the character or behavior of a person taking a stand on an issue rather than the issue itself. The statement "That fat slob wants higher taxes" is an example of this type of argument.
- Hasty generalizations – These are condemnations of a group based on the behavior of one person or part. An example of this type of argument is someone saying that all McDonald's restaurants are lousy because he or she had a bad experience at one location.
- Faulty causation – This is assigning the wrong cause to an event. An example is blaming a flat tire on losing a lucky penny rather than on driving over a bunch of nails.
- Bandwagon effect – This is the argument that if everybody else is doing something, it must be a good thing to do. The absurdity of this type of argument is highlighted by the question: "If everybody else is jumping off a cliff, should you jump, too?"

It is important for a reader to be able to identify various types of invalid arguments to prevent being deceived and making faulty conclusions.

Inductive reasoning and deductive reasoning

Inductive reasoning is using particulars to draw a general conclusion. The inductive reasoning process starts with data. For example, if every apple taken out of the top of a barrel is rotten, it can be inferred without investigating further that all the apples are probably rotten. Unless all data is examined, conclusions are based on probabilities. Inductive reasoning is also used to make inferences about the universe. The entire universe cannot be examined, but inferences can be made based on observations about what can be seen. These inferences may be proven false when more data is available, but they are valid at the time they are made if observable data is used.

- 20 -

Deductive reasoning is the opposite of inductive reasoning. It involves using general facts or premises to come to a specific conclusion. For example, if Susan is a sophomore in high school, and all sophomores take geometry, it can be inferred that Susan takes geometry. The word "all" does not allow for exceptions. If all sophomores take geometry, assuming Susan does too is a logical conclusion.

It is important for a reader to recognize inductive and deductive reasoning so he or she can follow the line of an argument and determine if the inference or conclusion is valid.

Theme

Theme is the central idea of a work. It is the thread that ties all the elements of a story together and gives them purpose. The theme is not the subject of a work, but what a work says about a subject. A theme must be universal, which means it must apply to everyone, not just the characters in a story. Therefore, a theme is a comment about the nature of humanity, society, the relationship of humankind to the world, or moral responsibility. There may be more than one theme in a work, and the determination of the theme is affected by the viewpoint of the reader. Therefore, there is not always necessarily a definite, irrefutable theme. The theme can be implied or stated directly.

Types of characters

Readers need to be able to differentiate between major and minor characters. The difference can usually be determined based on whether the characters are round, flat, dynamic, or static.

Round characters have complex personalities, just like real people. They are more commonly found in longer works such as novels or full-length plays.

Flat characters display only a few personality traits and are based on stereotypes. Examples include the bigoted redneck, the lazy bum, or the absent-minded professor.

Dynamic characters are those that change or grow during the course of the narrative. They may learn important lessons, fall in love, or take new paths.

Static characters remain the same throughout a story. Usually, round characters are dynamic and flat characters are static, but this is not always the case. Falstaff, the loyal and comical character in Shakespeare's plays about Henry IV, is a round character in terms of his complexity. However, he never changes, which makes him a reliable figure in the story.

Adjective, adverb, and conjunction

The definitions for these grammatical terms are as follows:
- Adjective – This is a word that modifies or describes a noun or pronoun. Examples are a *green* apple or *every* computer.
- Adverb – This is a word that modifies a verb (*instantly* reviewed), an adjective (*relatively* odd), or another adverb (*rather* suspiciously).

Conjunctions: There are three types of conjunctions:
- Coordinating conjunctions are used to link words, phrases, and clauses. Examples are and, or, nor, for, but, yet, and so.
- Correlative conjunctions are paired terms used to link clauses. Examples are either/or,
  neither/nor,
  if/then.
- Subordinating conjunctions relate subordinate or dependent clauses to independent ones.
  Examples are although, because, if, since, before, after, when, even though, in order that, and while.

Gerund, infinitive, noun, direct and indirect objects

The definitions for these grammatical terms are as follows:

Gerund – This is a verb form used as a noun. Most end in "ing." An example is: *Walking* is good exercise.

Infinitive – This is a verbal form comprised of the word "to" followed by the root form of a verb. An infinitive may be used as a noun, adjective, adverb, or absolute. Examples include:
- *To hold* a baby is a joy. (noun)
- Jenna had many files *to reorganize*. (adjective)
- Andrew tried *to remember* the dates. (adverb)
- *To be honest*, your hair looks awful. (absolute)

Noun – This is a word that names a person, place, thing, idea, or quality. A noun can be used as a subject, object, complement, appositive, or modifier.
Object – This is a word or phrase that receives the action of a verb.

A direct object states **to** whom/what an action was committed. It answers the question "to what?" An example is: Joan served *the meal*.

An indirect object states **for** whom/what an action was committed. An example is: Joan served *us* the meal.

Preposition, prepositional phrase, pronoun, sentence, and verb

The definitions for these grammatical terms are as follows:
- Preposition – This is a word that links a noun or pronoun to other parts of a sentence. Examples include above, by, for, in, out, through, and to.
- Prepositional phrase – This is a combination of a preposition and a noun or pronoun. Examples include across the bridge, against the grain, below the horizon, and toward the sunset.
- Pronoun – This is a word that represents a specific noun in a generic way. A pronoun functions like a noun in a sentence. Examples include I, she, he, it, myself, they, these, what, all, and anybody.

- Sentence – This is a group of words that expresses a thought or conveys information as an independent unit of speech. A complete sentence must contain a noun and a verb (I ran). However, all the other parts of speech can also be represented in a sentence.
- Verb – This is a word or phrase in a sentence that expresses action (Mary played) or a state of being (Mary is).

Capitalization and punctuation

Capitalization refers to the use of capital letters. Capital letters should be placed at the beginning of:
- Proper names (Ralph Waldo Emerson, Australia)
- Places (Mount Rushmore, Chicago)
- Historical periods and holidays (Renaissance, Christmas)
- Religious terms (Bible, Koran)
- Titles (Empress Victoria, General Smith)
- All main words in literary, art, or music titles (Grapes of Wrath, Sonata in C Major)

Punctuation consists of:
- Periods – A period is placed at the end of a sentence.
- Commas – A comma is used to separate:
- Two adjectives modifying the same word (long, hot summer)
- Three or more words or phrases in a list (Winken, Blinken, and Nod; life, liberty, and the pursuit of happiness)
- Phrases that are not needed to complete a sentence (The teacher, not the students, will distribute the supplies.)

Colons and semicolons

Colons – A colon is used to:
- Set up a list (We will need these items: a pencil, paper, and   an eraser.)
- Direct readers to examples or explanations (We have one chore left: clean out the garage.)
- Introduce quotations or dialogue (The Labor Department reported on unemployment: "There was a 3.67% increase in unemployment in 2010."; Scarlett exclaimed: "What shall I do?")

Semicolons – A semicolon is used to:
- Join related independent clauses (There were five major hurricanes this year; two of them hit Florida.)
- Join independent clauses connected by conjunctive adverbs (Popular books are often made into movies; however, it is a rare screenplay that is as good as the book.)
- Separate items in a series if commas would be confusing (The characters include: Robin Hood, who robs from the rich to give to the poor; Maid Marian, his true love; and Little John, Robin Hood's comrade-in-arms.)

Subject-verb agreement

A verb must agree in number with its subject. Therefore, a verb changes form depending on whether the subject is singular or plural. Examples include "I do," "he does," "the ball is," and "the balls are."

If two subjects are joined by "and," the plural form of a verb is usually used. For example: *Jack and Jill want* to get some water (Jack wants, Jill wants, but together they want).

If the compound subjects are preceded by each or every, they take the singular form of a verb. For example: *Each man and each woman brings* a special talent to the world (each brings, not bring).

If one noun in a compound subject is plural and the other is singular, the verb takes the form of the subject nearest to it. For example: Neither the *students* nor their *teacher was* ready for the fire drill.

Collective nouns that name a group are considered singular if they refer to the group acting as a unit. For example: The *choir is going* on a concert tour.

Syntax

Syntax refers to the rules related to how to properly structure sentences and phrases. Syntax is not the same as grammar. For example, "I does" is syntactically correct because the subject and verb are in proper order, but it is grammatically incorrect because the subject and verb don't agree.

There are three types of sentence structures:
- Simple – This type is composed of a single independent clause with one subject and one predicate (verb or verb form).
- Compound – This type is composed of two independent clauses joined by a conjunction (Amy flew, but Brenda took the train), a correlative conjunction (Either Tom goes with me or I stay here), or a semicolon (My grandfather stays in shape; he plays tennis nearly every day).
- Complex – This type is composed of one independent clause and one or more dependent clauses joined by a subordinating conjunction (Before we set the table, we should replace the tablecloth).

Types of paragraphs

Illustrative – An illustrative paragraph or essay explains a general statement through the use of specific examples. The writer starts with a topic sentence that is followed by one or more examples that clearly relate to and support the topic.

Narrative – A narrative tells a story. Like a news report, it tells the who, what, when, where, why, and how of an event. A narrative is usually presented in chronological order.

Descriptive – This type of writing appeals to the five senses to describe a person, place, or thing so that the readers can see the subject in their imaginations. Space order is most often used in descriptive writing to indicate place or position.

Process – There are two kinds of process papers: the "how-to" that gives step-by-step directions on how to do something and the explanation paper that tells how an event occurred or how something works.

Definition paragraph

A definition paragraph or essay describes what a word or term means. There are three ways the explanation can be presented:

Definition by synonym – The term is defined by comparing it to a more familiar term that the reader can more easily understand (A phantom is a ghost or spirit that appears and disappears mysteriously and creates dread).

Definition by class – Most commonly used in exams, papers, and reports, the class definition first puts the term in a larger category or class (The Hereford is a breed of cattle), and then describes the distinguishing characteristics or details of the term that differentiate it from other members of the class (The Hereford is a breed of cattle distinguished by a white face, reddish-brown hide, and short horns).

Definition by negation – The term is defined by stating what it is not and then saying what it is (Courage is not the absence of fear, but the willingness to act in spite of fear).

Types of essays

A comparison and contrast essay examines the similarities and differences between two things. In a paragraph, the writer presents all the points about subject A and then all the points about subject B. In an essay, the writer might present one point at a time, comparing subject A and subject B side by side.

A classification paper sorts information. It opens with a topic sentence that identifies the group to be classified, and then breaks that group into categories. For example, a group might be baseball players, while a category might be positions they play.

A cause and effect paper discusses the causes or reasons for an event or the effects of a cause or causes. Topics discussed in this type of essay might include the causes of a war or the effects of global warming.

A persuasive essay is one in which the writer tries to convince the audience to agree with a certain opinion or point of view. The argument must be supported with facts, examples, anecdotes, expert testimony, or statistics, and must anticipate and answer the questions of those who hold an opposing view. It may also predict consequences.

Purpose and audience

Early in the writing process, the writer needs to definitively determine the purpose of the paper and then keep that purpose in mind throughout the writing process. The writer needs to ask: "Is the purpose to explain something, to tell a story, to entertain, to inform, to argue a point, or some combination of these purposes?"

Also at the beginning of the writing process, the writer needs to determine the audience of the paper by asking questions such as: "Who will read this paper?," "For whom is this paper intended?," "What does the audience already know about this topic?," "How much does the audience need to know?," and "Is the audience likely to agree or disagree with my point of view?" The answers to these questions will determine the content of the paper, the tone, and the style.

Drafting, revising, editing, and proofreading

Drafting is creating an early version of a paper. A draft is a prototype or sketch of the finished product. A draft is a rough version of the final paper, and it is expected that there will be multiple drafts. Revising is the process of making major changes to a draft in regards to clarity of purpose, focus (thesis), audience, organization, and content.

Editing is the process of making changes in style, word choice, tone, examples, and arrangement. These are more minor than the changes made during revision. Editing can be thought of as fine tuning. The writer makes the language more precise, checks for varying paragraph lengths, and makes sure that the title, introduction, and conclusion fit well with the body of the paper.

Proofreading is performing a final check and correcting errors in punctuation, spelling, grammar, and usage. It also involves looking for parts of the paper that may be omitted.

Title and conclusion

The title is centered on the page and the main words are capitalized. The title is not surrounded by quotation marks, nor is it underlined or italicized. The title is rarely more than four or five words, and is very rarely a whole sentence. A good title suggests the subject of the paper and catches the reader's interest. The conclusion should flow logically from the body of the essay, should tie back to the introduction, and may provide a summary or a final thought on the subject. New material should never be introduced in the conclusion. The conclusion is a wrap-up that may contain a call to action, something the writer wants the audience to do in response to the paper. The conclusion might end with a question to give the reader something to think about.

Introduction

The introduction contains the thesis statement, which is usually the first or last sentence of the opening paragraph. It needs to be interesting enough to make the reader want to continue reading.

Possible openings for an introduction include:
- The thesis statement
- A general idea that gives background or sets the scene
- An illustration that will make the thesis more concrete and easy to picture
- A surprising fact or idea to arouse curiosity
- A contradiction to popular belief that attracts interest
- A quotation that leads into the thesis

Types of sentences

A declarative sentence makes a statement and is punctuated by a period at the end. An example is: The new school will be built at the south end of Main Street.

An interrogative sentence asks a question and is punctuated by a question mark at the end. An example is: Why will the new school be built so far out?

An exclamatory sentence shows strong emotion and is punctuated by an exclamation mark at the end. An example is: The new school has the most amazing state-of-the-art technology!

An imperative sentence gives a direction or command and may be punctuated by an exclamation mark or a period. Sometimes, the subject of an imperative sentence is you, which is understood instead of directly stated. An example is: Come to the open house at the new school next Sunday.

Parallelism, euphemism, hyperbole, and climax

Parallelism – Subjects, objects, verbs, modifiers, phrases, and clauses can be structured in sentences to balance one with another through a similar grammatical pattern. Parallelism helps to highlight ideas while showing their relationship and giving style to writing.

Examples are:
- Parallel words – The killer behaved coldly, cruelly, and inexplicably.
- Parallel phrases – Praised by comrades, honored by commanders, the soldier came home
- a hero.
- Parallel clauses – "We shall fight on the beaches, we shall fight on the landing grounds, we shall fight in the hills." (Winston Churchill)
- Euphemism – This is a "cover-up" word that avoids the explicit meaning of an offensive or unpleasant term by substituting a vaguer image. An example is using "expired" instead of "dead."
- Hyperbole – This is an example or phrase that exaggerates for effect. An example is the extravagant overstatement "I thought I would die!" Hyperbole is also used in tall tales, such as those describing Paul Bunyan's feats.
- Climax – This refers to the process of building up to a dramatic highpoint through a series of phrases or sentences. It can also refer to the highpoint or most intense event in a story.

Bathos, oxymoron, irony, and malapropism

Bathos – This is an attempt to evoke pity, sorrow, or nobility that goes overboard and becomes ridiculous. It is an insincere pathos and a letdown. It is also sometimes called an anticlimax, although an anticlimax might be intentionally included for comic or satiric effect.

Oxymoron – This refers to two terms that are used together for contradictory effect, usually in the form of an adjective that doesn't fit the noun. An example is: a "new classic."

Irony – This refers to a difference between what is and what ought to be, or between what is said and what is meant. Irony can be an unexpected result in literature, such as a twist of fate. For example, it is ironic that the tortoise beat the hare.

Malapropism – This is confusing one word with another, similar-sounding word. For example, saying a movie was a cliff dweller instead of a cliffhanger is a malapropism.

Transitional words and phrases

Transitional words are used to signal a relationship. They are used to link thoughts and sentences. Some types of transitional words and phrases are:
- Addition – Also, in addition, furthermore, moreover, and then, another
- Admitting a point – Granted, although, while it is true that
- Cause and effect – Since, so, consequently, as a result, therefore, thus
- Comparison – Similarly, just as, in like manner, likewise, in the same way
- Contrast – On the other hand, yet, nevertheless, despite, but, still
- Emphasis – Indeed, in fact, without a doubt, certainly, to be sure
- Illustration – For example, for instance, in particular, specifically
- Purpose – In order to, for this purpose, for this to occur
- Spatial arrangement – Beside, above, below, around, across, inside, near, far, to the left
- Summary or clarification – In summary, in conclusion, that is, in other words
- Time sequence – Before, after, later, soon, next, meanwhile, suddenly, finally

Pre-writing techniques

Pre-writing techniques that help a writer find, explore, and organize a topic include:
- Brainstorming – This involves letting thoughts make every connection to the topic possible, and then spinning off ideas and making notes of them as they are generated. This is a process of using imagination, uninhibited creativity, and instincts to discover a variety of possibilities.
- Freewriting – This involves choosing items from the brainstorming list and writing about them nonstop for a short period. This unedited, uncensored process allows one thing to lead to another and permits the writer to think of additional concepts and themes.
- Clustering/mapping – This involves writing a general word or phrase related to the topic in the middle of a paper and circling it, and then quickly jotting down related words or phrases. These are circled and lines are drawn to link words and phrases to others on the page. Clustering is a visual representation of brainstorming that reveals patterns and connections.

Listing and charting

Prewriting techniques that help a writer find, explore, and organize a topic include:
- Listing – Similar to brainstorming, listing is writing down as many descriptive words and phrases (not whole sentences) as possible that relate to the subject. Correct spelling and grouping of these descriptive terms can come later if needed. This list is merely intended to stimulate creativity and provide a vibrant vocabulary for the description of the subject once the actual writing process begins.

- Charting – This prewriting technique works well for comparison/contrast purposes or for the examination of advantages and disadvantages (pros and cons). Any kind of chart will work, even a simple two-column list. The purpose is to draw out points and examples that can be used in the paper.

Purpose of writing

Writing always has a purpose. The five reasons to write are:
- To tell a story – The story does not necessarily need to be fictional. The purposes are to explain what happened, to narrate events, and to explain how things were accomplished. The story will need to make a point, and plenty of details will need to be provided to help the reader imagine the event or process.
- To express oneself – This type of writing is commonly found in journals, diaries, or blogs. This kind of writing is an exercise in reflection that allows writers to learn something about themselves and what they have observed, and to work out their thoughts and feelings on paper.
- To convey information – Reports are written for this purpose. Information needs to be as clearly organized and accurate as possible. Charts, graphs, tables, and other illustrations can help make the information more understandable.
- To make an argument – This type of writing also makes a point, but adds opinion to the facts presented. Argumentative, or persuasive, writing is one of the most common and important types of writing. It should follow rules of logic and ethics.
- To explore ideas – This is speculative writing that is quite similar to reflective writing. This type of writing explores possibilities and asks questions without necessarily expecting an answer. The purpose is to stimulate readers to further consider and reflect on the topic.

Strategic arrangement

The order of the elements in a writing project can be organized in the following ways:
- Logical order – There is a coherent pattern in the presentation of information, such as inductive or deductive reasoning or a division of a topic into its parts.
- Hierarchical order – There is a ranking of material from most to least important or least to most important, depending on whether the writer needs a strong start or a sweeping finish. It can also involve breaking down a topic from a general form into specifics.
- Chronological order – This is an order that follows a sequence. In a narrative, the sequence will follow the time order of beginning to middle to end. In a "how to," the sequence will be step 1, step 2, step 3, and so on.
- Order defined by genre – This is a pre-determined order structured according to precedent or professional guidelines, such as the order required for a specific type of research or lab report, a resume, or an application form.
- Order of importance – This method of organization relies on a ranking determined by priorities. For example, in a persuasive paper, the writer usually puts the strongest argument in the last body paragraph so that readers will remember it. In a news report, the most important information comes first.
- Order of interest – This order is dependent on the level of interest the audience has in the subject. If the writer anticipates that reader knowledge and interest in the subject will be low, normal order choices need to be changed. The piece should

begin with something very appealing. This will hook the reader and make for a strong opening.

Beginning stages of writing

The following are the beginning stages of learning to write:

- Drawing pictures is the first written attempt to express thoughts and feelings. Even when the picture is unrecognizable to the adult, it means something to the child.
- The scribble stage begins when the child attempts to draw shapes. He or she may also try to imitate writing. The child may have a story or explanation to go with the shapes.
- Children have the most interest in learning to write their own names, so writing lessons usually start with that. Children will soon recognize that there are other letters too.
- Children are learning the alphabet and how to associate a sound with each letter. Reversing letters is still common, but instruction begins with teaching children to write from left to right.
- Written words may not be complete, but will likely have the correct beginning and end sounds/letters. Children will make some attempt to use vowels in writing.
- Children will write with more ease, although spelling will still be phonetic and only some punctuation will be used.

Journals

Writing in a journal gives students practice in writing, which makes them more comfortable with the writing process. Journal writing also gives students the opportunity to sort out their thoughts, solve problems, examine relationships and values, and see their personal and academic growth when they revisit old entries. The advantages for the teacher are that the students become more experienced with and accustomed to writing. Through reading student journals, the teacher can also gain insight into the students' problems and attitudes, which can help the teacher tailor his or her lesson plans. A journal can be kept in a notebook or in a computer file. It shouldn't be just a record of daily events, but an expression of thoughts and feelings about everything and anything. Grammar and punctuation don't matter since journaling is a form of private communication. Teachers who review journals need to keep in mind that they should not grade journals and that comments should be encouraging and polite.

Revising

Revising a paper involves rethinking the choices that were made while constructing the paper and then rewriting it, making any necessary changes or additions to word choices or arrangement of points. Questions to keep in mind include:

- Is the thesis clear?
- Do the body paragraphs logically flow and provide details to support the thesis?
- Is anything unnecessarily repeated?
- Is there anything not related to the topic?
- Is the language understandable?
- Does anything need to be defined?
- Is the material interesting?

Another consideration when revising is peer feedback. It is helpful during the revision process to have someone who is knowledgeable enough to be helpful and will be willing to give an honest critique read the paper.

Paragraph coherence

Paragraph coherence can be achieved by linking sentences by using the following strategies:
- Repetition of key words – It helps the reader follow the progression of thought from one sentence to another if key words (which should be defined) are repeated to assure the reader that the writer is still on topic and the discussion still relates to the key word.
- Substitution of pronouns – This doesn't just refer to using single word pronouns such as I, they, us, etc., but also alternate descriptions of the subject. For example, if someone was writing about Benjamin Franklin, it gets boring to keep saying Franklin or he. Other terms that describe him, such as that notable American statesman, this printer, the inventor, and so forth can also be used.
- Substitution of synonyms – This is similar to substitution of pronouns, but refers to using similar terms for any repeated noun or adjective, not just the subject. For example, instead of constantly using the word great, adjectives such as terrific, really cool, awesome, and so on can also be used.

Verbs

In order to understand the role of a verb and be able to identify the verb that is necessary to make a sentence, it helps to know the different types of verbs. These are:
- Action verbs – These are verbs that express an action being performed by the subject. An example is: The outfielder caught the ball (outfielder = subject and caught = action).
- Linking verbs – These are verbs that link the subject to words that describe or identify the subject. An example is: Mary is an excellent teacher (Mary = subject and "is" links Mary to her description as an excellent teacher). Common linking verbs are all forms of the verb "to be," appear, feel, look, become, and seem.
- Helping verbs – When a single verb cannot do the job by itself because of tense issues, a second, helping verb is added. Examples include: should have gone ("gone" is the main verb, while "should" and "have" are helping verbs), and was playing ("playing" is the main verb, while "was" is the helping verb).

Conjunctions

There are different ways to connect two clauses and show their relationship.

A coordinating conjunction is one that can join two independent clauses by placing a comma and a coordinating conjunction between them. The most common coordinating conjunctions are and, but, or, nor, yet, for, and so. Examples include: "It was warm, so I left my jacket at home" and "It was warm, and I left my jacket at home."

A subordinating conjunction is one that joins a subordinate clause and an independent clause and establishes the relationship between them. An example is: "We can play a game after Steve finishes his homework." The dependent clause is "after Steve finishes his homework" because the reader immediately asks, "After Steve finishes, then what?" The independent clause is "We can play a game." The concern is not the ability to play a game, but "when?" The answer to this question is dependent on when Steve finishes his homework.

Run-ons and comma splices

A run-on sentence is one that tries to connect two independent clauses without the needed conjunction or punctuation and makes it hard for the reader to figure out where one sentence ends and the other starts. An example is: "Meagan is three years old she goes to pre-school." Two possible ways to fix the run-on would be: "Meagan is three years old, and she goes to pre-school" or "Meagan is three years old; however, she goes to pre-school."

A comma splice occurs when a comma is used to join two independent clauses without a proper conjunction. The comma should be replaced by a period or one of the methods for coordination or subordination should be used. An example of a comma splice is: "Meagan is three years old, she goes to pre-school."

Fragment

A fragment is an incomplete sentence, which is one that does not have a subject to go with the verb, or vice versa. The following are types of fragments:
*   Dependent clause fragments – These usually start with a subordinating conjunction. An example is: "Before you can graduate." "You can graduate" is a sentence, but the subordinating conjunction "before" makes the clause dependent, which means it needs an independent clause to go with it. An example is: "Before you can graduate, you have to meet all the course requirements."
*   Relative clause fragments – These often start with who, whose, which, or that. An example is: "Who is always available to the students." This is a fragment because the "who" is not identified. A complete sentence would be: "Mr. Jones is a principal who is always available to the students."
*   The "ing" fragment lacks a subject. The "ing" form of a verb has to have a helping verb. An example is: "Walking only three blocks to his job." A corrected sentence would be: "Walking only three blocks to his job, Taylor has no need for a car."
*   Prepositional phrase fragments are ones that begin with a preposition and are only a phrase, not a complete thought. An example is: "By the time we arrived." "We arrived" by itself would be a complete sentence, but the "by" makes the clause dependent and the reader asks, "By the time you arrived, what happened?" A corrected sentence would be: "By the time we arrived, all the food was gone."
*   Infinitive phrase fragments have the same problem as prepositional phrase ones. An example is: "To plant the seed." A corrected sentence would be: "To plant the seed, Isaac used a trowel."

- 32 -

Speaking skills children should have

Children of elementary/intermediate school age should be able to:
- Speak at an appropriate volume, tone, and pace that is understandable and appropriate to the audience
- Pronounce most words accurately
- Use complete sentences
- Make eye contact
- Use appropriate gestures with speech
- Exhibit an awareness of audience and adjust content to fit the audience (adjust word choices and style to be appropriate for peers or adults)
- Ask relevant questions
- Respond appropriately when asked questions about information or an opinion, possibly also being able to provide reasons for opinions
- Speak in turn, not interrupt, and include others in conversations
- Provide a summary or report orally
- Participate in small and large group discussions and debates
- Read orally before an audience
- Conduct short interviews
- Provide directions and explanations orally, including explanations of class lessons

Viewing skills children should have

Children of elementary school age should be developing or have attained the ability to understand the importance of media in people's lives. They should understand that television, radio, films, and the Internet have a role in everyday life. They should also be able to use media themselves (printing out material from the Internet or making an audio or video tape, for example). They should also be aware that the purpose of advertising is to sell.

Children of intermediate school age should be developing or have attained the ability to obtain and compare information from newspapers, television, and the Internet. They should also be able to judge its reliability and accuracy to some extent. Children of this age should be able to tell the difference between fictional and non-fictional materials in media. They should also be able to use a variety of media, visuals, and sounds to make a presentation.

Listening skills children should have

Through the elementary/intermediate school years, children should develop the following listening skills:
- Follow oral instructions consistently
- Actively listen to peers and teachers
- Avoid creating distracting behavior or being distracted by the behavior of others most of the time
- Respond to listening activities and exhibit the ability to discuss, illustrate, or write about the activity and show knowledge of the content and quality of the listening activity
- Respond to listening activities and exhibit the ability to identify themes, similarities/differences, ideas, forms, and styles of activities

- Respond to a persuasive speaker and exhibit the ability to analyze and evaluate the credibility of the speaker and form an opinion describing whether they agree or disagree with the point made
- Demonstrate appropriate social behavior while part of an audience

Teaching viewing skills

Viewing skills can be sharpened by having students look at a single image, such as a work of art or a cartoon, and simply asking students what they see. The teacher can ask what is happening in the image, and then elicit the details that clue the students in to what is happening. Of course, there may be more than one thing happening. The teacher should also question the students about the message of the image, its purpose, its point of view, and its intended audience. The teacher should ask for first impressions, and then provide some background or additional information to see if it changes the way students look at or interpret the image. The conclusion of the lesson should include questions about what students learned from the exercise about the topic, themselves, and others.

Students are exposed to multiple images every day. It is important for them to be able to effectively interpret these images. They should be able to make sense of the images and the spoken and print language that often accompany them. Learning can be enhanced with images because they allow for quicker connections to prior knowledge than verbal information. Visuals in the classroom can also be motivational, can support verbal information, and can express main points, sometimes resulting in instant recognition.

Some of the common types of images that students see every day include: bulletin boards, computer graphics, diagrams, drawings, illustrations, maps, photographs, posters, book covers, advertisements, Internet sites, multimedia presentations, puppet shows, television, videos, print cartoons, models, paintings, animation, drama or dance performances, films, and online newscasts and magazines.

Activities at school that can be used to strengthen the viewing skills of students of varying ages include:
- Picture book discussions – Students can develop an appreciation of visual text and the language that goes with it through guided discussions of picture books that focus on the style and color of the images and other details that might capture a child's attention.
- Gallery walks – Students can walk around a room or hallway viewing the posted works of other students and hear presentations about the works. They can also view a display prepared by the teacher. Students are expected to take notes as they walk around, have discussions, and perhaps do a follow-up report.
- Puppet theater and drama presentations – Students can learn about plots, dialogue, situations, characters, and the craft of performance from viewing puppet or drama presentations, which also stimulate oral communication and strengthen listening skills. Discussions or written responses should follow performances to check for detail acquisition.

Classroom viewing center

A classroom viewing center should contain magazines, CD-ROMs, books, videos, and individual pictures (photographs or drawings).

Students should have a viewing guide that explains expectations related to the viewing center (before, during, and after using the center). For younger students, the teacher can ask questions that guide them through the viewing rather than expecting them to read the guidelines and write responses.

Before viewing, students should think about what they already know about the subject and what they want to learn from the viewing.

During the viewing, students should make notes about whatever interests them or is new to them.

After viewing, students could discuss or individually write down what they found to be the most interesting idea or striking image and explain why it caught their attention.

Important questions pertaining to viewing a narrative

A teacher should make students responsible for gaining information or insight from the viewing. Setting expectations increases student attention and critical thinking. As with any viewing, the students should consider what they already know about the topic and what they hope to gain by watching the narrative before viewing it. During the viewing, the students should take notes (perhaps to answer questions provided by the teacher).

After the viewing, students should be able to answer the following questions:
- What was the time period and setting of the story?
- Who were the main characters?
- How effective was the acting?
- What was the problem or goal in the story?
- How was the problem solved or the goal achieved?
- How would you summarize the story?
- What did you learn from the story?
- What did you like or dislike about the story or its presentation?
- Would you recommend this viewing to others?
- How would you rate it?

Learning by listening difficulties

It is difficult to learn just by listening because the instruction is presented only in spoken form. Therefore, unless students take notes, there is nothing for them to review. However, an active listener will anticipate finding a message in an oral presentation and will listen for it, interpreting tone and gestures as the presentation progresses. In group discussions, students are often too busy figuring out what they will say when it is their turn to talk to concentrate on what others are saying. Therefore, they don't learn from others, but instead come away knowing only what they already knew. Students should be required to respond directly to the previous speaker before launching into their own comments. This practice will force students to listen to each other and learn that their own responses will be better because of what can be added by listening to others.

Speaking

Volume – Voice volume should be appropriate to the room and adjusted according to whether or not a microphone is used. The speaker should not shout at the audience, mumble, or speak so softly that his or her voice is inaudible.

Pace and pronunciation – The speaker shouldn't talk so fast that his or her speech is unintelligible, nor should the speaker speak so slowly as to be boring. The speaker should enunciate words clearly.

Body language and gestures – Body language can add to or distract from the message, so annoying, repetitive gestures such as waving hands about, flipping hair, or staring at one spot should be avoided. Good posture is critical.

Word choice – The speaker should use a vocabulary level that fits the age and interest level of the audience. Vocabulary may be casual or formal depending on the audience.

Visual aids – The speaker should use whatever aids will enhance the presentation, such as props, models, media, etc., but should not use anything that will be distracting or unmanageable.

Listening and new language

Listening is a critical skill when learning a new language. Students spend a great deal more time listening than they do speaking, and far less time reading and writing than speaking. Two ways to encourage ESL students to listen are to:
- Talk about topics that are of interest to the ESL learner. Otherwise, students may tune out the speaker because they don't want to put in that much effort to learn about a topic they find boring.
- Talk about content or give examples that are easy to understand or are related to a topic that is familiar to ESL students. Culturally relevant materials will be more interesting to

Listening is not a passive skill, but an active one. Therefore, a teacher needs to make the listening experience as rewarding as possible and provide as many auditory and visual clues as possible. Three ways that the teacher can make the listening experience rewarding for ESL students are:
- Avoid colloquialisms and abbreviated or slang terms that may be confusing to the ESL listener, unless there is enough time to define them and explain their use.
- Make the spoken English understandable by stopping to clarify points, repeating new or difficult words, and defining words that may not be known.
- Support the spoken word with as many visuals as possible. Pictures, diagrams, gestures, facial expressions, and body language can help the ESL learner correctly interpret the spoken language more easily and also leaves an image impression that helps them remember the words.

- 36 -

Top down and bottom up

ESL students need to be given opportunities to practice both top-down and bottom-up processing. If they are old enough to understand these concepts, they should be made aware that these are two processes that affect their listening comprehension.

In top-down processing, the listener refers to background and global knowledge to figure out the meaning of a message. For example, when asking an ESL student to perform a task, the steps of the task should be explained and accompanied by a review of the vocabulary terms the student already understands so that the student feels comfortable tackling new steps and new words. The teacher should also allow students to ask questions to verify comprehension.

In bottom-up processing, the listener figures out the meaning of a message by using "data" obtained from what is said. This data includes sounds (stress, rhythm, and intonation), words, and grammatical relationships. All data can be used to make conclusions or interpretations. For example, the listener can develop bottom-up skills by learning how to detect differences in intonation between statements and questions.

Listening lesson steps

All students, but especially ESL students, can be taught listening through specific training. During listening lessons, the teacher should guide students through three steps:
- Pre-listening activity – This establishes the purpose of the lesson and engages students' background knowledge. This activity should ask students to think about and discuss something they already know about the topic. Alternatively, the teacher can provide background information.
- The listening activity – This requires the listener to obtain information and then immediately do something with that information. For example, the teacher can review the schedule for the day or the week. The students are being given information about a routine they already know, but need to be able to identify names, tasks, and times.
- Post-listening activity – This is an evaluation process that allows students to judge how well they did with the listening task. Other language skills can be included in the activity. For example, this activity could involve asking questions about who will do what according to the classroom schedule (Who is the lunch monitor today?) and could also involve asking students to produce whole sentence replies.

Helping ESL students by speaking

To help ESL students better understand subject matter, the following teaching strategies using spoken English can be used:
- Read aloud from a textbook, and then ask ESL students to verbally summarize what was read. The teacher should assist by providing new words as needed to give students the opportunity to practice vocabulary and speaking skills. The teacher should then read the passage again to students to verify accuracy and details.
- The teacher could ask ESL students to explain why the subject matter is important to them and where they see it fitting into their lives. This verbalization gives them speaking practice and helps them relate to the subject.

- Whenever small group activities are being conducted, ESL students can be placed with English-speaking students. It is best to keep the groups to two or three students so that the ESL student will be motivated by the need to be involved. English-speaking students should be encouraged to include ESL students in the group work.

Helping ESL students by reading

There are supplemental printed materials that can be used to help ESL students understand subject matter. The following strategies can be used to help ESL students develop English reading skills.
- Make sure all ESL students have a bilingual dictionary to use. A thesaurus would also be helpful.
- Try to keep content area books written in the ESL students' native languages in the classroom. Students can use them side-by-side with English texts. Textbooks in other languages can be ordered from the school library or obtained from the classroom textbook publisher.
- If a student lacks confidence in his/her ability to read the textbook, the teacher can read a passage to the student and have him or her verbally summarize the passage. The teacher should take notes on what the student says and then read them back. These notes can be a substitute, short-form, in-their-own-words textbook that the student can understand.

Helping ESL students with general strategies

Some strategies can help students develop more than one important skill. They may involve a combination of speaking, listening, and/or viewing. Others are mainly classroom management aids. General teaching strategies for ESL students include:
- Partner English-speaking students with ESL students as study buddies and ask the English-speaking students to share notes.
- Encourage ESL students to ask questions whenever they don't understand something. They should be aware that they don't have to be able to interpret every word of text to understand the concept.
- Dictate key sentences related to the content area being taught and ask ESL students to write them down. This gives them practice in listening and writing, and also helps them identify what is important.
- Alternate difficult and easy tasks so that ESL students can experience academic success.
- Ask ESL students to label objects associated with content areas, such as maps, diagrams, parts of a leaf, or parts of a sentence. This gives students writing and reading experience and helps them remember key vocabulary.

Social Studies

Maps

There are three basic types of maps:
- Base maps – Created from aerial and field surveys, base maps serve as the starting point for topographic and thematic maps.
- Topographic maps – These show the natural and human-made surface features of the earth, including mountain elevations, river courses, roads, names of lakes and towns, and county and state lines.
- Thematic maps – These use a base or topographic map as the foundation for showing data based on a theme, such as population density, wildlife distribution, hill-slope stability, economic trends, etc.

Scale is the size of a map expressed as a ratio of the actual size of the land (for example, 1 inch on a map represents 1 mile on land). In other words, it is the proportion between a distance on the map and its corresponding distance on earth. The scale determines the level of detail on a map. Small-scale maps depict larger areas, but include fewer details. Large-scale maps depict smaller areas, but include more details.

Time zones

Time is linked to longitude in that a complete rotation of the Earth, or 360° of longitude, occurs every 24 hours. Each hour of time is therefore equivalent to 15° of longitude, or 4 minutes for each 1° turn. By the agreement of 27 nations at the 1884 International Meridian Conference, the time zone system consists of 24 time zones corresponding to the 24 hours in a day. Although high noon technically occurs when the sun is directly above a meridian, calculating time that way would result in 360 different times for the 360 meridians. Using the 24-hour system, the time is the same for all locations in a 15° zone. The 1884 conference established the meridian passing through Greenwich, England, as the zero point, or prime meridian. The halfway point is found at the 180th meridian, a half day from Greenwich. It is called the International Date Line, and serves as the place where each day begins and ends on earth.

Cartography

Cartography is the art and science of mapmaking. Maps of local areas were drawn by the Egyptians as early as 1300 BC, and the Greeks began making maps of the known world in the 6th century BC. Cartography eventually grew into the field of geography.

The first step in modern mapmaking is a survey. This involves designating a few key sites of known elevation as benchmarks to allow for measurement of other sites. Aerial photography is then used to chart the area by taking photos in sequence. Overlapping photos show the same area from different positions along the flight line. When paired and examined through a stereoscope, the cartographer gets a three-dimensional view that can be made into a topographical map. In addition, a field survey (on the ground) is made to determine municipal borders and place names.

The second step is to compile the information and computer-draft a map based on the collected data. The map is then reproduced or printed.

Map and globe terms

The most important terms used when describing items on a map or globe are:
- Latitude and longitude are the imaginary lines (horizontal and vertical, respectively) that divide the globe into a grid. Both are measured using the 360 degrees of a circle.
- Coordinates – These are the latitude and longitude measures for a place.
- Absolute location – This is the exact spot where coordinates meet. The grid system allows the location of every place on the planet to be identified.
- Equator – This is the line at 0° latitude that divides the earth into two equal halves called hemispheres.
- Parallels – This is another name for lines of latitude because they circle the earth in parallel lines that never meet.
- Meridians – This is another name for lines of longitude. The Prime Meridian is located at 0° longitude, and is the starting point for measuring distance (both east and west) around the globe. Meridians circle the earth and connect at the Poles.
- Northern Hemisphere – This is the area above, or north, of the equator.
- Southern Hemisphere – This is the area below, or south, of the equator.
- Western Hemisphere – This is the area between the North and South Poles. It extends west from the Prime Meridian to the International Date Line.
- Eastern Hemisphere – This is the area between the North and South Poles. It extends east from the Prime Meridian to the International Date Line.
- North and South Poles – Latitude is measured in terms of the number of degrees north and south from the equator. The North Pole is located at 90°N latitude, while the South Pole is located at 90°S latitude.
- Tropic of Cancer – This is the parallel, or latitude, 23½° north of the equator.
- Tropic of Capricorn – This is the parallel, or latitude, 23½° south of the equator. The region between these two parallels is the tropics. The subtropics is the area located between 23½° and 40° north and south of the equator.
- Arctic Circle – This is the parallel, or latitude, 66½° north of the equator.
- Antarctic Circle – This is the parallel, or latitude, 66½° south of the equator.

Features of geographic locations

Physical features:
- Vegetation zones, or biomes – Forests, grasslands, deserts, and tundra are the four main types of vegetation zones.
- Climate zones – Tropical, dry, temperate, continental, and polar are the five different types of climate zones. Climate is the long-term average weather conditions of a place.

Cultural features:
- Population density – This is the number of people living in each square mile or kilometer of a place. It is calculated by dividing population by area.
- Religion – This is the identification of the dominant religions of a place, whether Christianity, Hinduism, Judaism, Buddhism, Islam, Shinto, Taoism, or Confucianism. All of these originated in Asia.
- Languages – This is the identification of the dominant or official language of a place. There are 12 major language families. The Indo-European family (which includes English, Russian, German, French, and Spanish) is spoken over the widest geographic area, but Mandarin Chinese is spoken by the most people.

Coral reefs

Coral reefs are formed from millions of tiny, tube-shaped polyps, an animal life form encased in tough limestone skeletons. Once anchored to a rocky surface, polyps eat plankton and miniscule shellfish caught with poisonous tentacles near the mouth. Polyps use calcium carbonate absorbed from chemicals given off by algae to harden their body armor and cement themselves together in fantastic shapes of many colors. Polyps reproduce through eggs and larvae, but the reef grows by branching out shoots of polyps. There are three types of coral reefs:
- Fringing reefs – These surround, or "fringe," an island.
- Barrier reefs – Over the centuries, a fringe reef grows so large that the island sinks down from the weight, and the reef becomes a barrier around the island. Water trapped between the island and the reef is called a lagoon.
- Atolls – Eventually, the sinking island goes under, leaving the coral reef around the lagoon.

Mountains

Mountains are formed by the movement of geologic plates, which are rigid slabs of rocks beneath the earth's crust that float on a layer of partially molten rock in the earth's upper mantle. As the plates collide, they push up the crust to form mountains. This process is called orogeny. There are three basic forms of orogeny:
- If the collision of continental plates causes the crust to buckle and fold, a chain of folded mountains, such as the Appalachians, the Alps, or the Himalayas, is formed.
- If the collision of the plates causes a denser oceanic plate to go under a continental plate, a process called subduction; strong horizontal forces lift and fold the margin of the continent. A mountain range like the Andes is the result.
- If an oceanic plate is driven under another oceanic plate, volcanic mountains such as those in Japan and the Philippines are formed.

Human interaction

Wherever humans have gone on the earth, they have made changes to their surroundings. Many are harmful or potentially harmful, depending on the extent of the alterations. Some of the changes and activities that can harm the environment include:
- Cutting into mountains by machine or blasting to build roads or construction sites
- Cutting down trees and clearing natural growth
- Building houses and cities

- Using grassland to graze herds
- Polluting water sources
- Polluting the ground with chemical and oil waste
- Wearing out fertile land and losing topsoil
- Placing communication lines cross country using poles and wires or underground cable
- Placing railway lines or paved roads cross country
- Building gas and oil pipelines cross country
- Draining wetlands
- Damming up or re-routing waterways
- Spraying fertilizers, pesticides, and defoliants
- Hunting animals to extinction or near extinction

Environmental adaptation

The environment influences the way people live. People adapt to environmental conditions in ways as simple as putting on warm clothing in a cold environment; finding means to cool their surroundings in an environment with high temperatures; building shelters from wind, rain, and temperature variations; and digging water wells if surface water is unavailable. More complex adaptations result from the physical diversity of the earth in terms of soil, climate, vegetation, and topography. Humans take advantage of opportunities and avoid or minimize limitations. Examples of environmental limitations are that rocky soils offer few opportunities for agriculture and rough terrain limits accessibility. Sometimes, technology allows humans to live in areas that were once uninhabitable or undesirable. For example, air conditioning allows people to live comfortably in hot climates; modern heating systems permit habitation in areas with extremely low temperatures, as is the case with research facilities in Antarctica; and airplanes have brought people to previously inaccessible places to establish settlements or industries.

Carrying capacity and natural hazards

Carrying capacity is the maximum, sustained level of use of an environment can incur without sustaining significant environmental deterioration that would eventually lead to environmental destruction. Environments vary in terms of their carrying capacity, a concept humans need to learn to measure and respect before harm is done. Proper assessment of environmental conditions enables responsible decision making with respect to how much and in what ways the resources of a particular environment should be consumed. Energy and water conservation as well as recycling can extend an area's carrying capacity.

In addition to carrying capacity limitations, the physical environment can also have occasional extremes that are costly to humans. Natural hazards such as hurricanes, tornadoes, earthquakes, volcanoes, floods, tsunamis, and some forest fires and insect infestations are processes or events that are not caused by humans, but may have serious consequences for humans and the environment. These events are not preventable, and their precise timing, location, and magnitude are not predictable. However, some precautions can be taken to reduce the damage.

Interpretation of the past

Space, environment, and chronology are three different points of view that can be used to study history. Events take place within geographic contexts. If the world is flat, then transportation choices are vastly different from those that would be made in a round world, for example. Invasions of Russia from the west have normally failed because of the harsh winter conditions, the vast distances that inhibit steady supply lines, and the number of rivers and marshes to be crossed, among other factors. Any invading or defending force anywhere must make choices based on consideration of space and environmental factors. For instance, lands may be too muddy or passages too narrow for certain equipment. Geography played a role in the building of the Panama Canal because the value of a shorter transportation route had to outweigh the costs of labor, disease, political negotiations, and equipment, not to mention a myriad of other effects from cutting a canal through an isthmus and changing a natural land structure as a result.

Interpretation of the present

The decisions that individual people as well as nations make that may affect the environment have to be made with an understanding of spatial patterns and concepts, cultural and transportation connections, physical processes and patterns, ecosystems, and the impact, or "footprint," of people on the physical environment. Sample issues that fit into these considerations are recycling programs, loss of agricultural land to further urban expansion, air and water pollution, deforestation, and ease of transportation and communication. In each of these areas, present and future uses have to be balanced against possible harmful effects. For example, wind is a clean and readily available resource for electric power, but the access roads to and noise of wind turbines can make some areas unsuitable for livestock pasture. Voting citizens need to have an understanding of geographical and environmental connections to make responsible decisions.

Spatial organization

Spatial organization in geography refers to how things or people are grouped in a given space anywhere on earth. Spatial organization applies to the placement of settlements, whether hamlets, towns, or cities. These settlements are located to make the distribution of goods and services convenient. For example, in farm communities, people come to town to get groceries, to attend church and school, and to access medical services. It is more practical to provide these things to groups than to individuals. These settlements, historically, have been built close to water sources and agricultural areas. Lands that are topographically difficult, have few resources, or experience extreme temperatures do not have as many people as temperate zones and flat plains, where it is easier to live. Within settlements, a town or city will be organized into commercial and residential neighborhoods, with hospitals, fire stations, and shopping centers centrally located. All of these organizational considerations are spatial in nature.

Themes of geography

The five themes of geography are:
- Location – This includes relative location (described in terms of surrounding geography such as a river, sea coast, or mountain) and absolute location (the specific point of latitude and longitude).
- Place – This includes physical characteristics (beaches, deserts, mountains, plains, and waterways) and human characteristics (features created by humans, such as architecture, roads, religion, industries or occupations, and food and folk practices).
- Human-environmental interaction – This includes human adaptation to the environment (using an umbrella when it rains), human modification of the environment (building terraces to prevent soil erosion), and human dependence on the environment for food, water, and natural resources.
- Movement –Interaction through trade, migration, communications, political boundaries, ideas, and fashions all fall under this theme.
- Regions – This includes formal regions (a city, state, country, or other geographical organization as defined by political boundaries), functional regions (defined by a common function or connection, such as a school district), and vernacular regions (informal divisions determined by perceptions or one's mental image, such as the "Far East").

Geomorphology

The study of landforms is call geomorphology or physiography, a science that considers the relationships between geological structures and surface landscape features. It is also concerned with the processes that change these features, such as erosion, deposition, and plate tectonics. Biological factors can also affect landforms. Examples are when corals build a coral reef or when plants contribute to the development of a salt marsh or a sand dune. Rivers, coastlines, rock types, slope formation, ice, erosion, and weathering are all part of geomorphology.

A landform is a landscape feature or geomorphological unit. These include hills, plateaus, mountains, deserts, deltas, canyons, mesas, marshes, swamps, and valleys. These units are categorized according to elevation, slope, orientation, stratification, rock exposure, and soil type. Landform elements include pits, peaks, channels, ridges, passes, pools, and plains.

The highest order landforms are continents and oceans. Elementary landforms such as segments, facets, and relief units are the smallest homogenous divisions of a land surface at a given scale or resolution.

Oceans, seas, lakes, rivers, and canals

Oceans are the largest bodies of water on earth and cover nearly 71% of the earth's surface. There are five major oceans: Atlantic, Pacific (largest and deepest), Indian, Arctic, and Southern (surrounds Antarctica).

Seas are smaller than oceans and are somewhat surrounded by land like a lake, but lakes are fresh water and seas are salt water. Seas include the Mediterranean, Baltic, Caspian, Caribbean, and Coral.

Lakes are bodies of water in a depression on the earth's surface. Examples of lakes are the Great Lakes and Lake Victoria.

Rivers are a channeled flow of water that start out as a spring or stream formed by runoff from rain or snow. Rivers flow from higher to lower ground, and usually empty into a sea or ocean. Great rivers of the world include the Amazon, Nile, Rhine, Mississippi, Ganges, Mekong, and Yangtze.

Canals are artificial waterways constructed by humans to connect two larger water bodies. Examples of canals are the Panama and the Suez.

Mountains, hills, foothills, valleys, plateaus, and mesas

The definitions for these geographical features are as follows:
- Mountains are elevated landforms that rise fairly steeply from the earth's surface to a summit of at least 1,000-2,000 feet (definitions vary) above sea level.
- Hills are elevated landforms that rise 500-2,000 feet above sea level.
- Foothills are a low series of hills found between a plain and a mountain range.
- Valleys are a long depression located between hills or mountains. They are usually products of river erosion. Valleys can vary in terms of width and depth, ranging from a few feet to thousands of feet.
- Plateaus are elevated landforms that are fairly flat on top. They may be as high as 10,000 feet above sea level and are usually next to mountains.
- Mesas are flat areas of upland. Their name is derived from the Spanish word for table. They are smaller than plateaus and often found in arid or semi-arid areas.

Plains, deserts, deltas, and basins

Plains are extensive areas of low-lying, flat, or gently undulating land, and are usually lower than the landforms around them. Plains near the seacoast are called lowlands.

Deserts are large, dry areas that receive less than 10 inches of rain per year. They are almost barren, containing only a few patches of vegetation.

Deltas are accumulations of silt deposited at river mouths into the seabed. They are eventually converted into very fertile, stable ground by vegetation, becoming important crop-growing areas. Examples include the deltas of the Nile, Ganges, and Mississippi River.

Basins come in various types. They may be low areas that catch water from rivers; large hollows that dip to a central point and are surrounded by higher ground, as in the Donets and Kuznetsk basins in Russia; or areas of inland drainage in a desert when the water can't reach the sea and flows into lakes or evaporates in salt flats as a result. An example is the Great Salt Lake in Utah.

Marshes, swamps, tundra and taiga

Marshes and swamps are both wet lowlands. The water can be fresh, brackish, or saline. Both host important ecological systems with unique wildlife. There are, however, some major differences. Marshes have no trees and are always wet because of frequent floods and poor drainage that leaves shallow water. Plants are mostly grasses, rushes, reeds, typhas, sedges, and herbs. Swamps have trees and dry periods. The water is very slow-moving, and is usually associated with adjacent rivers or lakes.

Both taiga and tundra regions have many plants and animals, but they have few humans or crops because of their harsh climates. Taiga has colder winters and hotter summers than tundra because of its distance from the Arctic Ocean. Tundra is a Russian word describing marshy plain in an area that has a very cold climate but receives little snow. The ground is usually frozen, but is quite spongy when it is not. Taiga is the world's largest forest region, located just south of the tundra line. It contains huge mineral resources and fur-bearing animals.

Humid continental climate, prairie climate, subtropical climate, and marine climate

A humid continental climate is one that has four seasons, including a cold winter and a hot summer, and sufficient rainfall for raising crops. Such climates can be found in the United States, Canada, and Russia. The best farmlands and mining areas are found in these countries.

Prairie climates, or steppe regions, are found in the interiors of Asia and North America where there are dry flatlands (prairies that receive 10-20 inches of rain per year). These dry flatlands can be grasslands or deserts.

Subtropical climates are very humid areas in the tropical areas of Japan, China, Australia, Africa, South America, and the United States. The moisture, carried by winds traveling over warm ocean currents, produces long summers and mild winters. It is possible to produce a continuous cycle of a variety of crops.

A marine climate is one near or surrounded by water. Warm ocean winds bring moisture, mild temperatures year round, and plentiful rain. These climates are found in Western Europe and parts of the United States, Canada, Chile, New Zealand, and Australia.

Physical and cultural geography

Physical geography is the study of climate, water, and land and their relationships with each other and humans. Physical geography locates and identifies the earth's surface features and explores how humans thrive in various locations according to crop and goods production.

Cultural geography is the study of the influence of the environment on human behaviors as well as the effect of human activities such as farming, building settlements, and grazing livestock on the environment. Cultural geography also identifies and compares the features of different cultures and how they influence interactions with other cultures and the earth.

Physical location refers to the placement of the hemispheres and the continents.

Political location refers to the divisions within continents that designate various countries. These divisions are made with borders, which are set according to boundary lines arrived at by legal agreements.

Both physical and political locations can be precisely determined by geographical surveys and by latitude and longitude.

Natural resources, renewable resources, nonrenewable resources, and commodities

Natural resources are things provided by nature that have commercial value to humans, such as minerals, energy, timber, fish, wildlife, and the landscape. Renewable resources are those that can be replenished, such as wind, solar radiation, tides, and water (with proper conservation and clean-up). Soil is renewable with proper conservation and management techniques, and timber can be replenished with replanting. Living resources such as fish and wildlife can replenish themselves if they are not over-harvested.

Nonrenewable resources are those that cannot be replenished. These include fossil fuels such as oil and coal and metal ores. These cannot be replaced or reused once they have been burned, although some of their products can be recycled.

Commodities are natural resources that have to be extracted and purified rather than created, such as mineral ores.

Uses of geography

Geography involves learning about the world's primary physical and cultural patterns to help understand how the world functions as an interconnected and dynamic system. Combining information from different sources, geography teaches the basic patterns of climate, geology, vegetation, human settlement, migration, and commerce. Thus, geography is an interdisciplinary study of history, anthropology, and sociology. History incorporates geography in discussions of battle strategies, slavery (trade routes), ecological disasters (the Dust Bowl of the 1930s), and mass migrations. Geographic principles are useful when reading literature to help identify and visualize the setting, and also when studying earth science, mathematics (latitude, longitude, sun angle, and population statistics), and fine arts (song, art, and dance often reflect different cultures). Consequently, a good background in geography can help students succeed in other subjects as well.

Areas covered by geography

Geography is connected to many issues and provides answers to many everyday questions. Some of the areas covered by geography include:
- Geography investigates global climates, landforms, economies, political systems, human cultures, and migration patterns.
- Geography answers questions not only about where something is located, but also why it is there, how it got there, and how it is related to other things around it.
- Geography explains why people move to certain regions (climate, availability of natural resources, arable land, etc.).
- Geography explains world trade routes and modes of transportation.
- Geography identifies where various animals live and where various crops and forests grow.
- Geography identifies and locates populations that follow certain religions.
- Geography provides statistics on population numbers and growth, which aids in economic and infrastructure planning for cities and countries.

Globe and map projections

A globe is the only accurate representation of the earth's size, shape, distance, and direction since it, like the earth, is spherical. The flat surface of a map distorts these elements. To counter this problem, mapmakers use a variety of "map projections," a system for representing the earth's curvatures on a flat surface through the use of a grid that corresponds to lines of latitude and longitude. Some distortions are still inevitable, though, so mapmakers make choices based on the map scale, the size of the area to be mapped, and what they want the map to show. Some projections can represent a true shape or area, while others may be based on the equator and therefore become less accurate as they near the poles. In summary, all maps have some distortion in terms of the shape or size of features of the spherical earth.

Map projections

There are three main types of map projections:
- Conical projection superimposes a cone over the sphere of the earth, with two reference parallels secant to the globe and intersecting it. There is no distortion along the standard parallels, but distortion increases further from the chosen parallels. A Bonne projection is an example of a conical projection, in which the areas are accurately represented but the meridians are not on a true scale.
- Cylindrical any projection in which meridians are mapped using equally spaced vertical lines and circles of latitude (parallels) are mapped using horizontal lines. A Mercator's projection is a modified cylindrical projection that is helpful to navigators because it allows them to maintain a constant compass direction between two points. However, it exaggerates areas in high latitudes.
- Azimuthal is a stereographic projection onto a plane so centered at any given point that a straight line radiating from the center to any other point represents the shortest distance. This distance can be measured to scale.

National Geographic Bee

Organizing place names into categories of physical features helps students learn the type of information they need to know to compete in the National Geographic Bee. The physical features students need to be knowledgeable about are:
- The continents (Although everyone has been taught that there are seven continents, some geographers combine Europe and Asia into a single continent called Eurasia.)
- The four major oceans
- The highest and lowest points on each continent (Mt. Everest is the highest point in the world; the Dead Sea is the lowest point.)
- The 10 largest seas (The Coral Sea is the largest.)
- The 10 largest lakes (The Caspian Sea is actually the largest lake.)
- The 10 largest islands (Greenland is the largest island.)
- The longest rivers (The Nile is the longest river.)

- Major mountain ranges
- Earth's extremes such as the hottest (Ethiopia), the coldest (Antarctica), the wettest (India), and the driest (Atacama Desert) places; the highest waterfall (Angel Falls); the largest desert (Sahara); the largest canyon (Grand Canyon); the longest reef (Great Barrier Reef); and the highest tides.

Sumer, Egypt, and the Indus Valley

These three ancient civilizations are distinguished by their unique contributions to the development of world civilization.

Sumer used the first known writing system, which enabled the Sumerians to leave a sizeable written record of their myths and religion; advanced the development of the wheel and irrigation; and urbanized their culture with a cluster of cities.

Egypt was united by the Nile River. Egyptians originally settled in villages on its banks; had a national religion that held their pharaohs as gods; had a central government that controlled civil and artistic affairs; and had writing and libraries.

The Indus Valley was also called Harappan after the city of Harappa. This civilization started in the 3rd and 4th centuries BC and was widely dispersed over 400,000 square miles. It had a unified culture of luxury and refinement, no known national government, an advanced civic system, and prosperous trade routes.

Early empires

The common traits of these empires were: a strong military; a centralized government; control and standardization of commerce, money, and taxes; a weight system; and an official language.

Mesopotamia had a series of short-term empires that failed because of their oppression of subject peoples.

Egypt also had a series of governments after extending its territory beyond the Nile area. Compared to Mesopotamia, these were more stable and long-lived because they blended different peoples to create a single national identity.

Greece started as a group of city-states that were united by Alexander the Great and joined to create an empire that stretched from the Indus River to Egypt and the Mediterranean coast. Greece blended Greek values with those of the local cultures, which collectively became known as Hellenistic society.

Rome was an Italian city-state that grew into an empire extending from the British Isles across Europe to the Middle East. It lasted for 1,000 years and became the foundation of the Western world's culture, language, and laws.

Deities of Greek and Roman mythology

The major gods of the Greek/Roman mythological system are:
- Zeus/Jupiter – Head of the Pantheon, god of the sky
- Hera/Juno – Wife of Zeus/Jupiter, goddess of marriage
- Poseidon/Neptune – God of the seas
- Demeter/Ceres – Goddess of grain
- Apollo – God of the sun, law, music, archery, healing, and truth
- Artemis/Diana – Goddess of the moon, wild creatures, and hunting
- Athena/Minerva – Goddess of civilized life, handicrafts, and agriculture
- Hephaestus/Vulcan – God of fire, blacksmith
- Aphrodite/Venus – Goddess of love and beauty
- Ares/Mars – God of war
- Dionysus/Bacchus – God of wine and vegetation
- Hades/Pluto – God of the underworld and the dead
- Eros/Cupid – Minor god of love
- Hestia/Vesta – Goddess of the hearth or home
- Hermes/Mercury – Minor god of gracefulness and swiftness

Chinese and Indian empires

While the Chinese had the world's longest lasting and continuous empires, the Indians had more of a cohesive culture than an empire system. Their distinct characteristics are as follows:
- China – Since the end of the Warring States period in 221 BC, China has functioned as an empire. Although the dynasties changed several times, the basic governmental structure remained the same into the 20th century. The Chinese also have an extensive written record of their culture which heavily emphasizes history, philosophy, and a common religion.
- India – The subcontinent was seldom unified in terms of government until the British empire controlled the area in the 19th and 20th centuries. In terms of culture, India has had persistent institutions and religions that have loosely united the people, such as the caste system and guilds. These have regulated daily life more than any government.

Middle Ages

The Middle Ages, or Medieval times, was a period that ran from approximately 500-1500 AD. During this time, the centers of European civilization moved from the Mediterranean countries to France, Germany, and England, where strong national governments were developing. Key events of this time include:
- Roman Catholicism was the cultural and religious center of medieval life, extending into politics and economics.
- Knights, with their systems of honor, combat, and chivalry, were loyal to their king. Peasants, or serfs, served a particular lord and his lands.
- Many universities were established that still function in modern times.
- The Crusades, the recurring wars between European Christians and Middle East Muslims, raged over the Holy Lands.

- One of the legendary leaders was Charles the Great, or Charlemagne, who created an empire across France and Germany around 800 AD.
- The Black Death plague swept across Europe from 1347-1350, leaving between one third and one half of the population dead.

Protestant Reformation

The dominance of the Catholic Church during the Middle Ages in Europe gave it immense power, which encouraged corrupt practices such as the selling of indulgences and clerical positions. The Protestant Reformation began as an attempt to reform the Catholic Church, but eventually led to the separation from it. In 1517, Martin Luther posted his *Ninety-Five Theses* on the door of a church in Saxony, which criticized unethical practices, various doctrines, and the authority of the pope. Other reformers such as John Calvin and John Wesley soon followed, but disagreed among themselves and divided along doctrinal lines. Consequently, the Lutheran, Reformed, Calvinist, and Presbyterian churches were founded, among others. In England, King Henry VIII was denied a divorce by the pope, so he broke away and established the Anglican Church. The Protestant reformation caused the Catholic Church to finally reform itself, but the Protestant movement continued, resulting in a proliferation of new denominations.

Renaissance

Renaissance is the French word for rebirth, and is used to describe the renewal of interest in ancient Greek and Latin art, literature, and philosophy that occurred in Europe, especially Italy, from the 14th through the 16th centuries. Historically, it was also a time of great scientific inquiry, the rise of individualism, extensive geographical exploration, and the rise of secular values.
Notable figures of the Renaissance include:
- Petrarch – An Italian scholar, writer, and key figure in northern Italy, which is where the Renaissance started and where chief patrons came from the merchant class
- Leonardo da Vinci – Artist and inventor
- Michelangelo and Raphael – Artists
- Desiderius Erasmus – Applied historical scholarship to the New Testament and laid the seeds for the Protestant Reformation
- Sir Thomas More – A lawyer and author who wrote *Utopia*
- Nicolò Machiavelli – Author of *Prince and Discourses*, which proposed a science of human nature and civil life
- William Shakespeare – A renowned playwright and poet

Industrial Revolution

The Industrial Revolution started in England with the construction of the first cotton mill in 1733. Other inventions and factories followed in rapid succession. The steel industry grew exponentially when it was realized that cheap, abundant English coal could be used instead of wood for melting metals. The steam engine, which revolutionized transportation and work power, came next. Around 1830, a factory-based, technological era was ushered into the rest of Europe. Society changed from agrarian to urban. A need for cheap, unskilled labor resulted in the extensive employment and abuse of women and children, who worked up to 14 hours a day, six days a week in deplorable conditions. Expanding populations brought crowded, unsanitary conditions to the cities, and the factories created air and water pollution. Societies had to deal with these new situations by enacting child labor laws and creating labor unions to protect the safety of workers.

Cross-cultural comparisons

It is important to make cross-cultural comparisons when studying world history so that the subject is holistic and not oriented to just Western civilization. Not only are the contributions of civilizations around the world important, but they are also interesting and more representative of the mix of cultures present in the United States. It is also critical to the understanding of world relations to study the involvement of European countries and the United States in international commerce, colonization, and development. Trade routes from ancient times linked Africa, Asia, and Europe, resulting in exchanges and migrations of people, philosophies, and religions, as well as goods. While many civilizations in the Americas thrived and some became very sophisticated, many eventually became disastrously entangled in European expansion. The historic isolation of China and the modern industrialization of Japan have had huge impacts on relations with the rest of the world. The more students understand this history and its effects on the modern world, the better they will able to function in their own spheres.

French explorers in the United States

The French never succeeded in attracting settlers to their territories. Those who came were more interested in the fur and fish trades than in forming colonies. Eventually, the French ceded their southern possessions and New Orleans, founded in 1718, to Spain. However, the French made major contributions to the exploration of the new continent, including:
- Giovanni da Verrazano and Jacques Cartier explored the North American coast and the St. Lawrence Seaway for France.
- Samuel de Champlain, who founded Quebec and set up a fur empire on the St. Lawrence Seaway, also explored the coasts of Massachusetts and Rhode Island between 1604 and 1607.
- Fr. Jacques Marquette, a Jesuit missionary, and Louis Joliet were the first Europeans to travel down the Mississippi in 1673.
- Rene-Robert de la Salle explored the Great Lakes and the Illinois and Mississippi Rivers from 1679-1682, claiming all the land from the Great Lakes to the Gulf of Mexico and from the Appalachians to the Rockies for France.

Spanish explorers in the United States

The Spanish claimed and explored huge portions of the United States after the voyages of Christopher Columbus. Among them were:
- Juan Ponce de Leon – In 1513, he became the first European in Florida; established the oldest European settlement in Puerto Rico; discovered the Gulf Stream; and searched for the fountain of youth.
- Alonso Alvarez de Pineda – He charted the Gulf Coast from Florida to Mexico in 1519. Probably the first European in Texas, he claimed it for Spain.
- Panfilo de Narvaez – He docked in Tampa Bay with Cabeza de Vaca in 1528, claimed Florida for Spain, and then sailed the Gulf Coast.

- Alvar Nuñez Cabeza de Vaca – He got lost on foot in Texas and New Mexico. Estevanico, or Esteban, a Moorish slave, was a companion who guided them to Mexico.
- Francisco Vásquez de Coronado – While searching for gold in 1540, he became the first European to explore Kansas, Oklahoma, Texas, New Mexico, and Arizona.
- Hernando De Soto – He was the first European to explore the southeastern United States from Tallahassee to Natchez.

Colonization of Virginia

In 1585, Sir Walter Raleigh landed on Roanoke Island and sent Arthur Barlow to the mainland, which they named Virginia. Two attempts to establish settlements failed. The first permanent English colony was founded by Captain John Smith in Jamestown in 1607.

The Virginia Company and the Chesapeake Bay Company successfully colonized other Virginia sites. By 1619, Virginia had a House of Burgesses. The crown was indifferent to the colony, so local government grew strong and tobacco created wealth. The First Families of Virginia dominated politics there for two centuries, and four of the first five United States presidents came from these families.

The Virginia Company sent 24 Puritan families, known as Pilgrims, to Virginia on the Mayflower. In 1620, it landed at Plymouth, Massachusetts instead. The Plymouth Plantation was established and survived with the help of natives. This is where the first Thanksgiving is believed to have occurred.

Colonization efforts in Massachusetts, Maryland, Rhode Island, and Pennsylvania

In 1629, 400 Puritans arrived in Salem, which became an important port and was made famous by the witch trials in 1692.

In 1628, the self-governed Massachusetts Bay Company was organized, and the Massachusetts Indians sold most of the land to the English. Boston was established in 1630 and Harvard University was established in 1636.

Maryland was established by Lord Baltimore in 1632 in the hopes of providing refuge for English Catholics. The Protestant majority, however, opposed this religious tolerance.

Roger Williams was banished from Massachusetts in 1636 because he called for separation of church and state. He established the Rhode Island colony in 1647 and had 800 settlers by 1650, including Anne Hutchinson and her "Antinomians," who attacked clerical authority.

In 1681, William Penn received a royal charter for the establishment of Pennsylvania as a colony for Quakers. However, religious tolerance allowed immigrants from a mixed group of denominations, who prospered from the beginning.

American Revolution

The English colonies rebelled for the following reasons:
- England was remote yet controlling. By 1775, few Americans had ever been to England. They considered themselves Americans, not English.
- During the Seven Years' War (aka French and Indian War) from 1754-1763, Americans, including George Washington, served in the British army, but were treated as inferiors.
- It was feared that the Anglican Church might try to expand in the colonies and inhibit religious freedom.
- Heavy taxation such as the Sugar and Stamp Acts, which were created solely to create revenue for the crown, and business controls such as restricting trade of certain products to England only, were burdensome.
- The colonies had no official representation in the English Parliament and wanted to govern themselves.
- There were fears that Britain would block westward expansion and independent enterprise.
- Local government, established through elections by property holders, was already functioning.

Important events leading up to the American Revolution

Over several years, various events and groups contributed to the rebellion that became a revolution:
- Sons of Liberty – This was the protest group headed by Samuel Adams that incited the Revolution.
- Boston Massacre – On March 5, 1770, soldiers fired on a crowd and killed five people.
- Committees of Correspondence – These were set up throughout the colonies to transmit revolutionary ideas and create a unified response.
- The Boston Tea Party – On December 6, 1773, the Sons of Liberty, dressed as Mohawks, dumped tea into the harbor from a British ship to protest the tea tax. The harsh British response further aggravated the situation.
- First Continental Congress – This was held in 1774 to list grievances and develop a response, including boycotts. It was attended by all the colonies with the exception of Georgia.
- The Shot Heard Round the World – In April, 1775, English soldiers on their way to confiscate arms in Concord passed through Lexington, Massachusetts and met the colonial militia called the Minutemen. A fight ensued. In Concord, a larger group of Minutemen forced the British to retreat.

Major turning points of the Revolution

The original 13 colonies were: Connecticut, Delaware, Georgia, Maryland, Massachusetts, New Hampshire, New Jersey, New York, North Carolina, Pennsylvania, Rhode Island, South Carolina, and Virginia. Delaware was the first state to ratify the constitution.
The major turning points of the American Revolution were:

- The actions of the Second Continental Congress – This body established the Continental Army and chose George Washington as its commanding general. They allowed printing of money and created government offices.
- "Common Sense" – Published in 1776 by Thomas Paine, this pamphlet calling for independence was widely distributed.
- The Declaration of Independence – Written by Thomas Jefferson, it was signed on July 4, 1776 by the Continental Congress assembled in Philadelphia.
- Alliance with France – Benjamin Franklin negotiated an agreement with France to fight with the Americans in 1778.
- Treaty of Paris – In 1782, it signaled the official end of the war, granted independence to the colonies, and gave them generous territorial rights.

Articles of Confederation and the Constitution

The Articles of Confederation, designed to protect states' rights over those of the national government and sent to the colonies for ratification in 1777, had two major elements that proved unworkable. First, there was no centralized national government. Second, there was no centralized power to tax or regulate trade with other nations or between states. With no national tax, the Revolution was financed by printing more and more money, which caused inflation.

In 1787, a convention was called to write a new constitution. This constitution created the three branches of government with checks and balances of power: executive, legislative, and judicial. It also created a bicameral legislature so that there would be equal representation for the states in the Senate and representation for the population in the House.

Those who opposed the new constitution, the Anti-Federalists, wanted a bill of rights included. The Federalist platform was explained in the "Federalist Papers," written by James Madison, John Jay, and Alexander Hamilton.

The Constitution went into effect in 1789, and the Bill of Rights was added in 1791.

Louisiana Purchase

The Louisiana Purchase in 1803 for $15 million may be considered Thomas Jefferson's greatest achievement as president. The reasons for the purchase were to gain the vital port of New Orleans, remove the threat of French interference with trade along the Mississippi River, and double the territory of the United States. The purchase both answered and raised new questions about the use of federal power, including the constitutionality of the president making such a purchase, Jefferson asking Congress for permission, and Jefferson taking the biggest federalist action up to that time, even though he was an anti-federalist.

Jefferson sent Meriwether Lewis and William Clark to map the new territory and find a means of passage all the way to the Pacific Ocean. Although there was no river that flowed all the way west, their expedition and the richness of the land and game started the great western migration of settlers.

War of 1812

A war between France and Britain caused blockades that hurt American trade and caused the British to attack American ships and impress sailors on them. An embargo against France and Britain was imposed by Jefferson, but rescinded by Madison with a renewed demand for respect for American sovereignty. However, Britain became more aggressive and war resulted. Native Americans under the leadership of Tecumseh sided with the British. The British captured Washington, D.C., and burned the White House, but Dolly Madison had enough forethought to save priceless American treasures, such as the Gilbert Stuart portrait of George Washington. Most battles, however, came to a draw. As a result, in 1815, when the British ended the war with France, they negotiated for peace with the United States as well under the Treaty of Ghent. A benefit of the war was that it motivated Americans to become more self-sufficient due to increased manufacturing and fewer imports.

Monroe Doctrine, Manifest Destiny, and Missouri Compromise

Three important political actions in the 19th century were:
- The Monroe Doctrine – Conceived by President James Monroe in 1823, this foreign policy warned European powers to cease colonization of Central and South America or face military intervention by the United States. In return, the United States would not meddle in the political affairs or standing colonies of Europe.
- The Missouri Compromise – In 1820, there were 11 free states and 11 slave states. The fear of a power imbalance between slave and free states when Missouri petitioned to become a slave state brought about this agreement. Maine was brought in as a free state; the southern border of Missouri was set as the northernmost line of any slave territory; and the western states could come in as free states, while Arkansas and Florida could be slave states.
- Manifest Destiny – This was a popular belief during the 1840s that it was the right and duty of the United States to expand westward to the Pacific. The idea became a slogan for the flood of settlers and expansionist power grabs.

Andrew Jackson

A number of important milestones occurred in American history during the presidency of Andrew Jackson. They included:
- Jackson's election is considered the beginning of the modern political party system and the start of the Democratic Party.
- Jeffersonian Democracy, a system governed by middle and upper class educated property holders, was replaced by Jacksonian Democracy, a system that allowed universal white male suffrage.
- The Indian Removal Act of 1830 took natives out of territories that whites wanted to settle, most notably the Trail of Tears that removed Cherokees from Georgia and relocated them to Oklahoma.
- The issue of nullification, the right of states to nullify any federal laws they thought unconstitutional, came to a head over tariffs. However, a strong majority vote in

Congress supporting the Tariff Acts cemented the policy that states must comply with federal laws.

Whig Party

The Whig Party existed from 1833 to 1856. It started in opposition to Jackson's authoritarian policies, and was particularly concerned with defending the supremacy of Congress over the executive branch, states' rights, economic protectionism, and modernization. Notable members included: Daniel Webster, Henry Clay, Winfield Scott, and a young Abraham Lincoln. The Whigs had four presidents: William Henry Harrison, Zachary Taylor, John Tyler (expelled from the party), and Millard Fillmore. However, the Whigs won only two presidential elections. Harrison and Taylor were elected in 1840 and 1848, respectively. However, both died in office, so Tyler and Fillmore assumed the presidency. In 1852, the anti-slavery faction of the party kept Fillmore from getting the nomination. Instead, it went to Scott, who was soundly defeated. In 1856, the Whigs supported Fillmore and the National American Party, but lost badly. Thereafter, the split over slavery caused the party to dissolve.

Important 19th century American writers

In the 19th century, American literature became an entity of its own and provided a distinct voice for the American experience. Some of the great writers from this time period were:

James Fenimore Cooper
He was the first to write about Native Americans, and was the author of the Leatherstocking series, which includes *The Last of the Mohicans* and *The Deerslayer*.

Ralph Waldo Emerson
He was an essayist, philosopher, and poet, and also the leader of the Transcendentalist movement. His notable works include "Self-Reliance" and "The American Scholar."

Nathaniel Hawthorne
This novelist and short story writer wrote *The Scarlet Letter*, *The House of Seven Gables*, "Young Goodman Brown," and "The Minister's Black Veil."

Herman Melville
He was a novelist, essayist, short story writer, and poet who wrote *Moby Dick, Billy Budd*, and "Bartleby the Scrivener."

Edgar Allan Poe
He was a poet, literary critic, and master of the short story, especially horror and detective stories. His notable works include "The Tell-Tale Heart," "The Pit and the Pendulum," "Annabel Lee," and "The Raven."

Harriet Beecher Stowe
She was an abolitionist and the author of *Uncle Tom's Cabin*.

Henry David Thoreau
He was a poet, naturalist, and Transcendentalist who wrote *Walden* and *Civil Disobedience*.

Walt Whitman
He was a poet, essayist, and journalist who wrote *Leaves of Grass* and "O Captain! My Captain!"

Important 19th Century social and religious leaders

Some of the important social and religious leaders from the 19th century were:

Susan B. Anthony
A women's rights and abolition activist, she lectured across the nation for suffrage, property and wage rights, and labor organizations for women.

Dorothea Dix
She created the first American asylums for the treatment of mental illness and served as the Superintendent of Army Nurses during the War Between the States.

Frederick Douglass
He was an escaped slave who became an abolitionist leader, government official, and writer.

William Lloyd Garrison
He was an abolitionist and the editor of the *Liberator*, the leading anti-slavery newspaper of the time.

Joseph Smith
He founded the Latter Day Saints in 1827 and wrote the Book of Mormon.

Horace Mann
He was a leader of the common school movement that made public education a right of all Americans.

Elizabeth Cady Stanton
With Lucretia Mott, she held the Seneca Falls Convention in 1848, demanding women's suffrage and other reforms. From the 1850s onward, she worked with Susan B. Anthony.

Brigham Young
He was the leader of the Mormons when they fled religious persecution, built Salt Lake City, and settled much of the West. He was the first governor of the Utah Territory.

Compromise of 1850, Fugitive Slave Law, Kansas-Nebraska Act, Bleeding Kansas, and the Dred Scott Case

The Compromise of 1850, calling upon the principle of popular sovereignty, allowed those who lived in the Mexican cession to decide for themselves whether to be a free or slave territory.

The Fugitive Slave Law of 1850 allowed slave owners to go into free states to retrieve their escaped slaves.

The Kansas-Nebraska Act of 1854 repealed the Missouri Compromise of 1820 to allow the lands from the Louisiana Purchase to settle the slavery issue by popular sovereignty. Outraged Northerners responded by defecting from the Whig Party and starting the Republican Party.

Bleeding Kansas was the name applied to the state when a civil war broke out between pro- and anti-slavery advocates while Kansas was trying to formalize its statutes before being admitted as a state.

The Dred Scott vs. Sandford case was decided by the Supreme Court in 1857. It was ruled that Congress had no authority to exclude slavery from the territories, which in effect meant that the Missouri Compromise had been unconstitutional.

Confederate States and Civil War leaders

The states that seceded from the Union to form the Confederacy were: South Carolina, North Carolina, Virginia, Florida, Mississippi, Alabama, Louisiana, Texas, and Tennessee. The slave-holding states that were kept in the Union were Delaware, Maryland, Kentucky, and Missouri.

Jefferson Davis of Mississippi, a former U. S. senator and cabinet member, was the president of the Confederacy.

Abraham Lincoln of Illinois was the President of the United States. His election triggered the secession of the south. He was assassinated shortly after winning a second term.

Robert E. Lee of Virginia was offered the position of commanding general of the Union Army, but declined because of loyalty to his home state. He led the Army of Northern Virginia and the central Confederate force, and is still considered a military mastermind.

Ulysses S. Grant of Ohio wasn't appointed to command the Union Army until 1864, after a series of other commanders were unsuccessful. He received Lee's surrender at the Appomattox Court House in Virginia in April, 1865, and went on to become President from 1869 to 1877.

Reconstruction

Reconstruction was the period from 1865 to 1877, during which the South was under strict control of the U.S. government. In March, 1867, all state governments of the former Confederacy were terminated, and military occupation began. Military commanders called for constitutional conventions to reconstruct the state governments, to which delegates were to be elected by universal male suffrage. After a state government was in operation and the state had ratified the 14th Amendment, its representatives were admitted to Congress. Three constitutional amendments from 1865 to 1870, which tried to rectify the problems caused by slavery, became part of the Reconstruction effort.

The 13th Amendment declared slavery illegal.

The 14th Amendment made all persons born or naturalized in the country U.S. citizens, and forbade any state to interfere with their fundamental civil rights.

The 15th Amendment made it illegal to deny individuals the right to vote on the grounds of race.

In his 1876 election campaign, President Rutherford B. Hayes promised to withdraw the troops, and did so in 1877.

Industrial changes

Important events during this time of enormous business growth and large-scale exploitation of natural resources were:
- Industrialization – Like the rest of the world, the United States' entry into the Industrial Age was marked by many new inventions and the mechanization of factories.
- Railroad expansion – The Transcontinental Railroad was built from 1865 to 1969. Railroad tracks stretched over 35,000 miles in 1865, but that distance reached 240,000 miles by 1910. The raw materials and manufactured goods needed for the railroads kept mines and factories very busy.
- Gold and silver mining – Mines brought many prospectors to the West from 1850 to about 1875, but mining corporations soon took over.
- Cattle ranching – This was a large-scale enterprise beginning in the late 1860s, but by the 1880s open ranges were being fenced and plowed for farming and pastures. Millions of farmers moved into the high plains, establishing the "Bread Basket," which was the major wheat growing area of the country.

Gilded Age

The Gilded Age, from the 1870s to 1890, was so named because of the enormous wealth and grossly opulent lifestyle enjoyed by a handful of powerful families. This was the time when huge mansions were built as summer "cottages" in Newport, Rhode Island, and great lodges were built in mountain areas for the pleasure of families such as the Vanderbilts, Ascots, and Rockefellers.

Control of the major industries was held largely by the following men, who were known as Robber Barons for their ruthless business practices and exploitation of workers: Jay Gould, railroads; Andrew Carnegie, steel; John D. Rockefeller, Sr., oil; Philip Danforth Armour, meatpacking; J. P. Morgan, banking; John Jacob Astor, fur pelts; and Cornelius Vanderbilt, steamboat shipping.

Of course, all of these heads of industry diversified and became involved in multiple business ventures. To curb cutthroat competition, particularly among the railroads, and to prohibit restrained trade, Congress created the Interstate Commerce Commission and the Sherman Anti-Trust Act. Neither of these, however, was enforced.

19th Century immigration trends

The population of the United States doubled between 1860 and 1890, the period that saw 10 million immigrants arrive. Most lived in the north. Cities and their slums grew tremendously because of immigration and industrialization. While previous immigrants had come from Germany, Scandinavia, and Ireland, the 1880s saw a new wave of immigrants from Italy, Poland, Hungary, Bohemia, and Greece, as well as Jewish groups from central and eastern Europe, especially Russia. The Roman Catholic population grew from 1.6 million in 1850 to 12 million in 1900, a growth that ignited an anti-Catholic backlash from the anti-Catholic Know-Nothing Party of the 1880s and the Ku Klux Klan.

Exploited immigrant workers started labor protests in the 1870s, and the Knights of Labor was formed in 1878, calling for sweeping social and economic reform. Its membership reached 700,000 by 1886. Eventually, this organization was replaced by the American Federation of Labor, headed by Samuel Gompers.

Progressive Movement

The Progressive Era, which was the time period from the 1890s to the 1920s, got its name from progressive, reform-minded political leaders who wanted to export a just and rational social order to the rest of the world while increasing trade with foreign markets. Consequently, the United States interfered in a dispute between Venezuela and Britain. America invoked the Monroe Doctrine and sided with Cuba in its independence struggle against Spain. The latter resulted in the Spanish-American Wars in 1898 that ended with Cuba, Puerto Rico, the Philippines, and Guam becoming American protectorates at the same time the United States annexed Hawaii. In 1900, America declared an Open Door policy with China to support its independence and open markets. In 1903, Theodore Roosevelt helped Panama become independent of Columbia, and then secured the right to build the Panama Canal. Roosevelt also negotiated the peace treaty to end the Russo-Japanese War, which earned him the Nobel Peace prize. He then sent the American fleet on a world cruise to display his country's power.

Age of Reform

To the Progressives, promoting law and order meant cleaning up city governments to make them honest and efficient, bringing more democracy and humanity to state governments, and establishing a core of social workers to improve slum housing, health, and education. Also during the Progressive Era, the national government strengthened or created the following regulatory agencies, services, and acts to oversee business enterprise.

Passed in 1906, the Hepburn Act reinforced the Interstate Commerce Commission. In 1902, Roosevelt used the Justice Department and lawsuits to try to break monopolies and enforce the Sherman Anti-Trust Act. The Clayton Anti-Trust Act was added in 1914.

From 1898 to 1910, the Forest Service guided lumber companies in the conservation and more efficient use of woodland resources under the direction of Gifford Pinchot.

In 1906, the Pure Food and Drug Act was passed to protect consumers from fraudulent labeling and adulteration of products.

In 1913, the Federal Reserve System was established to supervise banking and commerce. In 1914, the Fair Trade Commission was established to ensure fair competition.

Decade of Optimism

After World War I, Warren Harding ran for President on the slogan "return to normalcy" and concentrated on domestic affairs. The public felt optimistic because life improved due to affordable automobiles from Henry Ford's mass production system, better roads, electric lights, airplanes, new communication systems, and voting rights for women (19th Amendment, 1920). Radio and movies helped develop a national culture. For the first time, the majority of Americans lived in cities. Young people shortened dresses and haircuts, and smoked and drank in public despite Prohibition (18th Amendment, 1919).

Meantime, the Russian Revolution caused a Red Scare that strengthened the already strong Ku Klux Klan that controlled some states' politics. In 1925, the Scopes trial in Tennessee convicted a high school teacher for presenting Darwinian theories. The Teapot Dome scandal rocked the Harding administration. After Harding died in 1923, Calvin Coolidge became president. He was followed by Herbert Hoover, a strong proponent of capitalism under whom unregulated business led to the 1929 stock crash.

Great Depression

In the 1920s, the rich got richer. After World War I, however, farmers were in a depression when foreign markets started growing their own crops again. Increased credit buying, bank war debts, a huge gap between rich and poor, and a belief that the stock market would always go up got the nation into financial trouble. The Stock Market Crash in October, 1929 that destroyed fortunes dramatized the downward spiral of the whole economy. Banks failed, and customers lost all their money. By 1933, 14 million were unemployed, industrial production was down to one-third of its 1929 level, and national income had dropped by half.

Adding to the misery of farmers, years of breaking sod on the prairies without adequate conservation techniques caused the topsoil to fly away in great dust storms that blackened skies for years, causing deaths from lung disease and failed crops.

World Wars

World War I, which began in 1914, was fought by the Allies Britain, France, Russia, Greece, Italy, Romania, and Serbia. They fought against the Central Powers of Germany, Austria-Hungary, Bulgaria, and Turkey. In 1917, the United States joined the Allies, and Russia withdrew to pursue its own revolution. World War I ended in 1918.

World War II was truly a world war, with fighting occurring on nearly every continent. Germany occupied most of Europe and Northern Africa. It was opposed by the countries of the British Empire, free France and its colonies, Russia, and various national resistance forces. Japan, an Axis ally of Germany, had been forcefully expanding its territories in Korea, China, Indonesia, the Philippines, and the South Pacific for many years. When Japan attacked Pearl Harbor in 1941, the United States joined the Allied effort. Italy changed from the Axis to the Allied side mid-war after deposing its own dictator. The war ended in Europe in April, 1945, and in Japan in August, 1945.

World War I

When World War I broke out in 1914, America declared neutrality. The huge demand for war goods by the Allies broke a seven-year industrial stagnation and gave American factories full-time work. The country's sympathies lay mostly with the Allies, and before long American business and banking were heavily invested in an Allied victory. In 1916, Woodrow Wilson campaigned on the slogan "He kept us out of war." However, when the British ship the Lusitania was torpedoed in 1915 by a German submarine and many Americans were killed, Wilson had already warned the Germans that the United States would enter the war if Germany interfered with neutral ships at sea. Eventually, when it was proven that Germany was trying to incite Mexico and Japan into attacking the United States, Wilson declared war in 1917, even though America was unprepared. Nonetheless, America quickly armed and transferred sufficient troops to Europe, bringing the Allies to victory in 1918.

World War II

World War II began in 1939. As with World War I, the United States tried to stay out of World War II, even though the Lend-Lease program transferred munitions to Great Britain. However, on December 7, 1941, Japan attacked Pearl Harbor in Hawaii. Since Japan was an ally of Germany, the United States declared war on all the Axis powers. Although there was fighting in both Europe and the Pacific, the decision was made to concentrate on defeating Hitler first. Since it did not have combat within its borders, the United States became the great manufacturer of goods and munitions for the war effort. Women went to work in the factories, while the men entered the military. All facets of American life were centered on the war effort, including rationing, metal collections, and buying war bonds. The benefit of this production was an end to the economic depression. The influx of American personnel and supplies eventually brought victory in Europe in April of 1945, and in Asia the following August.

Cold War

After World War II, the Soviet Union kept control of Eastern Europe, including half of Germany. Communism spread around the world. Resulting fears led to:

- The Truman Doctrine (1947) – This was a policy designed to protect free peoples everywhere against oppression.
- The Marshall Plan (1948) – This devoted $12 billion to rebuild Western Europe and strengthen its defenses.
- The Organization of American States (1948) – This was established to bolster democratic relations in the Americas.
- The Berlin Blockade (1948-49) – The Soviets tried to starve out West Berlin, so the United States provided massive supply drops by air.
- The North Atlantic Treaty Organization (1949) – This was formed to militarily link the United States and western Europe so that an attack on one was an attack on both.

- The Korean War (1950-53) – This divided the country into the communist North and the democratic South.
- The McCarthy era (1950-54) – Senator Joseph McCarthy of Wisconsin held hearings on supposed Communist conspiracies that ruined innocent reputations and led to the blacklisting of suspected sympathizers in the government, Hollywood, and the media.

1960s

The 1960s were a tumultuous time for the United States. Major events included:
- The Cuban Missile Crisis (1961) – This was a stand-off between the United States and the Soviet Union over a build-up of missiles in Cuba. Eventually, the Soviets stopped their shipments and a nuclear war was averted.
- The assassinations of President Kennedy (1963), Senator Robert Kennedy (1968), and Dr. Martin Luther King, Jr. (1968).
- The Civil Rights Movement – Protest marches were held across the nation to draw attention to the plight of black citizens. From 1964 to 1968, race riots exploded in more than 100 cities.
- The Vietnam War (1964-73) – This resulted in a military draft. There was heavy involvement of American personnel and money. There were also protest demonstrations, particularly on college campuses. At Kent State, several students died after being shot by National Guardsmen.

Major legislation – Legislation passed during this decade included the Civil Rights Act, the Clean Air Act, and the Water Quality Act. This decade also saw the creation of the Peace Corps, Medicare, and the War on Poverty, in which billions were appropriated for education, urban redevelopment, and public housing.

Two presidents and two vice presidents

In a two-year time span, the United States had two presidents and two vice presidents. This situation resulted first from the resignation of Vice President Spiro T. Agnew in October of 1973 because of alleged kickbacks. President Richard M. Nixon then appointed House Minority Leader Gerald R. Ford to be vice president. This was accomplished through Senate ratification, a process that had been devised after Harry Truman succeeded to the presidency upon the death of Franklin Roosevelt and went through nearly four years of his presidency without a vice president. Nixon resigned the presidency in August of 1974 because some Republican party members broke into Democratic headquarters at the Watergate building in Washington, DC, and the president participated in covering up the crime. Ford succeeded Nixon, and had to appoint another vice president. He chose Nelson Rockefeller, former governor of New York.

Six basic principles of the Constitution

The six basic principles of the Constitution are:
- Popular Sovereignty – The people establish government and give power to it; the government can function only with the consent of the people.
- Limited Government – The Constitution specifies limits on government authority, and no official or entity is above the law.

- Separation of Powers – Power is divided among three government branches: the legislative (Congress), the executive (President), and the judicial (federal courts).
- Checks and Balances – This is a system that enforces the separation of powers and ensures that each branch has the authority and ability to restrain the powers of the other two branches, thus preventing tyranny.
- Judicial Review – Judges in the federal courts ensure that no act of government is in violation of the Constitution. If an act is unconstitutional, the judicial branch has the power to nullify it.
- Federalism – This is the division of power between the central government and local governments, which limits the power of the federal government and allows states to deal with local problems.

Classic forms of government

Forms of government that have appeared throughout history include:
- Feudalism – This is based on the rule of local lords who are loyal to the king and control the lives and production of those who work on their land.
- Classical republic – This form is a representative democracy. Small groups of elected leaders represent the interests of the electorate.
- Absolute monarchy – A king or queen has complete control of the military and government.
- Authoritarianism – An individual or group has unlimited authority. There is no system in place to restrain the power of the government.
- Dictatorship – Those in power are not held responsible to the people.
- Autocracy – This is rule by one person (despot), not necessarily a monarch, who uses power tyrannically.
- Oligarchy – A small, usually self-appointed elite rules a region.
- Liberal democracy – This is a government based on the consent of the people that protects individual rights and freedoms from any intolerance by the majority.
- Totalitarianism – All facets of the citizens' lives are controlled by the government.

Bill of Rights

The United States Bill of Rights was based on principles established by the Magna Carta in 1215, the 1688 English Bill of Rights, and the 1776 Virginia Bill of Rights. In 1791, the federal government added 10 amendments to the United States Constitution that provided the following protections:
- Freedom of speech, religion, peaceful assembly, petition of the government, and petition of the press
- The right to keep and bear arms
- No quartering of soldiers on private property without the consent of the owner
- Regulations on government search and seizure
- Provisions concerning prosecution
- The right to a speedy, public trial and the calling of witnesses
- The right to trial by jury
- Freedom from excessive bail or cruel punishment
- These rights are not necessarily the only rights
- Powers not prohibited by the Constitution are reserved to the states.

Amending the Constitution

So far, there have been only 27 amendments to the federal Constitution. There are four different ways to change the wording of the constitution: two methods for proposal and two methods for ratification:

- An amendment is proposed by a two-thirds vote in each house of Congress and ratified by three-fourths of the state legislatures.
- An amendment is proposed by a two-thirds vote in each house of Congress and ratified by three-fourths of the states in special conventions called for that purpose.
- An amendment is proposed by a national convention that is called by Congress at the request of two-thirds of the state legislatures and ratified by three-fourths of the state legislatures.
- An amendment is proposed by a national convention that is called by Congress at the request of two-thirds of the state legislatures and ratified by three-fourths of the states in special conventions called for that purpose.

National, concurrent, and state powers of government

The division of powers in the federal government system is as follows: National – This level can coin money, regulate interstate and foreign trade, raise and maintain armed forces, declare war, govern United States territories and admit new states, and conduct foreign relations.

Concurrent – This level can levy and collect taxes, borrow money, establish courts, define crimes and set punishments, and claim private property for public use.
State – This level can regulate trade and business within the state, establish public schools, pass license requirements for professionals, regulate alcoholic beverages, conduct elections, and establish local governments.

Delegated powers are those granted by the Constitution. There are three types:

- Expressed or enumerated powers – These are specifically spelled out in the Constitution. Implied – These are not expressly stated, but are reasonably suggested by the expressed powers.
- Inherent – These are powers not expressed by the Constitution but ones that national governments have historically possessed, such as granting diplomatic recognition.
- Powers can also be classified or reserved or exclusive. Reserved powers are not granted to the national government, but not denied to the states. Exclusive powers are those reserved to the national government, including concurrent powers.

Extending suffrage in the United States

Originally, the Constitution of 1789 provided the right to vote only to white male property owners. Through the years, suffrage was extended through the following five stages.

- In the early1800s, states began to eliminate property ownership and tax payment qualifications.
- By 1810, there were no more religious tests for voting. In the late 1800s, the 15th Amendment protected citizens from being denied the right to vote because of race or color.

- In 1920, the 19th Amendment prohibited the denial of the right to vote because of gender, and women were given the right to vote.
- Passed in 1961 and ratified in 1964, the 23rd Amendment added the voters of the District of Columbia to the presidential electorate and eliminated the poll tax as a condition for voting in federal elections. The Voting Rights Act of 1965 prohibited disenfranchisement through literacy tests and various other means of discrimination.
- In 1971, the 26th Amendment set the minimum voting age at 18 years of age.

Major Supreme Court cases

Out of the many Supreme Court rulings, several have had critical historical importance. These include:
- Marbury v. Madison (1803) – This ruling established judicial review as a power of the Supreme Court.
- Dred Scott v. Sandford (1857) – This decision upheld property rights over human rights in the case of a slave who had been transported to a free state by his master, but was still considered a slave.
- Brown v. Board of Education (1954) – The Court ruled that segregation was a violation of the Equal Protection Clause and that the "separate but equal" practice in education was unconstitutional. This decision overturned the 1896 Plessy v. Ferguson ruling that permitted segregation if facilities were equal.
- Miranda v. Arizona (1966) – This ruling made the reading of Miranda rights to those arrested for crimes the law. It ensured that confessions could not be illegally obtained and that citizen rights to fair trials and protection under the law would be upheld.

Famous speeches

Among the best-known speeches and famous lines known to modern Americans are the following:
- The Gettysburg Address – Made by Abraham Lincoln on November 19, 1863, it dedicated the battleground's cemetery.
- The Fourteen Points – Made by Woodrow Wilson on January 18, 1918, this outlined Wilson's plans for peace and the League of Nations.
- Address to Congress – Made by Franklin Roosevelt on December 8, 1941, it declared war on Japan and described the attack on Pearl Harbor as "a day which will live in infamy."
- Inaugural Address – Made by John F. Kennedy on January 20, 1961, it contained the famous line: "Ask not what your country can do for you, ask what you can do for your country."
- Berlin Address – Made by John F. Kennedy on June 26, 1963, it contained the famous line "Ich bin ein Berliner," which expressed empathy for West Berliners in their conflict with the Soviet Union.
- "I Have a Dream" and "I See the Promised Land" – Made by Martin Luther King, Jr. on August 28, 1963 and April 3, 1968, respectively, these speeches were hallmarks of the Civil Rights Movement.

- Brandenburg Gate speech – Made by Ronald Reagan on June 12, 1987, this speech was about the Berlin Wall and the end of the Cold War. It contained the famous line "Tear down this wall."

Primaries

The direct primary system is a means for members of a political party to participate in the selection of a candidate from their party to compete against the other party's candidate in a general election.

A closed primary is a party nominating election in which only declared party members can vote. Party membership is usually established by registration. Currently, 26 states and the District of Columbia use this system.

An open primary is a party nominating election in which any qualified voter can take part. The voter makes a public choice at the polling place about which primary to participate in, and the choice does not depend on any registration or previous choices.

A blanket primary, which allowed voters to vote in the primaries of both parties, was used at various times by three states. The Supreme Court ruled against this practice in 2000.

Important documents

Other than amendments to the Constitution, important Supreme Court decisions, and the acts that established the National Park system, the following are among the greatest American documents because of their impact on foreign and domestic policy:
- Declaration of Independence (1776)
- The Articles of Confederation (1777)
- The Constitution (1787) and the Bill of Rights (1791)
- The Northwest Ordinance (1787)
- The Federalist Papers (1787-88)
- George Washington's First Inaugural Address (1789) and his Farewell Address (1796)
- The Alien and Sedition Act (1798)
- The Louisiana Purchase Treaty (1803)
- The Monroe Doctrine (1823)
- The Missouri Compromise (1820)
- The Compromise of 1850
- The Kansas-Nebraska Act (1854)
- The Homestead Act (1862)
- The Emancipation Proclamation (1863)
- The agreement to purchase Alaska (1866)
- The Sherman Anti-Trust Act (1890)
- Theodore Roosevelt's Corollary to the Monroe Doctrine (1905)
- The Social Security Act (1935) and other acts of the New Deal in the 1930s; The Truman Doctrine (1947); The Marshall Plan (1948)
- The Civil Rights Act (1964)

Federal taxes

The four types of federal taxes are:
- Income taxes on individuals – This is a complex system because of demands for various exemptions and rates. Further, the schedule of rates can be lowered or raised according to economic conditions in order to stimulate or restrain economic activity. For example, a tax cut can provide an economic stimulus, while a tax increase can slow down the rate of inflation. Personal income tax generates about five times as much as corporate taxes. Rates are based on an individual's income, and range from 10 to 35 percent.
- Income taxes on corporations – The same complexity of exemptions and rates exists for corporations as individuals. Taxes can be raised or lowered according to the need to stimulate or restrain the economy.
- Excise taxes – These are taxes on specific goods such as tobacco, liquor, automobiles, gasoline, air travel, and luxury items, or on activities such as highway usage by trucks.
- Customs duties – These are taxes imposed on imported goods. They serve to regulate trade between the United States and other countries.

Currency system

The Constitution of 1787 gave the United States Congress the central authority to print or coin money and to regulate its value. Before this time, states were permitted to maintain separate currencies.

The currency system is based on a modified gold standard. There is an enormous store of gold to back up United States currency housed at Fort Knox, Kentucky.

Paper money is actually Federal Reserve notes and coins. It is the job of the Bureau of Engraving and Printing in the Treasury Department to design plates, special types of paper, and other security measures for bills and bonds. This money is put into general circulation by the Treasury and Federal Reserve Banks, and is taken out of circulation when worn out. Coins are made at the Bureau of the Mint in Philadelphia, Denver, and San Francisco.

Employment Act of 1946

The Employment Act of 1946 established the following entities to combat unemployment:
- The Council of Economic Advisers (CEA) – Composed of a chair and two other members appointed by the President and approved by the Senate, this council assists the President with the development and implementation of U.S. economic policy. The Council members and their staff, located in the Executive Office, are professionals in economics and statistics who forecast economic trends and provide analysis based on evidence-based research.
- The Economic Report of the President – This is presented every January by the President to Congress. Based on the work of the Council, the report recommends a program for maximizing employment, and may also recommend legislation.

- Joint Economic Committee (JEC) – This is a committee composed of 10 members of the House and 10 members of the Senate that makes a report early each year on its continuous study of the economy. Study is conducted through hearings and research, and the report is made in response to the president's recommendations.

Basic economic principles

Supply is the amount of a product or service available to consumers. Demand is how much consumers are willing to pay for the product or service. These two facets of the market determine the price of goods and services. The higher the demand, the higher the price the supplier will charge; the lower the demand, the lower the price.

Scarcity is a measure of supply in that demand is high when there is a scarcity, or low supply, of an item. Choice is related to scarcity and demand in that when an item in demand is scarce, consumers have to make difficult choices. They can pay more for an item, go without it, or go elsewhere for the item.

Money is the cash or currency available for payment. Resources are the items one can barter in exchange for goods. Money is also the cash reserves of a nation, while resources are the minerals, labor force, armaments, and other raw materials or assets a nation has available for trade.

Economic downturn

When a recession happens, people at all levels of society feel the economic effects. For example:
- High unemployment results because businesses have to cut back to keep costs low, and may no longer have the work for the labor force they once did.
- Mortgage rates go up on variable-rate loans as banks try to increase their revenues, but the higher rates cause some people who cannot afford increased housing costs to sell or suffer foreclosure.
- Credit becomes less available as banks try to lessen their risk. This decreased lending affects business operations, home and auto loans, etc.
- Stock market prices drop, and the lower dividends paid to stockholders reduce their income. This is especially hard on retired people who rely on stock dividends.
- Psychological depression and trauma may occur in those who suffer bankruptcy, unemployment, or foreclosure during a depression.

Positive economic effects

The positive economic aspects of abundant natural resources are an increase in revenue and new jobs where those resources have not been previously accessed. For example, the growing demand for oil, gas, and minerals has led companies to venture into new regions. The negative economic aspects of abundant natural resources are:
- Environmental degradation, if sufficient regulations are not in place to counter strip mining, deforestation, and contamination.
- Corruption, if sufficient regulations are not in place to counter bribery, political favoritism, and exploitation of workers as greedy companies try to maximize their profits.

- Social tension, if the resources are privately owned such that the rich become richer and the poor do not reap the benefits of their national resources. Class divisions become wider, resulting in social unrest.
- Dependence, if the income from the natural resources is not used to develop other industries as well. In this situation, the economy becomes dependent on one source, and faces potential crises if natural disasters or depletion take away that income source.

Two kinds of economies

Economics is the study of the buying choices that people make, the production of goods and services, and how our market system works. The two kinds of economies are command and market. In a command economy, the government controls what and how much is produced, the methods used for production, and the distribution of goods and services. In a market economy, producers make decisions about methods and distribution on their own. These choices are based on what will sell and bring a profit in the marketplace. In a market economy, consumers ultimately affect these decisions by choosing whether or not to buy certain goods and services. The United States has a market economy.

Market economy

The five characteristics of a market economy are:
- Economic freedom – There is freedom of choice with respect to jobs, salaries, production, and price.
- Economic incentives – A positive incentive is to make a profit. However, if the producer tries to make too high a profit, the consequences might be that no one will purchase the item at that price. A negative incentive would be a drop in profits, causing the producer to decrease or discontinue production. A boycott, which might cause the producer to change business practices or policies, is also a negative economic incentive.
- Competition – There is more than one producer for any given product. Consumers thereby have choices about what to buy, which are usually made based on quality and price. Competition is an incentive for a producer to make the best product at the best price. Otherwise, producers will lose business to the competition.
- Private ownership – Production and profits belong to an individual or to a private company, not to the government.
- Limited government – Government plays no role in the economic decisions of its individual citizens.

Production and economic flow

The factors of production are:
- Land – This includes not only actual land, but also forests, minerals, water, etc.
- Labor – This is the work force required to produce goods and services, including factors such as talent, skills, and physical labor.
- Capital – This is the cash and material equipment needed to produce goods and services, including buildings, property, tools, office equipment, roads, etc.
- Entrepreneurship – Persons with initiative can capitalize on the free market system by producing goods and services.

The two types of markets are factor and product markets. The factor market consists of the people who exchange their services for wages. The people are sellers and companies are buyers. The product market is the selling of products to the people who want to buy them. The people are the buyers and the companies are the sellers. This exchange creates a circular economic flow in which money goes from the producers to workers as wages, and then flows back to producers in the form of payment for products.

Economic impact of technology

At the start of the 21st century, the role of information and communications technologies (ICT) grew rapidly as the economy shifted to a knowledge-based one. Output is increasing in areas where ICT is used intensively, which are service areas and knowledge-intensive industries such as finance; insurance; real estate; business services, health care, and environmental goods and services; and community, social, and personal services. Meanwhile, the economic share for manufacturers is declining in medium- and low-technology industries such as chemicals, food products, textiles, gas, water, electricity, construction, and transport and communication services. Industries that have traditionally been high-tech, such as aerospace, computers, electronics, and pharmaceuticals are remaining steady in terms of their economic share.

Technology has become the strongest factor in determining per capita income for many countries. The ease of technology investments as compared to industries that involve factories and large labor forces has resulted in more foreign investments in countries that do not have natural resources to call upon.

Social studies skills and materials

For classes in history, geography, civics/government, anthropology, sociology, and economics, the goal is for students to explore issues and learn key concepts. Social studies help improve communication skills in reading and writing, but students need sufficient literacy skills to be able to understand specialized vocabulary, identify key points in text, differentiate between fact and opinion, relate information across texts, connect prior knowledge and new information, and synthesize information into meaningful knowledge. These literacy skills will be enhanced in the process, and will extend into higher order thinking skills that enable students to compare and contrast, hypothesize, draw inferences, explain, analyze, predict, construct, and interpret. Social studies classes also depend on a number of different types of materials beyond the textbook, such as nonfiction books, biographies, journals, maps, newspapers (paper or online), photographs, and primary documents.

Benefits of social studies

Social studies cover the political, economic, cultural, and environmental aspects of societies not only in the past, as in the study of history, but also in the present and future. Students gain an understanding of current conditions and learn how to prepare for the future and cope with change through studying geography, economics, anthropology, government, and sociology. Social studies classes teach assessment, problem solving, evaluation, and decision making skills in the context of good citizenship. Students learn about scope and sequence, designing investigations, and following up with research to collect, organize, and present information and data. In the process, students learn how to search for patterns and their meanings in society and in their own lives. Social studies build a positive self-concept within the context of understanding the similarities and differences of people. Students begin to understand that they are unique, but also share many feelings and concerns with others. As students learn that each individual can contribute to society, their self-awareness builds self-esteem.

Knowledge gained from social studies

Anthropology and sociology provide an understanding of how the world's many cultures have developed and what these cultures and their values have to contribute to society.

Sociology, economics, and political science provide an understanding of the institutions in society and each person's role within social groups. These topics teach the use of charts, graphs, and statistics.

Political science, civics, and government teach how to see another person's point of view, accept responsibility, and deal with conflict. They also provide students with an understanding of democratic norms and values, such as justice and equality. Students learn how to apply these norms and values in their community, school, and family.

Economics teaches concepts such as work, exchange (buying, selling, and other trade transactions), production of goods and services, the origins of materials and products, and consumption.

Geography teaches students how to use maps, globes, and locational and directional terms. It also provides them with an understanding of spatial environments, landforms, climate, world trade and transportation, ecological systems, and world cultures.

An important part of social studies, whether anthropology, sociology, history, geography, or political science, is the study of local and world cultures, as well as individual community dynamics. Students should be able to:
- Differentiate between values held by their own culture and communityand values held by other cultures and communities
- Recognize the influences of other cultures on their own cultureMajor social institutions and their roles in the students' communities
- Understand how individuals and groups interact to obtain food, clothing, and shelter
- Understand the role of language, literature, the arts, and traditions in a culture
- Recognize the role of media and technology in cultures, particularly in the students' own cultures
- Recognize the influence of various types of government, economics, the environment, and technology on social systems and cultures
- Evaluate the effectiveness of social institutions in solving problems in a community or culture
- Examine changes in population, climate, and production, and evaluate their effects on the community or culture

Objectives for social studies

A middle school or high school student should be able to:And distinguish between primary and secondary sources such as diaries, letters, photographs, documents, newspapers, media, and computer technologies

Evaluate sources with respect to their authenticity, authority, credulity, and possible bias

Recognize how someone's point of view can be influenced by nationalism, racism, religion, or culture and ethnicity

Construct time lines of key events, periods, and historically significant individualsAnd analyze the reasons for major shifts in national political boundaries

Address and reconcile different points of view through discussion, debate, or persuasive writing or speaking

Interpret information from a broad selection of research materials, such as encyclopedias, almanacs, dictionaries, atlases, and political cartoons

Apply cause and effect reasoning and chronological thinking to past, present, and future situations

Use maps, globes, graphs, charts, models, and databases to demonstrate spatial relationships and patterns

Inquiry-based learning

Facilitated by the teacher who models, guides, and poses a starter question, inquiry-based learning is a process in which students are involved in their learning. This process involves formulating questions, investigating widely, and building new understanding and meaning. This combination of steps asks students to think independently, and enables them to answer their questions with new knowledge, develop solutions, or support a position or point of view. In inquiry-based learning activities, teachers engage students, ask for authentic assessments, require research using a variety of resources (books, interviews, Internet information, etc.), and involve students in cooperative interaction. All of these require the application of processes and skills. Consequently, new knowledge is usually shared with others, and may result in some type of action. Inquiry-based learning focuses on finding a solution to a question or a problem, whether it is a matter of curiosity, a puzzle, a challenge, or a disturbing confusion.

Constructivist Learning and Information Seeking Behavior Theory

The Constructivist Learning Theory supports a view of inquiry-based learning as an opportunity for students to experience learning through inquiry and problem solving. This process is characterized by exploration and risk taking, curiosity and motivation, engagement in critical and creative thinking, and connections with real-life situations and real audiences.

The Information Seeking Behavior Theory purports that students progress through levels of question specificity, from vague notions of the information needed to clearly defined needs or questions. According to this theory, students are more successful in the search process if they have a realistic understanding of the information system and problem. They should understand that the inquiry process is not linear or confined to certain steps, but is a flexible, individual process that leads back to the original question.

Essential questions

Essential questions for learning include those that:
- Ask for evaluation, synthesis, and analysis – the highest levels of Bloom's Taxonomy
- Seek information that is important to know
- Are worth the student's awareness
- Will result in enduring understanding
- Tend to focus on the questions "why?" or "how do we know this information?"
- Are more open-ended and reflective in nature
- Often address interrelationships or lend themselves to multi-disciplinary investigations
- Spark curiosity and a sense of wonder, and invite investigation and activity
- Can be asked over and over and in a variety of instances
- Encourage related questions
- Have answers that may be extended over time
- Seek to identify key understandings
- Engage students in real-life, applied problem solving
- May not be answerable without a lifetime of investigation, and maybe not even then

Verifying research

Some sources are not reliable, so the student must have a means to evaluate the credibility of a source when doing research, particularly on the Internet. The value of a source depends on its intended use and whether it fits the subject. For example, students researching election campaigns in the 19th century would need to go to historical documents, but students researching current election practices could use candidate brochures, television advertisements, and web sites. A checklist for examining sources might include:
- Check the authority and reputation of the author, sponsoring group, or publication
- Examine the language and illustrations for bias
- Look for a clear, logical arrangement of information
- If online, check out the associated links, archives, contact ability, and the date of last update

Research methods

Social science research relies heavily on empirical research, which is original data gathering and analysis through direct observation or experiment. It also involves using the library and Internet to obtain raw data, locate information, or review expert opinion. Because social science projects are often interdisciplinary, students may need assistance from the librarian to find related search terms.

While arguments still exist about the superiority of quantitative versus qualitative research, most social scientists understand that research is an eclectic mix of the two methods. Quantitative research involves using techniques to gather data, which is information dealing with numbers and measurable values. Statistics, tables, and graphs are often the products. Qualitative research involves non-measurable factors, and looks for meaning in the numbers produced by quantitative research. Qualitative research takes data from observations and analyzes it to find underlying meanings and patterns of relationships.

Cultures and community relations

- An important part of social studies, whether anthropology, sociology, history, geography, or political science, is the study of local and world cultures, as well as individual community dynamics. Students should be able to:Values held by their own culture and communityValues held by other cultures and communities
- Recognize the influences of other cultures on their own cultureMajor social institutions and their roles in the students' communities
- Understand how individuals and groups interact to obtain food, clothing, and shelter
- Understand the role of language, literature, the arts, and traditions in a culture
- Recognize the role of media and technology in cultures, particularly in the students' own cultures
- Recognize the influence of various types of government, economics, the environment, and technology on social systems and cultures
- Evaluate the effectiveness of social institutions in solving problems in a community or culture
- Examine changes in population, climate, and production, and evaluate their effects on the community or culture

English Practice Test

Practice Questions

1. Which of the following students may need extra instruction and evaluation with respect to oral language skills?
   a. Rosa: whose first language is Spanish. Rosa speaks with a distinct accent and can be difficult to understand when speaking about a new or unfamiliar topic.
   b. Greer: who avoids oral assignments when possible. He avoids speaking up in class and only responds when called upon.
   c. Ashley: who often has trouble answering questions in class. Her responses are often off-topic. She also struggles with oral presentations, seeming to present a string of unrelated facts.
   d. Brett: who frequently becomes loud and disruptive whenever group work is assigned. He often becomes involved in heated discussions with classmates when discussing ideas.

2. Mr. Callas is introducing a unit on oral traditions from around the world. He wants his seventh-grade students to gain a better understanding of the relationship between written text and oral language, as well as increase their multi-cultural understanding. Which of the following assignments would be the most relevant?
   a. "Read Chapter 12 on Oral Traditions and complete the end-of-chapter review."
   b. "Select a poem or song from a culture around the world and recite it for the class."
   c. "Conduct a poll of twenty fellow students, asking about their family's country of origin. Present a graph or diagram of your results in class."
   d. "Choose a country to research and write a first-person narrative about a typical day in the life of one of its citizens. The narratives will be read in class."

3. Which of the following exercises would be the most appropriate tool for helping students evaluate the effectiveness of their own spoken messages?
   a. Discuss written and oral assignments in class before completing them. Once the assignments are completed, the teacher meets individually with each student to discuss the content and effectiveness of each student's work.
   b. Instruct students to present oral reports in class, which are then "graded" by classmates. A score of 1-10 is assigned based on students' perception of the reports' clarity. The student's average score determines his report's effectiveness.
   c. Ask each student to prepare an oral report and a content quiz that highlights the report's main idea. The student then uses classmates' scores on the reviews to determine his report's effectiveness.
   d. Put students into groups of three. Two students complete a role-playing assignment based on prompts provided by the teacher. The third student gives constructive feedback on how the other two can refine and clarify their speech.

Use the following information to answer the next two questions.

Mr. Gilbert teaches fourth graders whose reading skills range from emergent to advanced. He introduces an activity called "Book Buddies" in which his students are paired with emerging Kindergarten readers to practice reading beginner-level short books. He hopes they will gain confidence and increase their own reading skills through these visits. Mr. Gilbert's students pick their Book Buddies up once a week and read together for about half an hour.

4. What aspect of this program is most likely to increase all of the fourth-graders' oral language skills?
    a. Finding opportunities to explain unfamiliar ideas or sound out new words with the younger students.
    b. Spending time with younger students and being reminded of how much they have learned in the past three years.
    c. Being exposed to different kinds of reading texts.
    d. Practicing their decoding skills and increasing their vocabulary.

5. What might be the best way to adapt the Book Buddy program for fourth grade students who are still learning English?
    a. Exempt ESOL students from the program altogether so that they can practice reading with their primary teacher.
    b. Create some groups that have three Book Buddies: a skilled reader, an ESOL student, and a Kindergartener; this will allow the English language learner to listen, learn, and give guidance when he is able.
    c. Make no changes to the program and simply allow the younger students and the English language learner to help each other decode and compare ideas in their own way.
    d. Allow English language learners to listen to books on tape read by native English speakers with their Kindergarten partners.

6. Mr. Campbell begins each Language Arts lesson with the "Phrase of the Day." This phrase ranges from analogies to idioms to snippets of figurative language. His students use their journals to explain what they think the phrase means and to draw a picture, also. Mr. Campbell then reveals the phrase's true meaning, which the children record on the same page as their own interpretations. When he reviews these pages in the students' journals, Mr. Campbell is most likely to:
    a. Check to ensure that each student is diligently recording both their own interpretations and the correct interpretations.
    b. Use the mechanics and spelling errors within to help him design test questions and worksheets.
    c. Grade the pages for originality and humor.
    d. Use them to informally assess students' oral language skills.

7. Which of the following activities would incorporate the best use of technology to increase students' oral language skills?
   a. Students visit the school computer lab to work on math and science activities with software that utilizes voice-recognition technology in an interactive process.
   b. Students use an internet program and computer camera to converse with English-speaking students in other countries.
   c. Students can visit the classroom's Language Lab, in which there are tape recorders and CD players. Students can use these players to listen to novels, poetry, and other literary works on tape.
   d. A teacher videotapes a class discussion about a story and replays it for the students to watch and discuss.

8. Every year, students prepare with excitement for Historical Characters Day. Each student is expected to choose a character who was influential in years past and compose a report on why he was important. The students are permitted to dress up as their respective characters on the day on which the reports are turned in. This year, the teachers want to incorporate an aspect of this anticipated event that will more directly increase their students' oral communication skills. Of the options they have brainstormed, which of the following would be most helpful?
   a. Ask the students to read their reports aloud to the class.
   b. Require that the reports be memorized so that students can make better use of voice modulation and eye contact while presenting.
   c. Require the students to write why they chose their character and three interesting things they learned on a set note cards, and present what they have written to the class.
   d. Hold an election for the student with the most realistic costume and require students to give supporting evidence for their votes.

Use the information below to answer the questions 9 and 10:

A middle school teacher consistently includes "the Daily Chat" in her lesson plans, several times a week. Students are placed into pairs, with the occasional group of three. The teacher chooses one student during each chat with whom she will partner. During these conversations, students can pick a topic and discuss it for five to ten minutes. They are asked to use the following log sheet:

Date:
Name:
Partner's Name:

☐ My partner looked at me most of the time while we were speaking.
☐ My partner listened while I was speaking.
☐ My partner waited until I finished before taking his turn to speak.
☐ My partner enunciated while speaking (I understood the words he was saying).
☐ My partner explained himself well (I understood the ideas behind what he was saying).

9. Which skill is least likely to be improved by this activity?
   a. Active listening; students listen for the purpose of understanding and responding appropriately.
   b. Speaking clearly; students practice speaking in ways that can be easily heard and understood.
   c. Nonverbal communication skills; students communicate engagement in conversation through body language, etc.
   d. Oral conflict resolution; students can resolve disagreements using their verbal skills.

10. What is the most likely purpose for the teacher to partner with a new student during each Daily Chat?
   a. She wants to make sure that the students get positive feedback on a regular basis during skill-building exercises.
   b. She has found that there are almost always absent students, creating a space for her to function as a partner during days where one student lacks a partner.
   c. She recognizes the value of building oral communication skills with adults as well as peers.
   d. She wants to demonstrate how to resolve conflicts or common problems that students often face when attempting to communicate effectively.

11. The eighth-grade class will be holding class elections in the fall as part of an integrated Social Studies and English unit. The students will be studying government elections and modeling their process based on their studies. The candidates for Vice President and President will debate pre-determined issues in front of their class using modified rules found in formal debates (i.e. they are timed and will use a moderator). Which of the following exercises would be most beneficial to introduce in English class to help prepare each student for the debates?
    a. Watch recordings of Presidential and Vice Presidential debates from years past and model their speech from what they have heard.
    b. Create multiple opportunities for students to discuss the pre-determined issues in class, allowing for free-flowing dialogue and differing opinions.
    c. Students write their thoughts in short-essay format so that each section can be read aloud during the appropriate part of the debate.
    d. Students determine a position on each selected issue and assign it to a note card or small piece of paper. On each card, they record two to three reasons or supporting ideas for the opinion.

12. A teacher wants to work on her students' listening comprehension in addition to their reading comprehension, since she understands that the skills are interrelated. She has a series of short stories that she thinks the students will enjoy. Which of the following would be the best supplement to typical written comprehension exercises?
    a. Preview content and then read the stories aloud to the students. Assess listening comprehension through verbal and written questions.
    b. Ask the students to choose one story each to read aloud to a small group. Encourage the students to discuss what they have learned afterward.
    c. Assign each student a story to read and require them to write a report on it. Each student should then present his report based on what he has learned to the class.
    d. Have the students read stories aloud to the class, and create mock tests based upon the main ideas which they identify.

13. Ms. Walters wants to help her brand-new group of still-emergent fourth-grade students build comprehension skills. Which of the following exercises would be the best way to quickly gauge the students' current comprehension levels during the first week of class?
    a. Provide the students with instruction-level text to be read independently. Hold an in-class discussion about what happened in the story.
    b. Read a story aloud to the class and then ask each student to draw three pictures representing the beginning, middle and end of the story.
    c. Put students into group or pairs to read the story aloud. Each group then collaborates to answer the story review questions.
    d. Have each student re-tell the story to the class in his own words.

14. Which of the following strategies would not be helpful in building the word-identification skills of emergent readers?
    a. Allowing for invented spelling in written assignments or in class work.
    b. Reinforcing phonemic awareness while reading aloud.
    c. Using dictionaries to look up unfamiliar words.
    d. Studying and reviewing commonly-used sight words at the students' ability level.

15. Mrs. Harris is pleased that her fifth-graders are showing progress in their reading comprehension and writing skills. The students are performing very well on their written tests, evaluations, and homework. After the holiday break, she wants to design lessons that increase the students' literacy skills by incorporating multiple contexts. Which of the following might be the best way to do this?
   a. Read their next book aloud and discuss it in class.
   b. Have the students quiz one another in small groups on the content of their textbooks and other reading assignments.
   c. Read a play in class and allow the students to act it out for their peers following their unit test.
   d. Administer spelling and vocabulary tests orally to determine students' verbal skills.

16. Which of the following would be most useful in assessing and documenting students' language progress throughout a school year?
   a. An audio/video recording of each student reading the same text at the beginning of the year and again at the end of the year
   b. A portfolio including pre-tests, post-tests, vocabulary work, journal entries, writing assignments, group projects and other relevant work from throughout the year
   c. Score composites and details from state- and national-referenced exams or other standardized tests.
   d. A detailed narrative composed by the student's teacher, detailing strengths, weaknesses, and descriptions of the student's work.

17. Valeria is a bright sixth-grader who struggles with reading fluency. She comes from a predominantly Spanish-speaking home and has only lived in the United States for two years. Her teacher plans to use the guided oral reading strategy to help increase Valeria's reading skills. Which of the following would not be a part of this strategy?
   a. Valeria is partnered with another student who is also struggling with language fluency in class.
   b. Valeria's partner reads a given text aloud and then gives her a chance to read the text silently several times.
   c. Valeria reads the text aloud three to four times.
   d. Valeria's partner gives encouragement and feedback.

18. Mr. Waleran requires his students of all ability levels to write freely in their journals twice a week. While students are encouraged to use proper spelling and mechanics as much as possible, the purpose behind this activity is to encourage students to express themselves through writing without concern for grading parameters. How should he adapt this activity for Dimitri, who has several academic delays that keep him from reading and writing in legible or coherent ways?
   a. Allow Dimitri to dictate his thoughts to another student or teacher who will then record them into his journal in writing.
   b. Encourage Dimitri to draw pictures in his journal that represent his thoughts, and encourage him to use the words he knows to label or describe the pictures.
   c. Tell Dimitri to keep an audio journal at home, using a personal tape recorder.
   d. Require Dimitri to attempt to write in complete sentences as much as he can, and then edit the journal together for spelling and mechanical errors.

19. A teacher reads to her students at least once a week. This month, she plans to read poetry to her class. The students will then discuss what they have heard for the rest of each class period. What is this teacher's most likely purpose in designing these lessons?
    a. To give students a break from extensive reading requirements.
    b. To build phonological awareness, specifically of rhyming words.
    c. To teach students that there is more to literature than prose.
    d. To increase students' listening skills while exposing them to new kinds of literature.

20. Mrs. Taylor is working with a diverse group of fifth-graders. She introduces a lesson and project that students can work on once they have finished their regular class work. Students may visit a section of the classroom where they can listen to a lesson via headphones on ancient Egyptian hieroglyphics and look at various library books on the subject. Students are then expected to create their own hieroglyphics that they can use to tell a short story. Which of the following skills is not built with this project?
    a. Understanding of various kinds of written expression, including non-alphabetic languages.
    b. Building multi-cultural awareness that will increase understanding between students of different backgrounds.
    c. Reading for purposes of information or new knowledge (i.e. 'reading to learn').
    d. Exposure to various media to build literacy skills across all levels of reading ability.

21. Each week, a teacher asks one student to bring in a recording of his favorite song and a written version of the lyrics. The students listen to the song and receive a copy of the lyrics. They discuss these words as either one large group or in small groups. What are these students probably learning from this exercise?
    a. Students are learning about the lives of their peers indirectly by listening to each student's favorite song; they can begin to understand each other by the meaning behind the song lyrics.
    b. Students are learning that they are very diverse in many ways: they have different musical tastes and prefer many different styles of music and expression.
    c. Students are learning that it is very difficult to communicate freely when bound by various musical traits such as rhyming, rhythm, and phrasing.
    d. Students are learning that literacy skills do not just pertain to schoolwork. These skills allow students to understand and communicate meanings through a variety of ways, including music and lyrics.

22. A teacher notices that one of her students is inconsistent with recalling his letter-sounds. He may remember a particular sound or blend one day and read it correctly; however, the next day, he may not be able to produce the same sound. What should she do?
    a. Immediately refer the student to the appropriate professional for educational testing since it is likely that he is exhibiting early signs of a learning difference or disability.
    b. Recognize that children all learn at different rates and that learning and producing letter-sounds involve multiple mental processes. Give the student as much time as he needs to internalize the sounds and produce them correctly.
    c. Provide the student with targeted instruction in letter-sound correspondence, using a schema such as Alphabet Action, in which letter-sounds are associated with physical actions (e.g., C is for Catch). Set a time frame after which, if the student does not improve, to begin the procedure for special-needs testing.
    d. Hold a conference with the child's parents and encourage them to seek outside tutoring or professional assistance with his reading skills.

23. Mrs. Bundy has three groups of students in her fifth-grade English class: those who want to answer every question, those who only speak when spoken to, and those who never speak at all. She is making plans for upcoming lessons and thinks about the last group of children who never speak up in class. What is important for Mrs. Bundy to know and do with respect to these students?
   a. Know that some students are simply quiet and do not feel comfortable speaking up in class. As long as the children are completing their work accurately, do not be concerned about them.
   b. Speak with those students after or before class. Let them know how important it is to express themselves in class, because that is part of what building literacy is all about.
   c. Make a point to speak directly to those students who talk less in class. Limit the amount of time the more verbal students can speak in class and require the quieter students to answer more direct questions and prompts.
   d. Place students who don't speak up in class together for group work. Make a point to spend time with those groups to give guidance and encouragement as they express their ideas verbally.

24. Some of the students in Mr. Smith's fourth-grade class cannot decode words well enough to read fluently in class. He knows they are well behind grade level and that he needs to provide them with activities that will allow them to be successful, building skills and confidence at the same time. Which activity would be best for this purpose?
   a. Enlist the parents' help by sending home a weekly list of sight words that the students can practice and memorize, decreasing the need to decode when they read.
   b. Show the students how to create words out of movable alphabet tiles or magnetic letters, building (encoding) words as they sound them out.
   c. Provide the children with early childhood readers that contain only very simple words so that the children will not feel badly as they read.
   d. Allow those children having trouble to stop each time they reach a challenging word and sound it out carefully, recording it to a list that will be studied for homework.

25. Which of the following statements is true regarding the relationship of reading fluency to reading comprehension?
   a. Reading fluency and reading comprehension should be considered separate, equally valuable skills that can be taught independently of one another.
   b. Reading comprehension is an important component of achieving a level of overall reading fluency.
   c. Reading fluency refers to a set of skills that should be continually improved upon, so that students can consistently comprehend that which they read.
   d. Reading comprehension and reading fluency are so intertwined that a child struggling in one area is often incapable of making progress in the other.

26. Abi, a fifth-grader, is reading aloud to his teacher during one-on-one reading time. His teacher uses this time to evaluate ongoing fluency and comprehension skills. Following today's reading, Abi's teacher determines that he needs practice with words that begin with digraphs. Which of the following sets of words would most likely be part of this assignment?
   a. Chicken, Shells, That
   b. Were, Frame, Click
   c. Sponge, Think, Blank
   d. Packed, Blistered, Smoothed

27. Which of the following generally would not be expected of an eighth-grader?
   a. Identify grade-level vocabulary words and be able to decode their roots, prefixes, and suffixes, as well as non-English words that are commonly used in English writing (e.g. phenomenon, charisma, etc.).
   b. Analyze literary works and identify common themes in various pieces of literature.
   c. Understand different points of view in literature (e.g. omniscient, subjective)
   d. Explain how media messages are reflective of the literature in cultures from which they originate.

Use the following information to answer question 28:

Susannah wrote the following journal entry on her happiest memory during journal time:

I lov going on picnics with my mom and dad. We et sandwitches and lemanad and somtyms mom and dad drink coffee. we play gams and haf fun.

28. Which of the following reading skills might be most helpful for Susannah?
   a. Decoding work focusing on silent ending phonemes.
   b. Sight word drills and practice.
   c. Reading aloud to a partner who gives constructive feedback.
   d. More spelling practice using original sentences.

29. A teacher writes four sentences on the board and instructs his students to copy the sentences from the board into their notebooks. They must underline words with prefixes and capitalize those with suffixes. Words with prefixes and suffixes though be underlined and capitalized. Which sentence is correct?
   a. The PRINCE declared his undying love for the PRINCESS.
   b. Add two cups of PRECOOKED chicken to the soup.
   c. This loud, loud noise is very DISPLEASING.
   d. The bookkeeper examined every page of the rare play.

30. Which of the following computer activities/games would be most beneficial during media time for students who are working on reading fluency?
   a. Students can select from a variety of high-interest texts and read aloud what they see on the screen.
   b. Students hear high-frequency sight and vocabulary words in their headphones and get points for "zapping" (clicking) the correct matching word on their screen.
   c. Students practice typing in a keyboarding program to build their speed and accuracy in writing reports and papers.
   d. Students can surf a limited and pre-approved number of internet sites to read on subjects of their choosing.

31. A teacher is fortunate to have many parent volunteers for the current school year, giving him parental help at least three times a week. He wants to utilize these volunteers in a way that will not only take into account their limited training, but will most benefit students. Which option should he choose?
    a. Ask each parent to speak to the class about what kinds of literacy skills they use each day in their careers.
    b. Enlist parents to help grade papers and presentations using a rubric.
    c. Ask parents to listen to his students read challenging but manageable texts, one at a time, helping students identify and sound out unfamiliar words.
    d. Primarily utilize parents' for non-instructional tasks, such as making copies, organizing the class library, monitoring the classroom during test time, etc.

32. Which of the following aspects of oral reading is the most important accompaniment to speed and accuracy?
    a. Vocal expression based on punctuation and content.
    b. Volume of the reader's/speaker's voice.
    c. Interest level of the text to be read aloud.
    d. Consistently increasing the number of words read aloud per minute.

33. Which of the following activities is widely used in building students' reading fluency?
    a. Sole focus on phonetic instruction.
    b. Repeated oral readings combined with feedback.
    c. Participation in vocabulary-building activities.
    d. Utilizing speed-reading techniques often used in adult literacy courses.

34. In monitoring a group of elementary-age students' reading fluency, which of the following students may need extra or specialized instruction?
    a. A student who reads an unfamiliar text more slowly than he reads a familiar text.
    b. A student reading an independent-level text, finding approximately 1 in 25 words difficult to read.
    c. A student reading an instructional-level text, finding approximately 1 in 5 words difficult to read.
    d. A student who scores a 70% on a comprehension test.

35. Which of the following reading assignments would be most appropriate as a context for teaching students how to preview information to improve comprehension?
    a. A written version of a popular movie that most of the students have seen outside of class.
    b. A reading assignment from the students' science class that they will be tested on next month.
    c. A novel the students read in English class last year.
    d. A set of poems that will be studied next month during Poetry Week.

36. A sixth-grade teacher is preparing to begin a unit in which students will be reading a novel in class. She plans to use the novel to teach her students specific strategies to improve and monitor their reading comprehension. Which of the following techniques would likely be taught during class?
   a. Discuss story elements such as exposition, climax and resolution.
   b. Demonstrate the practice of stopping at the end of chapters to summarize and review the content.
   c. Ask students to complete a review sheet before taking the unit test.
   d. Practice decoding unfamiliar words throughout the book by using knowledge of frequently-used root words.

37. A teacher notices that her new student, Carl, has a hard time answering questions related to comprehension during class and has scored low on comprehension quizzes and worksheets. What would be the most logical first step in determining how to help Carl?
   a. Encourage Carl to read all assigned texts at least twice before class to help him understand what he has read.
   b. Provide Carl with story maps of what he will be reading to assist his comprehension visually.
   c. Ask Carl to read aloud with his teacher individually so that she can ensure that he is reading with expected accuracy and speed (i.e., fluently).
   d. Modify Carl's class work so that he is able to work on easier comprehension material until his skills are brought up to speed.

38. Which of the following would be the best strategy for helping eighth-grade students choose books that they will read independently and use to write book reports?
   a. Provide two choices from which the students can pick that you know everybody can understand.
   b. Allow students to freely pick their books, but require that they read a few pages aloud to you in order to ensure that the reading level is neither too easy nor too difficult based on their abilities.
   c. Encourage the students to read a book that contains unfamiliar words and idioms so that they will be challenged to use context clues, dictionaries and other sources to build comprehension.
   d. Establish no parameters on book selection to encourage free choice and promote students' excitement about the project.

39. Which of the following students is not performing "at grade level" and may warrant academic support or testing?
   a. Karishma, seventh grade, looks panicked and becomes very quiet when asked to state her opinion about a particular subject in class discussions and rarely raises her hand when a question about text comprehension is posed.
   b. Lynne, fifth grade, is able to comprehend most of what she reads in plays and in fiction, but sometimes has trouble understanding poetry.
   c. Barron, sixth grade, can read fluently aloud and often recall concrete facts, but is rarely able to draw conclusions, make inferences, or understand figurative language.
   d. Sebastien, eighth grade, lacks motivation to read much of what is assigned in class and frequently fails to complete his homework; he often contributes intelligently to class discussions.

Use the following information to answer questions 40 and 41:

> Autumn must be the most enchanting season of all. The wind takes on a chill that, when inhaled, ____ with the scent of ____ wood to lightly and singe your throat! Statuesque ____ seem to erupt into ____ blooms of colors seen ____ no other time, except _____ inside boxes of children's ____. For many people, the ____ of camping, cookouts, sports, ____ school creates warm, tingling ____ of security as the _____ slowly turns from Summer _____ Fall. There is no other day in the year like the first day of Autumn.

40. The passage above is an example of what kind of reading comprehension assessment?
    a. Vocabulary Memorization Test
    b. Cloze Individual Assessment
    c. Student Response Form
    d. Figurative Language Assessment

41. In determining his students' reading comprehension levels, a teacher uses the above passage. He finds that about half of Anne's answers make sense in the blanks. Which answer choice describes the level at which Anne is reading the text?
    a. instructional level
    b. independent level
    c. frustration level
    d. novice level

42. Which of the following practices would assist students in constructing meaning from a fictional text written long before the students were born?
    a. After the text is read for homework, students discuss any aspects of the story that they did not understand or that were unfamiliar to them.
    b. Students individually visualize scenery and events in the text as they read.
    c. The class makes a list of unfamiliar words in the text and looks them up in the dictionary as the text is read.
    d. Before the text is assigned, students learn about pertinent historical events or aspects of culture that informed the writing of the text.

43. Which of the following strategies would be most appropriate for increasing comprehension before reading a chapter book without pictures?
    a. Previewing the chapter titles and identifying questions that would be answered by reading.
    b. Predicting the ending of the story after reading the introduction and first chapter of the book.
    c. Discussing what the students have heard from other individuals about the story.
    d. Researching and reading book reviews to get an idea of what experts have said about the story.

44. Which of these sets of factors would most greatly affect a student's reading comprehension in class and on tests?
   a. Oral language development, written language development and eating a healthy breakfast.
   b. Word analysis skills, sight word knowledge and ability to monitor understanding.
   c. Vocabulary development, sight word knowledge and reference skills.
   d. Prior knowledge, good classroom participation and academic performance in other subjects.

45. A teacher assigns a project in which students must compare excerpts from the Charles Dickens novel they are reading in class and an article from the week's newspaper. The teacher has chosen a specific passage from the novel. The students can choose the newspaper excerpts, as long as they are of similar lengths. The students must then write a short essay comparing the two. What is this teacher hoping to show her students?
   a. That Dickens' writing style is journalistic and that he informed much of what is considered to be current journalistic philosophy.
   b. That there are links between the students' lives and what they read in class; the relationships are there if they make an effort to see them.
   c. That you can compare even two unlike things.
   d. That there are distinct differences between the way meaning is constructed in daily life and in literature; different processes must be applied.

46. A seventh-grade teacher wants to encourage her students to read more for pleasure. She knows that the students' comprehension, vocabulary and writing skills will also be improved by reading more frequently. What is the best way to increase the amount of time students spend reading for pleasure?
   a. Assign "extra-credit" in which students can write a book report on a favorite book they read as a child.
   b. Increase the number of books and poems included in each unit of study.
   c. Ask the students to read a text of their choosing (e.g., a magazine, comic book, internet source, novel) each week and present to the class what they enjoyed about it.
   d. Have each student make a list of books they would like to read someday and then create a timeline for when they want to complete each one.

47. Students in Mr. Carmen's class receive a list of words each month that make up their spelling and vocabulary work. They are expected to write the words in original sentences to help them remember spellings and meanings of each one. Mr. Carmen also, however, wants to build the students' vocabulary using indirect learning styles. Which of the following would not contribute to learning vocabulary indirectly?
   a. Assigning more complex "bonus words" each month that can be written and defined for extra credit.
   b. Expecting students to read a weekly newspaper.
   c. Watching an instructional-level video in class and discussing any unknown words.
   d. Asking students to complete a series of short interviews with adults in their lives.

48. Which of the following vocabulary activities would best prepare students for a unit on imagery and figurative language?
    a. A class discussion on the difference between literal and inferential comprehension.
    b. A worksheet on synonyms and antonyms.
    c. A set of word games (e.g., crosswords, word searches) involving adjectives and adverbs.
    d. A vocabulary quiz

Use the following information to answer questions 49 and 50:
    A class considers the paragraph below:

> Sarah and Kelly grinned at one another conspiratorially as they approached Dad, who was quietly reading his paper in the living room. "Dad, we'd like to ride our bikes down to Emil's house today," giggled Kelly. She glanced at her sister and shifted her weight from foot to foot. Dad appeared to think this over for a moment and replied, "Sure, that's fine with me!" The girls scampered to get their bikes and were soon on their way. With the children gone, Dad noticed how peaceful and quiet the house sounded. His reverie was quickly interrupted as he heard Mom calling from upstairs, "okay, everybody, I told you at breakfast that I need as much help as I can get to help me give the dog a bath, clean the house and finish the laundry today!" Dad groaned, knowing that he had been conned!

49. Which method would be best for helping students determine the meaning of the word "reverie" in the next to last sentence?
    a. Using context clues
    b. Making an educated guess
    c. Decoding the prefix, root, and suffix of the word
    d. Previewing and reviewing

50. Which of the following questions, when assigned as an in-class writing topic, would allow the teacher to monitor the children's inferential comprehension?
    a. What do you think the girls plan to do at Emil's once they arrive?
    b. What does it mean to say that Dad had been "conned?"
    c. Why is it important for everyone to help Mom with the chores?
    d. What did Dad enjoy so much while he was reading?

51. Which of the following choices shows the correct type of text matched with an appropriate strategy for increasing reading comprehension?
    a. Popular magazine: critical analysis/deconstruction
    b. Literary novel: key concept synthesis
    c. Persuasive essay: journaling over time, recording personal thoughts about the reading
    d. Chapter from science textbook: text outlining with vocabulary and main ideas

52. Students in an eighth grade class examine this vocabulary list on Monday. Which literary genre is likely to be introduced this week?

Vocabulary:
Narrative
Heroism
Ancient
Martyr
Duality
Supernatural
Deity
Culture

    a. Historical Fiction
    b. Poetry
    c. Mythology
    d. Drama

53. Which question below applies most closely to data analysis skills for Mrs. Layton's fifth-graders?

Our Hobbies	
Reading	8
Soccer	4
Dance	3
Art	10
Music	9
Video Games	2

    a. How many students in all reported their hobbies in this chart?
    b. Which of these hobbies is the best use of time for students?
    c. What kind of activities do the students enjoy most: physical or artistic?
    d. What is the numeric difference between the most popular and least popular hobby?

54. Which of the following practices is the best use of technology to increase reading comprehension and literacy skills?
    a. Encourage the use of tape recorders in class, by which students can record classroom conversations and lessons to be reviewed during homework and study time.
    b. Accessing a specific website online that shows children how to use graphic organizers for the stories and texts which they are reading in class.
    c. Allowing students who have completed their class work to play games or spend monitored time online.
    d. Asking students to read articles on various comprehension skills and provide a post-test to measure how well they can apply specific skills.

55. Which of the following approaches would be best for scaffolding students' peer interactions regarding classroom and independent reading?
    a. Incorporating debates into class time in which students are assigned an argument and must debate its merits with another student.
    b. Encourage students to form book groups outside of the classroom in which they select and discuss books of interest.
    c. Free discussion across the entire classroom in which students raise their hands to share thoughts and are called upon by the teacher.
    d. Dividing students into small groups of three or four and discussing comprehension/opinion questions, monitored by the teacher.

Use the following information to answer question 56:
Look at an excerpt from the worksheet assigned to a group of sixth graders.

   Match the numbers to the corresponding letter.

   1. Victor spends about an hour every day helping his grandmother around the house.
   2. Stella is always quick to smile and talk with new students at school.
   3. Jorge did not read the directions that came with his brand new telescope.
   4. Faye has been enjoying the weekend art classes she just began.

   ___a. He does not see or learn as much as he could.
   ___b. They have grown much closer and have a stronger relationship.
   ___c. She has begun to teach her little sister some of the things she has learned.
   ___d. She is well-respected among all the students.

56. What particular skill does this set of questions address?
    a. Distinguishing fact from opinion
    b. Relationship of main and supporting ideas
    c. Understanding cause and effect
    d. Sequencing in a story

57. Mr. Garson's sixth-grade class is working on a creative writing assignment in which they imagine themselves living a "day in the life" of a person from another country. This project is intended to help his students understand different points of view. Mr. Garson is surprised that Kim, who moved to Houston from China last year, is struggling to complete the assignment. She is composing very slowly compared to her classmates. How should he help Kim?

     a. Allow Kim to write freely in her first language and then ask her English as a Second Language teacher help her translate the assignment into English.

     b. Suggest that Kim simply write about a day in her own life, since she probably understands the lives of those different from her.

     c. Allow Kim to choose another topic that she is more comfortable with to write creatively about.

     d. Pair Kim with another English-language learner to assist her with completing the assignment.

58. Ms. Carroll teaches Social Studies to sixth- and seventh-grade students. She recently assigned a written report for homework. Many of the students turned in reports that were difficult to read due to phonetic and incorrect spelling. When Ms. Carroll speaks with the Language Arts teachers on her team, they tell her that the same students typically achieve very high scores on their spelling tests. Students are given a word list at the beginning of each week to be studied, and then tested on some of the words each week (the teacher reads words aloud to be recorded on an answer sheet). Which of the following is most likely to be the reason for discrepancy in spelling skills between tests and assignments?

     a. When they must concentrate on other grammar and writing skills, the students forget what they have learned for their spelling tests.

     b. The students' handwriting skills are poor, leading to unclear words and inadvertent spelling mistakes.

     c. The students have determined a way to cheat on spelling tests, knowing exactly which words to study beforehand, and do not learn the entire list.

     d. The students memorize only specific words for the week; they have not had the opportunity to develop their spelling skills within the context of writing assignments.

59. What might be the best method for informally assessing students' writing development and skills?

     a. Create a rule that mistakes on class work can always be corrected for extra credit.

     b. Make time for journaling in class during which students can write freely without being graded on mechanics, spelling, or structure.

     c. Create a class website upon which students can write content and post comments to one another.

     d. Occasionally ask the students' other teachers how they are doing with writing assignments.

Use the following information to answer questions 60 and 61:

Dear Grandma,

Hello, how are you doing? How are grandpa and Daisy? Daisy is such a cute Dog she is growing up really fast. I just started Middle School last month, I stay late on Tusdays and Thursdays so I can practice with the Team and go to meetings. I wasn't too sure how it would work out for me when I started. there is a lot more homework and lots of new, older kids. but I am starting to get used to the homework and have met some cool, new friends. I am really looking forward to visting you and grandpa during Thanksgiving. I also joined the soccer team and the drama club. thank you so much for the art set you sent me for my birthday. I have already used it to do some skeches and some sculpting! Please make the Pumpkin Pie that I like so much! Okay, that's about all I have to say right now. Write me back if you can I'll see you soon! Love, Chris

60. A sixth-grade class is instructed to write letters to family members describing daily life that will be sent out via the post office. The teacher notices several writing errors that are common across the writing samples. If this letter is a primary example of these writing errors, which set is most salient?

a. Organization of ideas, capitalization and punctuation
b. Contractions, punctuation, and writing style
c. Capitalization, spelling and use of passive voice
d. Writing style, organization of ideas, and use of active voice

61. Which lesson would not be helpful in addressing the primary issues in the students' writing?

a. Direct instruction on organizing ideas.
b. Practice with peer-editing for punctuation and capitalization errors.
c. Correcting sentences that incorrectly use passive voice.
d. Review of commonly-made spelling and capitalization mistakes.

62. Ms. Trent plans to create a rubric that will help her grade her middle-schoolers' writing samples. She wants to make sure that she is consistent across time and between various students who write with different styles. Which of the following would be most important for her to do in order to help build her students' writing skills?

a. Be sure to include every possible aspect of the writing process so that no detail is left out, as different students have different strengths.
b. Share the rubric with students so that they can monitor their own understanding of the writing process as they complete their assignments.
c. Use clear, simple language so that there is no confusion at a later date about what was intended.
d. Divide each segment of the rubric into its own category and assign equal point values—the purpose of which will be to help students understand that each aspect of the writing process is of equal value.

63. All of the following approaches are important for building students' writing skills in conjunction with one another, except:
    a. Discussing the various purposes for writing, including self-expression, narration, story-telling, persuasion and explanation.
    b. Exercises and activities that isolate and build students' writing skills, including grammar, spelling, mechanics, etc.
    c. Creating multiple and various opportunities for students to feel more at ease with the process, diminishing fear or discomfort with it.
    d. Maintaining a sequential approach to teaching writing, allowing all students to excel at one level or in one context before moving on to another.

64. What is the primary grammatical problem with this student's paragraph?

> Each of the kids in our class love to play games. Our favorite game, Hide and Go Seek, are fun and easy to play anywhere you go. The people in our class really enjoys getting to spend time with friends.

    a. punctuation
    b. subject-verb agreement
    c. word choice
    d. split infinitives

Consider the following scenario to answer question 65:

> A teacher provides some guidelines for her students who are having trouble with the Revision step of the writing process:
>
> > Take your time
> > Read very carefully, line by line
> > Use the proper symbols for specific revisions

65. What should she add to this list for students who are struggling with writing?
    a. If you find a mistake, re-write the whole sentence again.
    b. Ask a family member or friend to read your writing and suggest any revisions you ought to make.
    c. Read the paper once to correct only one convention at a time; re-reading multiple times helps eliminate mistakes.
    d. Write your paper carefully the first time around so that you do not have to spend much time in revision.

66. What activity would be most helpful to the students in the Revision step of the writing process?
    a. Provide extra direct instruction or lectures in the specific areas with which the students are struggling.
    b. Correct the students' writing and then require them to re-write their original pieces using proper grammar, spelling, etc.
    c. Place the students into pairs and have them correct each other's essays or papers to vary instruction and alleviate aversion to revision.
    d. Pull sentences from older students' writing and project it on the overhead. Use these samples to guide students in correcting them as a group.

67. All of the following are standard expectations of a child upon entering sixth grade (middle school), except for one. Which one is not a standard expectation of a child entering sixth grade?

    a. Identify and correctly spell words that are known as "commonly misspelled words," such as their/they're/there.

    b. Identify various points of view in a text, including first-person, third-person, etc.

    c. Compose poetry employing techniques such as figurative language, alliteration, onomatopoeia, etc.

    d. Understands the meanings and uses of various parts of speech in reading and writing: verbs, nouns, adjectives, pronouns, conjunctions, adverbs, prepositions, etc.

68. For students who have access to word processors in class, which phase of the writing process would be most appropriate to require the use of pencil and paper?

    a. Prewriting

    b. Drafting

    c. Publishing

    d. Presenting

Use the following information to answer questions 69 and 70:

The following conversation took place after class as a sixth-grade teacher handed Alex his most recent book report.

Mrs. Blaine: "Alex, I think you did an excellent job on the first part of your book report. You really picked up on a lot of the details in the plot—what a great memory you have! But what about the second part of the assignment? I didn't see anything about whether or not you liked the book with reasons for your opinion?"

Alex: "Yea...I just wasn't really sure what to write on that part, so I left it blank."

Mrs. Blaine: "Can you tell me now how you felt about the book?"

Alex: "It was alright, I guess. It was pretty good. It was boring at first, but I liked the way it ended."

Mrs. Blaine: "And why is that?"

Alex: "It was cool how the burglar was someone you knew all along; the author gave you clues and stuff throughout the story and you could try to solve the mystery while you were reading it."

Mrs. Blaine: "I understand. I liked that part of the story, too. Getting started on work like this can be challenging at first. <u>But it is important that you begin to learn this skill because you will use it over and over again in school and in your eventual career</u>. Let's talk about some ways to help you get going."

Alex: "Okay...sounds good."

69. What skill is Mrs. Blaine referring to in the underlined sentence?
    a. Understanding his feelings.
    b. Completing assignments thoroughly without leaving any information out.
    c. Stating an opinion or thesis and supplying supporting evidence.
    d. Writing even when you are unsure about the topic or instructions.

70. What would be the best way for Mrs. Blaine to help Alex build his skills in this area?
    a. Have Alex write his opinions and each supporting idea on paper plates or pieces of cardstock and show him how to move them around and arrange them in logical order on a large table or the floor.
    b. Have Alex explain his opinions and supporting ideas to her while she writes them down for him; he can then re-write them into the body of his report.
    c. Have Alex participate in extra lessons that let him explore his feelings about or reactions to various media, including books.
    d. Have Alex review each assignment with her before he turns it in to ensure that he has not left anything out.

71. Mr. Benton is in the process of grading the first writing assignments of the year for his eighth-grade students. He is a bit overwhelmed at the volume of errors in grammar, usage and overall composition he finds in almost every student's writing. Mr. Benton wants to use a systematic approach to building his students' writing skills, beginning by giving the students a clear and simple method to apply to their work. His goal is that the students can take part in analyzing and monitoring their own progress. What should he do?
    a. Show his students an outline of the six common writing traits and ask the students to evaluate their own skills within each trait. Teacher and student can use this evaluation to establish a plan for working on the skills that need the most help.
    b. Assign each student a writing buddy. The students can meet during writing assignments to edit one another's work. They can then separate to make the suggested revisions.
    c. Encourage the students to grade their own work using a rubric provided to them. Meet with the student to determine where they believe they need the most help and focus class work around those areas.
    d. Teach the students that most writing assignments can be composed using the five-paragraph essay model. Invest class time and homework in perfecting the model that includes thesis, evidence, and conclusions.

The following scenario is used to answer question 72:

> Mrs. Matson's 6th graders are chatting during snack time and she overhears the following conversation:
>
> Ellie: I hate how my mom always asks me how my day was, every single day! And then she gets mad when I say it's fine. But it really IS fine almost every day!
>
> Brynn: Oh, I know! My dad always wants to know what my reading is about, but sometimes I just don't feel like talking about it. It takes long enough to read it without talking about it.
>
> Jon: You have it easy. My mom AND dad help me with my homework every night, and then they give me extra work to do!

72. Mrs. Matson would like to not only give students a chance to voice their feelings about the changing communications with their parents, but also help them find a way to channel those feelings into something positive. Which project would be best for allowing students a positive way to communicate with their parents about what is happening in school?
   a. Encourage the students to talk to their parents about everything that is happening in school; after all, their parents only want to help them.
   b. After talking about this issue, ask the students to write short pieces about their schoolwork and experiences during the day and compile them into a newsletter to be sent home every two weeks.
   c. Help the students write letters to their parents, telling them how they feel about the issue
   d. Tell students to keep a log of their activities in the classroom and throughout the day to be shown to parents on a daily or weekly basis.

Use the following scenario to answer question 73:

> A middle-school teacher has written several questions on the chalk board to assist students in revising their most recent essays.
>
>> Do you know the meanings of all the vocabulary in your essay?
>> Did you use any major words (besides articles like a, an, and, the) more than three times?
>> Do you like the way your writing sounds when you read it aloud?
>> Does all the language used make sense?

73. Judging by the questions above, which writing trait is this teacher encouraging her students to work on today?
   a. sentence fluency
   b. ideas and development
   c. writing conventions
   d. word choice

Read the persuasive writing excerpt below to answer question 74:

"Why Peace is Important"
Peace is important to our lives. We have to have peace because we can't be fighting all the time. When people fight, they can't do anything else. It also makes everybody else feel upset and angry because they have to listen to the fighting. If you want to have peace you can talk to the person and try to get them to agree with you and say you are sorry if you do something wrong.

74. How could a teacher help this student develop his persuasive writing skills, based on this initial attempt?
   a. Continue to give positive reinforcement; this student has a good understanding of the persuasive structure.
   b. Introduce the use of a graphic organizer or flow chart to help the student organize his main idea and supporting evidence in a logical way.
   c. Encourage the student to include more details in his writing to make it more interesting and more personal.
   d. Focus primarily on the editing and revising processes to correct writing conventions, usage, and grammar.

75. A Language teacher is introducing a new writing topic to her class. She asks them to pretend that the person they are writing to or for is "an alien from outer space." What type of writing is she probably introducing?
   a. Fantasy/fiction
   b. Poetry
   c. Persuasive essay
   d. How-to article

76. Ms. Burns' fourth-graders are working very hard at building writing skills on many levels. They have come a long way with their knowledge of the six traits of writing, as well as their confidence in their own abilities. Some of the students have trouble finding their own unique "voices" when writing, probably because they are working so hard to maintain accurate grammar, spelling, organization, and continuity of ideas. How can Ms. Burns help the students inject their own personalities and voices into their writing without sacrificing correctness?
   a. Explain that they should always be sure to include personal opinions and insights to make the writing interesting.
   b. Project overhead examples of good writing that appropriately utilizes personal voice and lead a discussion about them in class.
   c. Guide students to select only topics with which they are very knowledgeable and explain that it is never a good idea to write about something that is unfamiliar to them.
   d. Teach students to imagine themselves as a new character every time they write--they should write from the point of view of that individual, phrasing things the way that person or character would if they were speaking.

Read the excerpt below to answer question 77:

> I like sweets. Cookies, cake and ice cream are very sweet and good. I like to eat these things after school or after I eat. Sweet tastes are the best for me and I do not like salty food. When I eat dessert, I feel so good and happy. My mom says that I should not eat too many sweets or I will get cavities, so I have to brush my teeth after eating them.

77. Which activity would benefit this student's writing skills the most?
   a. Make "word bulletin boards" with the student to help her build vocabulary to make her writing more interesting.
   b. Practice with editing other students' writing to familiarize her with writing conventions.
   c. Grammar exercises, specifically subject-verb agreement.
   d. Encouraging her to select a more challenging writing topic to stretch her skill level.

78. Mr. Talbot's class has an opportunity to begin writing letters to students in France who are learning English, just as Mr. Talbot's class is learning French. He knows that this will be an excellent opportunity for the students to work on letter-writing as well as build their language skills. What other writing skill can he use this opportunity to strengthen in his students?
   a. He can help them work through the five-step writing process and the six traits of writing; letter-writing is an excellent exercise for bringing all of those traits and steps together.
   b. He can teach them the proper formatting of letters and the etiquette of writing a good letter.
   c. He can teach them to consider their audience when writing by talking about what they know of their pen pals' lives, what they would find interesting, and how to communicate effectively with others who are not like themselves.
   d. He can teach his students about the importance of proper writing conventions like punctuation, grammar, and spelling, because their pen pals are still learning English.

79. An eighth-grade teacher assigns an end-of-the-year project for her English students. The students are placed into groups and instructed to make an "ad campaign" that includes a print ad, a television/radio commercial, and a persuasive essay. What is the teacher's most likely primary objective?
   a. To equip students with practical, real-life job experience in a competitive world.
   b. To allow students to apply concepts they have learned about audience, point of view, media messages, etc.
   c. To incorporate the use of technology into a unit of study.
   d. To encourage students to work cooperatively in groups.

80. A sixth-grade teacher begins class by showing a series of inkblot images, one by one, on pieces of cardstock. She asks her students to number their papers from 1-20 and write down what they think each image depicts. After the exercise, she asks for a few volunteers to explain what they saw in each inkblot. What do you think this teacher is attempting to convey?

a. That visual images can be interpreted differently, depending on the individual viewer.
b. That cultural symbols are typically universal and are inherent in our cultural mindset.
c. That psychological differences are often misconstrued as mental illness.
d. That it is important not to confirm understandings of visual images with peers before determining their meaning.

81. After reading Shakespeare's Romeo and Juliet in class, students watch the most recent Hollywood film version, starring Leonardo DiCaprio. Their teacher leads a class discussion after the film. Which of the following essay topics would be most helpful in challenging students to analyze how visual media affects their perceptions of a piece of literature?

a. Discuss your favorite character in the film version of Romeo and Juliet, and give at least three reasons to back up your opinion.
b. Which version of Romeo and Juliet did you like better, and why?
c. Compare the film with the play and point out at least four instances in which portions of the play were left out of the film version.
d. Describe the setting of the film and discuss why you think the film's director chose to portray the play in modern times.

Consider the picture below for answering question 82:

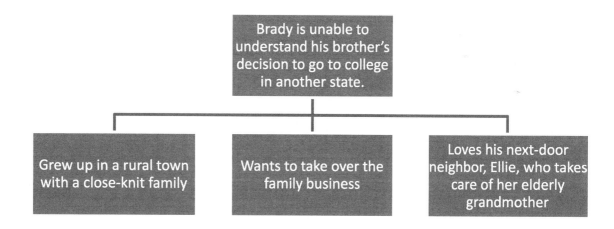

82. Mr. James created a poster featuring this chart to accompany his class instruction for the day. He will be showing students how to organize information into text organizers to help themselves understand what they have read. What other skill might this kind of organizer build as well?

    a. Constructing a paragraph
    b. Answering literature-based multiple-choice questions
    c. Character analysis
    d. Writing conventions

83. Mr. Ank has a game he plans to play with his middle school English students today. He has recorded several commercials from television and will play them without sound for the students. After each silent commercial, the students will share their ideas about what product the commercial is advertising. Following this game, the class will participate in a follow-up discussion and exercise. What is the likely purpose of Mr. Ank's game?

    a. To turn his students into savvy consumers.
    b. To help students understand how visual images affect meaning and understanding.
    c. To demonstrate how students can use visual images in their own schoolwork.
    d. To introduce variation into his instruction and give the kids a fun activity.

Use the drawing below to answer question 84.

84. A teacher plans to use the drawing above to explain story elements. Each point on the line represents an element of the story. Which choice matches the point on the chart with the smiling face above it?

    a. Rising Action
    b. Exposition
    c. Resolution
    d. Climax

85. Mrs. Gilbert, an English teacher, and Ms. Dudley, an Art teacher, are working together to create an integrated unit of study for their common students. The students will be studying King Tut, reading various accounts of his life, both fiction and non-fiction. Ms. Dudley will be guiding the students through various art projects related to the time period in which King Tut lived (e.g., making papyrus). Which choice provides an example of an additional project or lesson that will address visual interpretation and decoding skills?

     a. The students participate in Ancient Egypt Day and can dress up as characters or historical figures from the appropriate time period.

     b. The students visit a local museum exhibit on Ancient Egypt and keep a log of visual images and representations they see. The class discusses those images and their meanings during both classes.

     c. The students write stories about the lives of Ancient Egyptians and draw illustrations to go along with their writing.

     d. The students watch a movie about King Tut and create free-writing pieces based on what they have seen.

86. Mrs. Canas has had a parent offer to visit her fifth-grade class and provide a sign language seminar. The parent is fluent in American Sign Language and would like to offer her skills to benefit the students. Mrs. Canas thinks the seminar will be very interesting and provide a unique way to hone her students' listening and expressive skills. Which choice identifies another language skill set that would indirectly benefit from this seminar?

     a. Students' understanding of how visual messages, including body language, facial expression, and signs inform verbal communication and ideas.

     b. Students' fine motor skills and hand-eye coordination.

     c. Students' respect for other cultures, specifically the non-hearing community.

     d. Students' ability to communicate with other peers and adults in their community.

87. An eighth-grade class will be watching a mystery film in English class over the next two days. Throughout the story, the camera will often focus on objects or clothing that are colored bright red. These objects are always related to clues that lead the character toward solving the mystery. What literary device is the students' teacher planning to introduce in this context?

     a. Media deconstruction

     b. Color imagery

     c. Alliteration

     d. Symbolism

88. Middle school students at Ms. Kelso's school are expected to complete a large independent study project to be presented at the end of the second term. The project is the culmination of reading research, writing a paper, and the final element of publishing, or presentation. The students can choose how they present their work and are instructed to use visual aids. Which of the following would be a helpful guideline for Ms. Kelso to offer her students?

    a. Whenever possible, use pictures, video, music, charts and graphs to supplement your presentation for the purpose of keeping your audience's interest.
    b. Think about any parts of your paper that might be hard to explain. Choose a visual aid to help you show your audience the concept, and then use your words to explain it.
    c. Select the most interesting photographs from your research, create color photocopies, and pass them throughout the class during your presentation.
    d. Use your main ideas and supporting evidence to create a Power-point slideshow, making note-taking and organization simple and clear.

89. Which of the following visual images would be most appropriate for teaching students about how media images influence their perceptions and attitudes?

    a. a photograph found in a journalistic magazine, such as Time
    b. an illustration or diagram found in the students' own Social Studies textbook
    c. a political cartoon found in the newspaper
    d. a non-political cartoon found in another section of the newspaper

Use the following information to answer questions 90 and 91:

> A middle school class is working through the process of creating a research project. Since this kind of assignment is completely new, their teacher provides direct instruction and practice assignments to help the students approach the large project.

90. Which of the following approaches would increase a middle-school student's preliminary research skills?

    a. Assign and analyze a research paper on a topic of the student's choosing.
    b. Require students to submit a separate outline before completing a research paper.
    c. Require students to turn in note cards containing relevant information on each source they will use in an upcoming research project.
    d. Pre-test on several subjects to determine which area or discipline to explore.

91. What is the first point at which the teacher should meet individually to talk with the student?

    a. After the student first chooses a topic
    b. After the student turns in research note cards
    c. After the student completes the initial outline
    d. After the rough draft has been turned in

92. An eighth-grade teacher notices that her students perform very well on scheduled tests in class, but struggle with pop quizzes or other in-class assignments that involve recalling information. In discussing this issue with other teachers on her team, she finds that this is a pattern across all disciplines. What would be the best way to help students retain information on a daily or weekly basis in the absence of the motivation of an upcoming test?
   a. Devote the first few minutes of class on previewing information and tasks and the last few minutes of each class summarizing highlights from class work and homework reading.
   b. Increase the frequency of pop quizzes in hopes that the students will begin to study at home more often.
   c. Give the students a study guide before each quiz so they know what will be tested.
   d. Allow the students to work on the quizzes in groups so that they can help each other with memory and recall.

Use the following scenario to answer question 93:

   Mr. Katz draws these diagrams on the board at the beginning of English class. Janie and Katherine are the two main characters in the book which his class is currently reading.

Janie's Character Traits		Katherine's Character Traits	
1. Bossy		1. Kind to others	
2.		2.	
3.		3.	
	Same	Different	
Janie	1. 2. 3.	1. 2. 3.	
Katherine	1. 2. 3.	1. 2. 3.	

93. Based on the above diagram, what concept do you think Mr. Katz plans to teach?
   a. Structural Text Analysis
   b. Compare/Contrast
   c. Inferential Comprehension
   d. Use of Graphic/Text Organizers

94. Mrs. Costanza's eighth-grade students bring up some concerns during class time. They complain that their teachers are assigning too much reading for homework and that they are worried that they will never be able to retain the information for tests. Some students say that they don't know how to predict what information is important and what is not. What can Mrs. Costanza do to help them?
    a. Encourage students to allow enough time when studying to effectively memorize all the necessary information in the texts and assigned readings.
    b. Teach the students the SQ3R (Survey, Question, Read, Recite/Write, and Review) method.
    c. Ask other eighth-grade teachers to provide study guides that will outline exactly what will be on each test.
    d. Discuss the importance of taking detailed notes in class and asking relevant questions during class discussions.

95. Ana Velasquez's eighth-grade class at Jones Middle School is beginning a unit in which they will be expected to complete a research project. They will choose from a list of topics and then write a report. Each student is required to have a bibliography that includes at least one entry each from the following sources: the internet, library books, newspaper articles, and magazine articles. Which of the following topics would be the best choice for Ana?
    a. Day in the Life of the Velasquez family
    b. Hurricane Katrina
    c. The History of Jones High School
    d. How to get your homework done faster!

Use the following information to answer questions 96 and 97:

A teacher is talking with her students about the best way to retain information learned during a unit or course of study. She wants them to be prepared for high school and college, during which they will rely primarily on their class notes to study for tests and prepare papers. She describes these steps:

1. Read all assigned material before class. Make notes on any new vocabulary, questions or ideas you have as you read.
2. Take notes in class based on discussions and lectures.
3. Before the test, review your notes and assigned readings, spending more time on those segments which you remember the least.

96. In step #2, the teacher shows her students how to divide their note pages in half, using one side of the paper for main ideas or questions, and the other side for details relating to those larger concepts. What is the likely purpose of her demonstration?
   a. To help students understand cause and effect relationships, which will assist them in other disciplines such as History and Science.
   b. To emphasize the difference between main ideas and details. This emphasis will support an upcoming lesson on constructing a five-paragraph essay with a main idea and supporting evidence.
   c. To help students be more orderly and write neatly when it comes to taking notes, which will in turn make studying for tests and papers much easier.
   d. To show students how they can begin to organize their information and understanding about a subject as they take notes, constructing meaning from a large amount of information.

97. What step should be included at #3 to supplement her instruction?
   a. Meet with a partner for any information you failed to write down during class.
   b. Take an audio recorder with you in order to record everything discussed in lectures and class.
   c. Review your notes periodically; at least once a week.
   d. Read all assigned material at least once more in its entirety.

98. An eighth-grade teacher plans to deliver a test on a book recently read and discussed in class. He plans to include some short answers, multiple choice, fill-in-the-blanks, and 2-3 essay questions. The students are familiar with multiple-choice and fill-ins, but are not accustomed to short answers and essays. He wants to scaffold their attempts to study the large amount of material. What should he do?
   a. Make the test "open-notes."
   b. Provide a copy of the questions ahead of time so that the students can formulate their answers.
   c. Provide several sessions of written practice and instruction with similar short-answer and essay questions, and discuss the students' answers afterward.
   d. Allow the students to re-take the test if they struggle the first time around.

99. Sully is struggling to write his eighth-grade research report. His writing is full of great ideas and generalizations, but few supporting details and little evidence. When his teacher suggests that he needs to provide more supporting information, he looks blankly at her. How can she help him understand this concept and improve his paper?

    a. Tell Sully that his writing topic is too broad, and ask him some guiding questions to narrow it down. These questions could include: "what is most important to you about this subject?" and "what do you most want your readers to learn about?"

    b. As much as it will be frustrating for Sully, explain to him that sometimes it is easiest to start from scratch when a paper does not fit the appropriate format. Instruct him to use his previous paper to make a new outline for a new paper. Help him make the outline in great detail and then encourage him to simply use his previous paper as a source for details when writing the newer version.

    c. Use a graphic organizer that contains two columns: "ideas" and "details/evidence." Guide Sully to pick his top three or four main ideas and fill in the right hand side with appropriate details and information. Encourage him to use this exercise to revise his paper by adding in his evidence and eliminating any information that is not listed on his graphic organizer.

    d. Help him brainstorm a list of facts about his topic from memory and his research. Show Sully how to take his ideas one by one, adding at least two facts or details after each idea. Instruct him to make sure that each idea has supporting evidence and details.

100. Mrs. Bray's students have been performing poorly on in-class quizzes, lately. She gives them notice that there will be quizzes in class, although she does not tell them when they will take place. How can she help improve the students' performance without giving them direct insight about the quiz dates or material?

    a. Provide more opportunities for taking tests and quizzes in order to lower anxiety and increase familiarity with the format.

    b. Talk with the students about how they are preparing for quizzes and suggest alternatives that match the intended outcomes of the quiz.

    c. When covering potential quiz information emphasize and indirectly communicate that students should pay close attention.

    d. Send a note home to parents asking them to study with their children in anticipation of the quizzes.

Answers and Explanations

1. C: Oral language skills can be distinguished from specific speech characteristics exhibited by some children. Many students like Rosa, whose first language is not English, will speak with an accent and may be less clear when speaking about a topic that is unfamiliar. In fact, even those who are not English Language Learners may exhibit difficulty speaking on new topics. Greer may avoid oral assignments or speaking in class for a number of reasons, such as self-consciousness. This student could be helped by evaluating oral language skills in a one-on-one environment or by introducing peer scaffolding to help reduce anxiety. Brett's demeanor in group assignments may also be due to social characteristics rather than oral skills; it would be important to evaluate his skills in various contexts. Ashley, however, shows marked problems communicating orally both in class discussion and in prepared assignments. She would benefit from specific instruction related to presenting ideas orally.

2. D: Choice "a" would be appropriate for class work or homework, but is less likely than other choices to provide a deep understanding of the relationships between oral and spoken word. Choice "b" would address multicultural interest, but would not require interpretation since only recitation is assigned. Choice "c" could allow students to learn more about their classmates' backgrounds, but would require more specific parameters to ensure that both the multicultural and oral learning outcomes were achieved. Choice "c" also does not address the assumption that the classmates' family backgrounds are diverse, which may not be the case. Choice "d" requires students to use their research skills to learn more about another culture. By assigning a first-person narrative, Mr. Callas encourages the students to imagine life from the perspective of another person. This assignment also requires the student to make the transition from research to written assignment to spoken word.

3. C: Each answer can be an effective tool in teaching students to build oral language skills. The question makes clear that the objective is to help students evaluate their own oral language skills, which will assist them in both spoken and written assignments. The only answer choice that involves the student himself evaluating his message is answer "c." When the student prepares a review/quiz based upon important information, he or she will be more able to speak specifically to that information. When classmates complete the review, the student can identify any patterns in the questions' answers that give clues as to how well those main ideas were communicated. In this way, the student can evaluate how effective the oral presentation was, without relying on classmates or the teacher.

4. A: Even for the older students who are a bit behind grade level, having a chance to help a younger student can increase their confidence and oral skills. Students are challenged to explain and give feedback to the Kindergarteners and will have to think about how best to explain ideas to another person. By pairing the older students with younger ones, they have a chance to be the "teachers," and must consider their purpose and audience when speaking. Regardless of the older student's reading abilities, he or she can build their confidence and skill in oral language by helping a younger student with basic reading skills.

5. B: The purpose of this exercise is for the older students to build their confidence and oral language skills by helping to teach younger students. By doing this, older students build their skills by thinking critically about how to help a new reader understand basic reading

skills. In Choice "a", the English language learner may build reading skills, but will not have a chance to build confidence or oral skills, which are just as important to their language development. In Choice "c", the English language learner may lose confidence in attempting to meet program standards without the necessary language skills. In Choice "d", students practice listening skills, which would only indirectly build oral skills. Choice "b" allows students to learn not only by listening, but by having a chance to explain or assist when he or she has the requisite skills to do so. A skilled student is also there to assist when needed.

6. D: The "Phrase of the Day" appears from the question prompt to be dedicated to certain types of oral language, including analogies and idioms. By asking the students to record interpretations in an informal way (through pictures or the students' own words), he will have insight as to their perceptions about common language. He also directly builds the students' oral language skills by giving them the correct meaning of the phrase with which the students can compare their original answers. In this way, Mr. Campbell assesses and builds skills without the use of a formal test or quiz.

7. B: Oral language skills incorporate speaking, listening, and knowledge of conventional language. In Choice "a", students would be limited to a very specific vocabulary in order to work with the science and math programs, and would not have opportunities to increase their knowledge of language. In Choice "c", students are practicing their listening skills, but are not required to speak or think critically about what they have heard. Choice "d" does involve technology and class discussions; however, the benefit of watching the discussion on tape is relatively unclear. In Choice "b", students not only have a chance to build their speaking and listening skills, but also increase their knowledge of other cultures and ways of speaking.

8. C: In choices "a" and "b," students are primarily using written language in order to present to the class. They are required to use what they have composed as the text for their oral presentations. In Choice "c", students have the chance to learn how to prioritize information they have read and written, and also learn to modify the written word to create an oral presentation based upon specific parameters. This exercise highlights the differences between the written and spoken word. Choice "d" does not necessarily involve all of the students and less directly increases the students' oral skills in a relevant way.

9. D: In this activity, students are practicing a variety of skills related to communication. By analyzing the log sheet, it is apparent that students are expected to work on their conversational skills, including listening and speaking. Choice "a" refers to those points on the log sheet that relate to listening while another person is speaking. Choice "c" also pertains to listening skills, specifically with eye contact and other behaviors that let the student know that his partner was listening and making an effort to understand. Choice "b" refers to the ability to speak clearly (each word can be clearly understood) and effectively (the ideas behind the words make sense to the listener). Choice "d" could potentially come to fruition; however, conflict resolution is not specifically addressed in this activity.

10. C: Oral language skills are almost un-quantifiable because they cover a multitude of competencies. Vocabulary, enunciation, listening, body language, comprehension and many other skills directly affect a student's communicative ability. This particular activity primarily focuses on peer interactions. However, conversing with adults provides opportunities for students to learn new vocabulary and ways of speaking. Choices "a," " b" and "d" are possible outcomes or functions of the teacher's partnering with a new student

during each conversation. However, teachers must keep in mind that it is just as important for students to converse with adults in a context that allows them to learn from observation as well as participation.

11. D: In the debate process, it is important for students to take a position and support it with evidence or arguments in order to make their claims effective. Choice "d" requires students to formulate their opinions and supporting arguments, and helps them reduce extraneous information and create "reminders" for their talking points on notecards. Choice "c" requires students to prepare their arguments but encourages reading aloud during the debate rather than actually speaking directly to their opponent or to the crowd. Choice "c" fails to help students distinguish between written language and oral language and their occasionally separate purposes. Choice "b" creates opportunities for informal debate, but does not teach students the parameters for formal debating. Choice "a" is similarly informal and does not familiarize students with the preparation process with respect to formulating arguments, opinions, or preparing to speak in front of a large audience.

12. A: In Choice "a", the teacher guides previewing of information to show students how to put themselves in the right frame of mind to listen carefully for meaning. Students are then able to listen in a guided way based upon the previewing. By varying the type of comprehension assessment, the teacher will get a better understanding of what the students learned. Choice "b" is a good exercise, but does not provide for direct instruction by the teacher or a particularly skilled student. In Choice "c", students are focusing more upon reading comprehension than listening since they must read the story to themselves and then write a report. There is then no way to gauge what they have learned. The final choice would be useful, but does not include teacher-guided previewing, which is very helpful in building comprehension.

13. B: At the start of a new school year, a teacher will likely choose to engage in a series of exercises to help her understand her students' current ability levels. These exercises must provide opportunities for evaluation of the whole class, rather than a select few students. In Choice "a", the teacher is not likely to get a lot of information from each student during class discussion, since not all children may participate. An instruction-level text may also prove too difficult for some students to read without guidance from a fluent reader. Choice "c", while a good exercise for peer-assisted reading, would not provide the teacher chances to evaluate each student's comprehension at once. Choice "d" would be very time-consuming; it would also cause students to influence each other's comprehension (e.g. the students going first may influence the comprehension of those re-telling the story later). Choice "b" allows the teacher to evaluate the students' independent comprehension levels with one assignment.

14. A: Emergent readers are those who are not yet reading fluently (with appropriate speed and accuracy). Choice "b" refers to the practice of reviewing relationships between letters and sounds, which is vital to building reading skills. Choice "c" would help students build vocabulary retention by requiring them to find unfamiliar words in the dictionary. This practice causes the student to analyze and retain spelling of unfamiliar words, as well as reinforces dictionary/reference skills. Choice "d" addresses the fact that many words in the English language are irregularly spelled and cannot be decoded with conventional phonetic instruction. While invented spelling described in Choice "a" may be permitted in emergent readers, this practice is not likely to build specific reading skills.

15. C: Literacy skills encompass a variety of contexts: written, verbal, comprehension, vocabulary, grammar, spelling, etc. Designing class work that touches on these multiple contexts must allow the children to increase not only skills that can be measured on tests or written work. Reading a play gives students a chance to touch on comprehension, vocabulary, and grammar; acting the play out creates the opportunity for increased comprehension and oral interpretation. Each of the alternate answers focuses on one specific aspect of literacy skills, without incorporating multiple contexts.

16. B: Assessment is an ongoing process that involves formal testing and a host of other methods. Students are working at any given time in the school year on a multitude of skills sets, and all of these skills are interrelated and developing simultaneously at different rates. It is impossible to ever provide a "snapshot" of a student's abilities, because each student develops in a unique and complex manner. Choice "a" would only offer insight into a student's reading fluency. Choice "c" would show how a student could perform on standardized tests; however, many factors such as anxiety and test-taking speed affect those scores. Choice "d" relies on the teacher to interpret the student's strengths and weaknesses and would require an almost impossible attention to detail. Choice "b" includes both formal and informal assessments as well as giving insight into writing, vocabulary and other skill sets in a comprehensive portfolio.

17. A: Those who are familiar with the guided oral reading strategy will note that the struggling student must be paired with a fluent and skilled partner. If you are not familiar with this strategy, all of the answer choices could conceivably be a part of the oral reading strategy and appear to be related to one another. However, one choice does not make sense after reading all four options. In answer choices "b" and "d," Valeria's partner is required to read the text aloud and offer correction or feedback when Valeria reads aloud. If Valeria is paired with another struggling student (as suggested in Choice "a", neither "b" nor "d" would prove effective in building her reading fluency.

18. B: Mr. Waleran's purpose is to encourage students to express themselves in written words, interpreting their thoughts into writing. However, there are often children who cannot write well enough to create coherent or legible works. In these cases, it is still possible for students to express themselves in writing. Choice "b" allows Dimitri to express himself by drawing, which will likely make him feel more comfortable with the activity. He will also have the chance to use words he does know and incorporate them into his work. As his skills grow, he can gradually transition into more formal writing. Choices "a" and "c" allow Dimitri to explore his thoughts, but do not build his writing skills. Choice "d" will, in all likelihood, become a chore for Dimitri and reinforce his struggles with reading and writing.

19. D: Part of building literacy skills is showing students how to listen effectively to various types of texts: narrative, poetry, informative, etc. In order to become competent in a variety of literacy skills, students must be able to listen for information and for pleasure/experience. This teacher is not only exposing them to poetry, but creating a forum in which they can actively listen and then discuss what they have experienced or learned. The scenario given in Choice "a" could possibly be true, as could Choice "c". But it is less likely that the teacher would devote an entire month of reading and listening to a specific type of text simply to give her students a break or to make a point about poetry versus prose. Choice "b" assumes that the poetry she reads will rhyme, which is not always the case.

20. B: Mrs. Taylor's project introduces students to an ancient form of expression that was written, but not based upon alphabetic principles, like English. This project is applicable to all levels of readers, as it incorporates various kinds of media to assist comprehension. Students are required to listen and read for information so that they can apply what they have learned to creating their own hieroglyphics. In Choice "b", the answer suggests that what is learned about hieroglyphics will assist students in understanding those with different backgrounds. However, hieroglyphics are not used in any widespread way today, and are much less helpful in building multicultural awareness than perhaps a lesson on modern Egyptian culture or writing.

21. D: Teachers should try to avoid shallow notions of what it means to provide cultural or multi-cultural education; in Choice "a", we cannot presume to understand another person by listening to his favorite music or watching a favorite movie. In Choice "b", there is also the assumption that there is a variety of musical tastes in the class, which may not be the case. In fact, if many students pick the same song, it is possible to use that choice to open up dialogue about what they lyrics mean and why they are so popular with the class. Choice "c" is posed in direct opposition to Choice "d". However, Choice "d" suggests what most teachers know to be true: literacy skills are not just important for schoolwork and class work; students must be able to take meaning from a variety of different sources in order to grow into educated adults. Music is an important medium through which students can express themselves and learn about the world around them through comprehension and listening skills.

22. C: All children learn their letter-sound correspondences at different rates. This particular child may simply be showing his teacher that he has not quite mastered this skill set yet. However, the inconsistence with producing the sounds could possibly be a signal that he needs specialized instruction. It is impossible, however, to know exactly what is going on without providing specialized instruction and giving that instruction time to improve skills. Choice "a" suggests an immediate referral for special-needs testing, which may be unnecessary and too soon in this scenario. Choice "b" states that all children learn differently which is certainly true, but does not provide a plan for helping the child improve. In the final choice, the parents may become needlessly alarmed and spend extra money in a situation where the intervention may not be necessary or even helpful. Choice "c" provides specific instruction in the deficient skill and acknowledges that the child may improve on his own; but if he needs it, extra help can be found.

23. D: Students are expected to be able to express themselves verbally and build upon one another's ideas in class as they complete fourth and fifth grades. However, many students lack the confidence or skills to participate in class discussions or conversations. Rather than leave those students to their own devices, as suggested in choices "a" and "b" a teacher must help instruct the students on how to communicate orally in situations where they can be successful. Choice "c" would require the students to speak out more, but might not alleviate issues with preparedness or confidence as would Choice "d" which allows students to feel more comfortable and get the teacher's guidance.

24. B: This prompt focuses not only on reading fluency skills, but also on the issue of the young reader's confidence. It is very common for students who feel unsuccessful at reading to avoid the skill altogether. The teacher in this question realizes something important: it is vital to build a student's confidence with reading as he or she builds skill. In choice "a" there

is a faulty assumption that a student could ever memorize enough words to eliminate the need to decode. While some students with processing disorders or different learning styles do rely more heavily on sight words, this practice should not be solely relied upon. In choice "c" the students will likely feel negatively about being asked to read young children's books; their lack of confidence may be reinforced by this plan. In choice "d" students may also be frustrated by the extra work they are required to do without any evidence of success with this practice. In Choice "b", students can build their fluency skills by creating words with various sounds, which is often easier for students than decoding as they are learning to read. As their knowledge of letter-sound relationships grows, they will become better at decoding words they see on the page. Allowing students to encode will also provide them with more chances to feel successful as they learn.

25. C: Reading fluency is defined as a set of skills including speed, accuracy and inflection when reading words on a page. Reading comprehension generally refers to the ability to understand what is being read. Both sets of skills are important, and reading fluency is vital to comprehension, which is the ultimate goal of the practice of reading. It is possible, even common, to isolate skills for the purpose of skill-building or to compensate for areas in which a student is struggling; however, all skills are inter-related. Children can make progress in some aspects of reading while still working on more difficult areas. Based on these ideas, choices "a" and "d" can be ruled out as possible answers. Comprehension is typically not classified as being part of fluency skills, which eliminates Choice "b". Reading fluency should be considered a vital part of overall reading skills: fluency must be improved so that, ultimately, the student can comprehend what is being read more fully.

26. A: It is important to evaluate specific reading skills, such as phonemic awareness, in a variety of contexts. Reading aloud with Abi allowed his teacher to notice that he consistently misread words beginning with digraphs. Digraphs are sounds in which two distinct letters, when combined, produce a single third sound (e.g. when "s" and "h" produce the "-sh" sound). Blends are words in which two letters produce a third sound which is a combination of both sounds put together (e.g. "b" and "l" combined to make "b"). The only set of words consisting only of digraphs is choice set "a."

27. D: The first three choices are all required standards to be met by eighth-graders. Students at this grade level should, of course, be able to identify grade-level words and understand the phonemes and elements within them. Students at this level should also be familiar with words that cannot necessarily be decoded with typical approaches, but that they will encounter on a regular basis (such as phenomenon or charisma). Eighth-graders should also be able to identify and explain similarities in different kinds of texts, as stated in Choice "b", and differences in points of view, as described in Choice "c". However, an extensive knowledge of cultural literature and its effect on media is required to meet the standard in Choice "d". This type of knowledge base, in addition to advanced deconstruction skills mentioned in Choice "d", is more typical of work done in grades 9-12.

28. A: In the passage, Susannah misspells seven words. Six of these misspelled words, when spelled correctly, have silent letter-sounds (phonemes). If Susannah misspells a particular pattern of words in her writing, she may have difficulty reading the same kinds of words independently. While sight word practice Choice "a" would certainly be helpful, teaching Susannah the concept of a "silent e" would be more effective than instructing her to learn similar words by memorizing them out of context. Choices "c" and "d" are also helpful in

building reading skills; however, neither of them targets the specific type of word with which Susannah is struggling.

29. C: In Choice "a", the word prince is capitalized, though it does not have a suffix. The word undying is underlined, but should also be capitalized since it has both a prefix and a suffix. If you continue to apply the instructions given by the teacher, you will find that each sentence contains at least one mistake. Choice "c" contains a word with the root "please," which also has both a prefix and a suffix. Therefore, it is correctly underlined and capitalized.

30. B: Reading fluency refers to the speed, inflection and accuracy with which students read, either orally or silently. In order to read fluently, students must be able to decode, or break down into segments, words that adhere to the common rules of the English alphabet. For those words that are not easily decoded, students must build their vocabulary of "sight words," which are recognized without the need to decode. In Choice "a", students may or may not be reading fluently or accurately, since the computer program does not monitor how the student reads. In Choice "c", keyboarding practice bears no direct relationship to reading fluency. In Choice "d", again, the computer is simply a source for text, but does not build any specific fluency skill. In Choice "b", students are exposed to sight words and vocabulary in a fun way. Using a computer program allows for an unlimited supply of relevant words and for accurate scoring.

31. C: In Choice "a", parents would take up an inordinate amount of class time discussing literacy, without necessarily building any skills. This choice would also rely on the assumption that parents could speak effectively about this topic. Choice "b" would create inconsistency in grading, since there is interpretation and expertise required even in using a grading rubric. Choice "d" would certainly make the teacher's job easier to manage. However, Choice "c" allows parents with limited training to help students build reading fluency by reading challenging texts and building accuracy and speed. This choice satisfies both of the teacher's needs: taking into account the parents' limited training and helping the students most directly.

32. A: True fluency not only involves reading accurately and with appropriate speed, but using vocal inflection to communicate punctuation and emotion. Many students possess fluency with respect to accuracy or speed, but do not reflect interest or comprehension in their vocal modulation. Choice "b" suggests that volume is most important; however, volume can be considered a part of vocal expression. Choice "c" does not guarantee that the student will read with appropriate inflection or accuracy since interest level does not dictate fluency. At a certain point, students should not continue to increase their reading speed, as reading too quickly negatively affects comprehension. Therefore, Choice "d" is incorrect.

33. B: Much research points to the fact that students can increase their speed, accuracy and inflection when they engage in repeated readings of various texts. By reading assigned pieces more than once, they have a chance to apply feedback which they have received so that they make fewer mistakes and read more quickly. Students will struggle if they are only exposed to phonetic rules, without working on automatic word recognition or practice activities, as is suggested in Choice "a". Applying the same logic to vocabulary, it is necessary to rule out Choice "c". Choice "d" is not a widely accepted method for building reading fluency for student readers in traditional schools.

34. C: Generally speaking, students will read more slowly when introduced to texts and material that is new; speed increases with each subsequent reading. Hence, answer A) describes a normal child's reading pattern. When reading material independently, a student should not find more than approximately 1 in 20 words to be "difficult to read." Therefore, answer "b" is incorrect. Answer "d" refers to a comprehension test, which is not specifically related to the monitoring of fluency skills. This answer can be ruled out based upon its irrelevance. However, a student reading instructional-level material should find no more than 1 in 10 words difficult to read. Therefore, a student finding 1 in 5 questions difficult on an instructional-level test may need extra help or a text more appropriate for his age level.

35. B: Previewing information is a method by which students can work to improve their own unguided reading comprehension. During the previewing process, students consider the topic at hand, what they already know about it, and what they would like to learn or believe they will learn. Previewing helps students to approach reading for the purpose of comprehension ("reading to learn") and retention. In Choice "a", students will already be familiar with the text if they have already seen the movie; therefore, their previewing will be affected by familiarity with the text. The same is true for Choice "c", as the students have already read the novel. In Choice "d", previewing the poetry will indeed increase familiarity with the poems. However, reading poetry is typically not a process that involves "reading to learn." Instead, poetry is more often approached as a pleasure-reading activity or an opportunity for literary analysis. Allowing students to preview science material helps them actively learn to read for information and will aid them in other subjects.

36. B: The object of this unit is to teach students to monitor their own comprehension as they read longer and longer texts. The only choice that involves students analyzing their own understanding is Choice "b". This practice shows students logical points in the text to pause and ask themselves whether or not they understand that which they have read. Summarizing will help them identify main points in the story. Choice "b" is also the only choice that allows the teacher to directly instruct her students on comprehension while reading the book in class.

37. C: Many factors can affect a student's ability to understand what he or she is reading. Building comprehension skills is an ongoing process and can be made difficult if a student lacks the appropriate level of reading fluency. If he or she cannot read accurately or with enough speed, he or she will have much more trouble with comprehension than the average student. It is important to identify any decoding or vocabulary problems that might be affecting comprehension first; if those can be solved, comprehension skills may naturally increase as reading fluency increases.

38. B: The key word in this question is "independently." Students will be required to read a book on their own, synthesize the information they have found, pick out relevant main ideas, and then write about all those things. This multi-step process will require that the students be interested enough in their individual books to complete it, and that the students are actually capable of reading their books. Choice "b" allows students some choice, but ensures that the challenge level is appropriate. In Choice "a", more advanced students may find the process tedious if the books are too easy. Choice "c" suggests that students read books which are challenging, requiring additional comprehension work on top of that which is already assigned. The purpose of the project is to understand and synthesize information; selecting a difficult text may prove too much for some students. It is rarely a good idea to eliminate parameters whatsoever on book choice, because students could choose books which they are incapable of reading, or which would be too easy to challenge them.

39. C: Barron demonstrates the ability to read the words on a page, but struggles with several comprehension skills consistently. There is a pattern to Barron's issues: he has a hard time comprehending anything not stated literally in the text. Karishma may or may not have a hard time forming an opinion; we cannot tell as the prompt only says that she is uncomfortable speaking up in class, which seems to be a confidence problem rather than an academic one. Lynne appears to comprehend different genres of literature, which is a grade-level expectation, and it is common for students to have a bit more trouble with one particular genre. Sebastien is not unusual, as he is capable of intelligent contributions and comprehension, but primarily lacks interest. His is a problem of motivation rather than an academic struggle; he would possibly benefit from a wider text selection or a special project.

40. B: Cloze technique refers to the process of selecting a text to present to a student and deleting various words according to a pattern. Every fifth word has been omitted in this passage. The objective of a cloze-style assessment is to assess and increase reading comprehension. This type of assessment is unique in that there is no "correct" answer— students are only expected to use the context clues to fill in words that make sense in the blanks. If they have been able to create meaningful answers, then the exercise should be deemed a success. Choices "a" and "d" are not generally accepted forms of reading comprehension assessment. Choice "c" is an oft-used form of assessment which utilizes prepared questions and students' responses and should not be confused with the cloze-style technique.

41. A: There are differences in the way reading levels are assigned across research and history. These levels can apply to a variety of assessments, including reading fluency, comprehension, word identification and the like. However, it can be generally agreed upon that there are three broad reading levels: frustration, instructional, and independent. Frustration level indicates that the material is too difficult for the student and may create frustration or disappointment while reading. Frustration level typically refers to various assessment scores of below 40%. Instructional level refers to text that can be used for the improvement of reading skills, wherein a student can get about half of his answers correct, whether identifying words, answering questions, etc. Instructional level ranges from approximately 41% to 60%. Any score above an approximate 60% should be considered independent reading material for the student.

42. D: Teachers know that students are often expected to read works written long ago and whose relevance may not be immediately apparent. It is important that students have the information required to understand how the text was created. In Choice "d", students have the opportunity to learn about the socio-historical context in which the author created the piece. Armed with knowledge about the story's context, students can categorize and comprehend any of its aspects that would ordinarily be unclear. Students can also use this knowledge to find similarities and differences between aspects of their own lives and the context of the characters in the story. In choices "a"and "b," students are given the responsibility of determining what is important or unclear in the story. However, without understanding the work's context, students may not even be aware of the relevant information in the text, or may incorrectly interpret some events in the story. In Choice "c", the sole focus is on vocabulary, which may neglect other important characteristics of the writing.

43. A: In a longer text with chapter titles, these titles can give students an understanding of what the book might be about and allows it to be broken into regular increments. Creating questions that the students can answer during their reading will give them points at which they can stop and think about what they comprehend. In Choice "b", the students would be taught to focus primarily on the ending, which neglects the rest of the aspects of the text. Choices "c" and "d" could inappropriately influence the students' comprehension by causing them to rely on other people's opinions rather than on their own understanding.

44. B: There are many, many factors that affect reading comprehension in various proportions, depending on the student. Generally speaking, students must be able to recognize vocabulary, decode unfamiliar words, and monitor their own understanding in order to comprehend a given text. In Choice "a", all of these factors could affect comprehension; written language development and breakfast, however, are probably less important than the set of factors in Choice "b". In Choice "c", the factors seem to relate primarily to a student's understanding of the words in the text—vocabulary, sight words, and the ability to look up words. However, students must understand more than simply the words on the page; they must understand the relationships between the words and the underlying meaning of the whole text. In Choice "d", classroom participation and performance in other subjects does not necessarily indicate or affect comprehension skills.

45. B: Comprehension is a process of creating meaning from that which a student reads, sees, hears, or experiences. The tools for comprehending are similar across genres. The teacher has specifically chosen a passage and wants the students to compare, not contrast, the pieces. Dickensian writing is not generally considered to be journalistic, as suggested in Choice "a". Choice "c" is correct—you can in fact compare even unlike things. However, Choice "b" provides a richer backdrop for showing students how to link that which they read in school to their own lives and use the same tools to comprehend and take meaning from whatever they read.

46. C: Reading for pleasure is an important part of building students' literacy for life. Often, the more parameters that are established around reading, the less students are apt to read for fun. By removing limitations and requirements on the experience of reading, teachers will increase the likelihood that students can enjoy it. Choice "a" does involve books which the students enjoyed, but would not increase the amount of time spent reading for pleasure, as the books have already been read. Choice "b" simply increases the amount of time spent reading for class, but may or may not be enjoyable for the students. Choice "d" establishes a plan for reading for fun, but does not ensure that the students will adhere to the timeline created. Choice "c" removes the limits on what the students can read and is inclusive of students who may not already like to read by allowing them to choose the type of material. Students also have a chance to discuss the different kinds of elements in texts that they enjoy and share them with the class.

47. A: Choice "b" creates opportunities for students to encounter words they might not read on a daily basis at school or while reading for pleasure. They are likely to employ context clues or dictionaries as a means of understanding the main ideas. Choices "c" and "d" are two different methods to expose students to new and unfamiliar words by hearing them in an instructional context and in conversation with adults. Both choices would create opportunities for indirect vocabulary building as means to understand larger ideas. Choice "a" extends the vocabulary assignment by adding harder words. This strategy would likely

increase the number of words a student has learned; however, it would do so by direct instruction (words are directly assigned to be learned by students).

48. C: During the unit on imagery and figurative language, students will learn about how sensory experience can be translated into writing. In order to understand and apply these concepts, students will need an ever-increasing bank of descriptive words which they can identify and define. Choices "a," "b" and "d" would certainly be useful as supplements to this particular unit. However, Choice "c" most accurately addresses the question prompt in that it is an activity that directly increases relevant vocabulary skills. Word games engage students' interest, while building their knowledge of words they will encounter in their studies of imagery and figurative writing.

49. A: The text at hand contains several clues as to the meaning of this word, including the use of the words "peaceful" and "quiet" in the preceding sentence. Students may also recognize that Mom's requests for help with undesirable household chores interrupted Dad's peaceful, quiet 'reverie." Choice "a" is the specific method that would be most appropriate for determining the word's meaning; Choice "b" is a less reliable or systematic way of doing the same thing. Choice "c" would not be helpful in this case since "reverie" is not a word that can be decoded in a traditional manner. Choice "d" would not offer a realistic solution to this question since previewing and reviewing are more helpful in increasing comprehension of informative texts, rather than vocabulary words.

50. B: Inferential comprehension refers to a student's ability to understand ideas not explicitly contained in the text. By reading the paragraph, the student should ideally be able to understand that the girls knew they were getting out of helping with chores, because they grinned at one another conspiratorially and left immediately after gaining permission to do so. Mom also comments that she told everybody at breakfast that they'd need to help her out, which Dad has clearly forgotten. There are enough clues in the paragraph to help the reader understand what is happening without stating it in an obvious way. There are no clues to help the reader answer questions "a" or "c," In question Choice "d", the answer (peace and quiet) is stated explicitly, and would refer to literal comprehension instead of inferential comprehension.

51. D: When students read textual information for another subject, they are expected to pick out important words and concepts and retain them. By outlining the text, the student can keep track of the overall framework of information, as well as word definitions and main ideas. In Choice "a", the primary purpose for reading is likely entertainment. In Choice "b", a more appropriate reading comprehension strategy would not focus on key concepts at the expense of the literary style and tools. In Choice "c", it would be correct to analyze a persuasive essay for main ideas and supportive evidence, rather than an extended free-writing exercise.

52. C: The vocabulary list gives clues as to the type of text the students will be reading. Historical fiction is not likely to contain stories of deities or the supernatural, although the other vocabulary words might match. Poetry is not always considered as narrative text; nor would it necessarily explore culture or dualities (although those are possibilities). Drama, there again, is a possible match for this list, but does not match as well as Choice "c", mythology. Mythology encompasses many stories, typically ancient in origin, that explain and describe aspects of culture. Myths across cultures carry as many similarities as they do

differences. Common in mythology are stories of duality, gods and goddesses, heroism, and more.

53. C: The goal of this exercise is to help students learn to interpret data in the form of a chart. This skill is vital to increasing overall comprehension skills and test-taking ability. However, we are not given much information regarding this chart other than types of hobbies and how many students in a particular group reported enjoying them. Therefore, we cannot make a judgment about Choice "a"—we do not know if some students reported enjoying more than one hobby, keeping us from answering that question accurately. Choice "b" offers students a chance to form personal opinions about a given topic, which is not the purpose of this exercise. Choice "d" would be more appropriate for building math skills while incorporating reading skills. Choice "c", however, requires students to analyze the types of hobbies, categorize them into physical exercise or artistic pursuits, and then answer the question.

54. B: Technology should not be relied upon to teach comprehension skills, but can be helpful in providing supplements to classroom instruction. In Choice "a", this particular practice can be very helpful for some students who have trouble recalling what is discussed in class. Choice "c" sets up a reward system to encourage students to finish their work but will not directly increase any specific skill. Choice "d" relies on students to pull comprehension-building information from articles, instead of providing them with direct instruction or explanation. Choice "b" provides interactive tools that will help students organize information that they have read, which is an important comprehension skill.

55. D: The key word in this question is "scaffolding," which refers to a practice of supporting and guiding learners with respect to a particular skill. Talking about reading is an important part of building literacy skills, but is rarely helpful without direct instructions on how to do it respectfully and properly. In Choice "a", students are required to support a particular idea in a relatively high-stress format, in front of other students. Some students may struggle with this exercise while they are learning. Choice "b" removes the teacher or any type of guide from the discussion, which exempts students from direct instruction or scaffolding. Choice "c" may eliminate some students who are not confident speaking in front of large groups, and limits how much students can share at one time. Choice "d" gives students a safe, smaller group within which to discuss reading and also provides teacher moderation and discussion guides.

56. C: In this question, it is best to actually approach the exercise as the student would, reading through the choices and contemplating their relationships. Matching numbers 2 and 4 are easiest to do first because they include girls' names and can be matched with the lettered choices with female pronouns ("she"). Some of the choices could be categorized as facts or opinions, but not so consistently that Choice "a" would make sense. It would be impossible to assert accurately that these choices are main and supporting ideas without more information or sentences to prove this, as suggested in Choice "b". Choice "d" would also require more information to be considered a possible answer to this question. Choice "c" fits best, establishing a valid effect (letters) for each cause (numbers).

57. A: Mr. Garson's assignment is intended to expand his students' understanding of other people's points of view. Creative writing is a constructive process that requires many kinds of thought processes. In Choice "b", Mr. Garson would be undermining Kim's chance to think creatively and would constitute lowering his expectations of her due to the language

- 120 -

barrier. In Choice "c", he cannot guarantee that Kim would choose a topic that would encourage her to think creatively about different perspectives. In Choice "d", collaborating with another English-language learner would not likely speed up the process of writing; it also may short-circuit her own creative thinking due to the influence of another person's thoughts. Choice "a" allows Kim to focus on the creative constructive process without the issues associated with writing in a new language. Kim will achieve the intended outcome of the assignment, saving translation and language issues to be dealt with separately with the guidance of a trained teacher.

58. D: The students in this scenario are only given the opportunity to memorize a specific set of words each week. However, they have not been given a chance to stretch their spelling skills through various styles of teaching and assignments. Therefore, their knowledge of spelling conventions and irregular spelling will be limited to their word lists. However, writing requires a more expansive spelling skill set and must be practiced in a variety of styles in order to solidify them. In order to build spelling skills in writing, students must have opportunities to practice their spelling while writing, perhaps by using words in original sentences, learning word groups, reviewing words before and after the weekly tests, etc.

59. B: Because writing is an ongoing developmental process, it is important to monitor students' development in various ways over time. During journal time, students can write freely without concern for being graded on various aspects of their work. This freedom will likely enhance their willingness to explore their ideas. This process allows the teacher to understand which rules of conventional writing have carried over into the students' long-term memories and skill sets. Ideally, students will continually add new writing skills to their free journaling, indicating that their writing instruction is improving their skills without the students needing to consciously apply them. Journaling also allows students to practice that which they have learned without paying undue attention to parameters for grading.

60. A: This letter is difficult to follow because it is not organized according to main ideas and supporting sentences. The letter also displays inconsistent capitalization and punctuation within the body. In Choice "b", the reference to writing style is vague and can be viewed subjectively. Teachers are responsible for teaching writing conventions; however, it is important to teach proper grammar without criticizing the student's specific ideas or style. In choices "c" and "d" references to misuse of active and passive voice are irrelevant to this particular writing passage.

61. C: Organization, punctuation, and capitalization are the primary issues with this piece of writing and the letters written by the class. While there are only a few spelling errors, it is always helpful to review commonly made mistakes, as well as discuss capitalization rules. However, the student in this case does not misuse passive or active verbs. Passive voice refers to the over-use of "to be" verbs and to sentences in which the subject is acted upon, most often including passive participles (i.e., verbs in the –ed form). For instance, a sentence stating that "he robbed a bank" is normally preferable to "the bank was robbed." Therefore, Choice "c" would not be as helpful as the other lesson choices in this case.

62. B: Writing is a complex, subjective process which will never be graded identically amongst teachers. The best teachers, however, know that students write more clearly and more accurately when they know that which is expected of them. In Choice "a", the inclusion

of so many details may be confusing and cause the grading process to take too long. Choice "c" is certainly an important action to consider, but will probably not directly affect the students' writing skills. Choice "d" may communicate a certain point, but again, will not necessarily improve the students' skills; it will only affect the grading process. Choice "b" will engage the students actively in the writing process and in the building of skills. They will be able to analyze the rubric and determine how well they understand the assignment and whether or not they may need more practice or help in a particular area.

63. D: Writing is a skill that evolves over time because it is so complex and involves multiple skill sets. Because so many skills are important in writing, it is impossible to apply the same sequence to each new writer. Choice "a" is important for all writers, beginning to advanced, since writing, like reading, is a skill they will use across many contexts. Choice "b" gives students practice with the various aspects of the writing process that often prove difficult for new writers, especially when they are attempting to build content and write accurately at the same time. In Choice "c", students can diminish their fear or lack of motivation for writing because they will be able to explore it in a variety of ways. Choice "d", however, may create the problem of boredom for more advanced students and cause writing progress to be very slow for those still learning.

64. B: In the first sentence, the compound subject of the sentence is "each of the kids." This compound subject with a propositional phrase (of the kids) may trick students into thinking that the subject is plural, making the verb "love." But based on the singular subject, "each," the verb should be "loves." In the second sentence, the subject, "game," should change the verb to "is" instead of the plural "are." In the third sentence, the subject is compound with a prepositional phrase (in our class), but the verb should be singular, "enjoy." The punctuation suggested in Choice "a" and the word choice in Choice "c" is correct in the paragraph. There are no split infinitives.

65. B: Often, it helps writers to show their papers to a trusted friend or family member who is unfamiliar with the piece. A fresh set of eyes can identify errors that the student does not see while revising. Choice "a" creates unnecessary work for the student when only certain corrections need to be made. Choice "c" also requires a lot of work that may turn students off of the process of revision. Choice "d" describes most students' approach to revising their papers. There are, however, many processes at work when creating written pieces and it is very difficult to develop and write your ideas without making mistakes.

66. D: In Choice "a", the teacher is providing remedial instruction or extra help, but is not sharpening the actual skills needed to revise. Many students can perform well on mechanics worksheets and exercises, but have trouble with the process of re-reading and revising. Choice "b" is not correct for the same reason. Choice "c" relies upon the students themselves to identify and correct others' grammar, which may not be consistent or accurate. The final choice helps students practice the re-reading and identification skills needed to revise a piece of writing.

67. A: Curriculum standards are important for determining when specific skills should be introduced and mastered. While most literacy skills evolve simultaneously, there is an applicable sequence that should guide teaching. Choices "b" through "d" are all general expectations for fifth-grade students. All students do not master every skill included in order to matriculate, but effort to expose them to each skill should be made. Choice "a" is a

standard that students generally do not master until seventh or eighth grade, unless they are provided with specialized instruction at an earlier time and on a consistent basis.

68. A: In the writing process, the prewriting phase includes actions such as brainstorming, story mapping, and jotting down ideas. Most students need to organize their ideas before beginning to draft, or writing. It often helps students to organize their ideas with the use of drawings or diagrams instead of in a linear fashion. By requiring them to use pencil and paper in this phase of the writing process, teachers create an opportunity for students to use different tools to organize their ideas. Once the writing and publishing phases begin, it is appropriate to allow the use of word processors to that the students' work is legible for revision.

69. C: It is obvious when Mrs. Blaine first comments on Alex's report that he does well with literal comprehension and memory, but has trouble identifying and discussing his opinion about the book. Alex, like many students, is not confident in his ability to clearly state an idea and back it up with supporting evidence or ideas from what he has read. This is the skill she is suggesting he will need to use again and again. Alex has an opinion, that the book was "boring at first," but he "liked the way it ended." He knows how he feels about the book, but does not know how to explain his opinion in writing. Therefore, answer Choice "a" is inaccurate. Choices "b" and "c" are both likely to be necessary for Alex at some point, but are unlikely to be the most important skill Mrs. Blaine mentions.

70. A: Alex is having trouble expressing a logical argument in writing. However, he has an opinion about the book to get him started. By having him write each idea on separate items, Alex can use tangible objects to represent his thoughts. He can then move them around as he thinks through how they are related to one another. In this way, he can start to structure his thoughts with the help of visual aids, rather than attempting to do this abstractly. The remaining three choices might assist Alex with certain assignments, but will not give him concrete tools to help him organize his thoughts and write them in a clear, concise way.

71. A: Mr. Benton wants to use a clear-cut approach to writing, involving students in the process. As a teacher, Mr. Benton should know that there are six commonly agreed-upon writing traits: idea development, organization, voice, word choice, sentence fluency and conventions. These traits encompass the majority of writing skills that students will learn over the course of their studies. In Choice "a", not only does Mr. Benton provide students with this framework for thinking about writing, but helps them prioritize their needs in building their skills. The students can then work from the plan devised from that initial meeting. In choices "b" and "c", students are left primarily to their own devices to build their writing skills. However, if most of the students are struggling with writing (as suggested in the question prompt), it would not be advisable to leave the writing instruction to the students themselves. Choice "d" provides faulty information--there are many types of writing that would not be written in the five-paragraph style or format.

72. B: Part of teaching older students is helping them give voice to what is happening in their lives and connecting that voice to what they are learning in class. In Choice "b", students not only have a voice, but can channel that voice into a particular type of writing. In this case, they will be writing journalistically. They also have a chance to turn their frustration into a positive activity that will give parents the information they would like to know. In Choice "a", the students do not build any particular writing skills, nor does the problem get solved for parents or students. In Choice "c", the students would have a chance

to write about their feelings, but this does not eliminate the issue of parents wanting to know what is happening at school. Choice "d" only serves to make more work for the students, without building their writing skills.

73. D: The first two questions suggest that the primary focus of this exercise is word choice and vocabulary. The third question refers to the sound of the words chosen, and could also pertain to Choice "a", sentence fluency. The fourth question would work with choices "a," "c" or "d". But taken together, the questions point strongly to the concept of word choice. Choice "a", sentence fluency, refers to the way the words in sentences work together. Choice "b" refers to the way the students' ideas are developed in the paper. Choice "c" encompasses writing conventions such as punctuation, spacing, and capitalization.

74. B: In persuasive writing, the writer must introduce an opinion or statement about which he or she must provide supporting evidence. The paragraph or paper should start with the main idea and then segue into separate but related supporting details. In this writing sample, the student's ideas are written sequentially, as the student might think about them mentally. Introducing a visual aid to help him separate his primary idea and the ideas that give reasons for it may help him develop the piece into a longer, more logical argument. He already includes personal details and ideas that make the piece interesting to read, contrary to Choice "c". Choice "d" suggests that the student may have many grammatical and conventional corrections to make, which is not correct. While it is always important to encourage, as stated in Choice "a", Choice "b" would be the most direct, concrete way to assist this student in developing his skills.

75. D: When teachers talk to their students about writing, it is important to remember that young writers often leave out important details or information vital to its coherence. Students must learn to communicate clearly through writing and include all pertinent information. The teacher uses the metaphor of the alien from outer space to emphasize this point—an alien would have no prior knowledge that would aid comprehension, therefore the writer must be very thorough. This concept is important in all writing, but would be especially important in explaining to another person how to do something. In Choice "d", a student would choose a favorite activity, sport, or task and explain in a methodical way how to complete or participate in it. Neglecting any piece of information would make the piece irrelevant.

76. B: Many aspects of writing are difficult to teach directly. There are not as many specific exercises that show students how to write in their own voices without being overly colloquial or even incorrect. Students must always be working toward adhering to writing conventions, but also making that which they write personal and interesting. Part of "voice" is personal expression and making writing relevant to the intended audience. Often, the best way to show the students how to do this is to show them that which has already been done well and discuss why the writing is good. The students can use this discussion to improve their own writing through emulation. Choice "a" suggests that personal opinions are always relevant to one's writing, which is not always the case, depending on the type of assignment. In Choice "c", students would be very limited should they only choose subjects with which they are familiar--they would rarely have a chance to grow. The final choice would encourage students to speak in someone else's voice, which would create variety, but would not grow their ability to speak as themselves in any relevant or interesting way.

77. A: Reading this excerpt, it becomes apparent that the student is using a limited writing vocabulary. The words "sweet" or "sweets" are used three times; "like" is used three times as well. The sentences feel very repetitive because many words are used again and again. Working with students to build their vocabulary is one of the most helpful ways to build writing skills. The more words in a student's repertoire, the more interesting and lively his writing will be. Despite the vocabulary deficit, the student's writing conventions and grammar are actually quite good in this excerpt. Choice "d" suggests that the student needs to stretch his writing skill by choosing more challenging topics, but we do not know from this piece whether or not the student is working at an appropriate level of challenge.

78. C: Choice "a" is misleading, as writing a letter is a specific format and kind of exercise; it is not typically considered a catch-all exercise for learning the five-step process or the six traits of writing. While every writing exercise can be a backdrop for these skills, Choice "a" is not the most accurate answer. If you read the question prompt carefully, you see that it is already acknowledged that this opportunity will be a good exercise for showing students how to write a letter well. Therefore, Choice "b" is redundant. Choice "d" is true; students should be careful of their writing conventions so that their writing is easier to read, yet Choice "c" is the skill than can be most directly applied when writing to students of another language and culture; the audience actually encompasses Choice "d", as students would determine in thinking about their French pen pals that they might have a hard time reading English, and that they should be cognizant of that fact.

79. B: By the eighth grade, students should begin to understand the purposes and effectiveness of various media. If the students have been learning about how to deconstruct media messages, they have likely been studying ideas about audience, point of view, and persuasive language. Assigning a project in which the students are guided to think through these concepts will solidify their understanding of how media messages are created. Each of the other answers, "a," "b" and "d" will likely be accomplished through the completion of this project. However, it is not likely that the teacher has designed such a specific kind of assignment in order to increase her students' real-life job skills, as not all of them will go into media-related fields described in Choice "a". Choice "c" assumes that technology will be used in the assignment, although it is possible for students to create the ads and essays without the use of computers or other technology. Choice "d" could be accomplished by any number of assignments and is less likely to be the primary intended outcome.

80. A: Inkblot images are often used to gain insight into an individual's thoughts. The teacher clearly understands that different people will interpret these images in various ways. She asks the students to write their questions down so that they will not be influenced by others' interpretations. While some visual symbols are universal, most images are not inherent as suggested in Choice "b". Choice "c" could possibly be true, but would be irrelevant to a group of sixth graders in most circumstances. Choice "d" supposes that students should confer with one another before forming their own opinions, which should not be a rule of thumb. By allowing students to interpret the messages individually and then share their perceptions, the teacher will demonstrate that the individual's point of view will affect his understanding of visual images.

81. D: Students typically enjoy watching film versions of literature, especially when the text is challenging to read. An important part of media consumption is building skills to deconstruct the embedded ideas and messages. The teacher in this scenario wants the students to think about how the structure and content of the film affects their

understanding of a classic story. In choices "a" and "b", students are assigned to state their opinions about certain aspects of the film or play, but are not asked to critically analyze a specific message. Choice "c" simply creates a rather tedious assignment that will yield a rote list of examples. Choice "d" targets the unique setting of the film and encourages students to think about why the film's creators might have chosen to adapt the story in such a way, which is likely to suggest that the content of the story is relevant to people in any era or setting.

82. A: Mr. James is showing students the difference between a main idea (or concept) and its supporting evidence (or details). He has taken an element of a story and provided three details or character traits that provide proof of his claim. The organization of the graph helps students see the relationship between in the ideas, in addition to hearing it. This skill can be directly applied to either constructing meaning from a text or creating a well-planned paragraph. Choice "b" may not always be true, depending on the kind of questions asked. Choice "c" assumes that characters in texts can always be broken down into smaller components. Choice "d" refers to aspects of writing such as punctuation, grammar, spelling, etc.

83. B: Students are expected to have a variety of skills with respect to viewing, representing, and analyzing visual/media images by the time they enter high school. They should be able to understand visual imagery and how it affects or creates meaning. Students must also learn to deconstruct the messages they see and create their own for the purposes of communicating their own ideas. Choice "a" would, perhaps, be the goal of a consumerism or economics class, but is not the best choice for this scenario. This game would create understanding in students about different types of visual images, but they are not likely to be the same images used in their schoolwork at this juncture. Choice "d" is certainly true; the children will likely enjoy the game. However, Choice "b" most closely matches the educational requirements and standards laid out for students of this age.

84. D: Generally speaking, the following story elements take place in sequential order:
Exposition: refers to background information and actions in a story that describe the setting, characters, etc.
Rising action: events in the plot that lead up to the critical event or turning point
Climax: critical event, dramatic scene, or turning point in the story
Falling action: resulting events and actions following the conflict
Resolution: all actions and events are resolved and addressed
Teaching students about the plot elements they can find in most stories will help them develop many skills, including comparisons/contrasts, plot analysis, reading comprehension, etc.

85. B: Ancient Egypt provides a rich backdrop for a myriad of literacy skills. Students can develop their visual literacy skills in a number of ways, even using material and studies that date back thousands of years. In Choice "a", students are creating visual images with costume and dress, but no method for decoding those messages is stated in the answer choice. Drawing illustrations focuses on the same skill: creation of visual images, but no decoding or discussion of those images. In Choice "d", students could build their visual literacy skills if they were to discuss the visual images or representations in the film, but this activity is not included in the answer choice. In the correct answer, B), students are exposed to various representations and exhibits regarding the material in question and

then have a chance to discuss and uncover meaning in what they have seen, with the guidance of the teachers.

86. A: If you read the question prompt carefully, you will notice that the question refers specifically to language skills. While Choice "c" is important and would likely result from the exercise, it does not signify a specific language skill. Students' motor skills are not likely to significantly improve over the course of one day, eliminating Choice "b". In Choice "d", the assumption that other individuals in the community would be able to interpret sign language is incorrect. But the seminar would indeed provide an opportunity for students to learn about how visual representations affect meaning. Using sign language allows them to hone listening and expression skills simultaneously, as well as to learn how to decode non-verbal expressions.

87. D: In literature and in media, storytellers often use the color red to symbolize a number of concepts: red can signal importance, danger, love, or simply draw the viewer or reader to the particular object in question. The question prompt tells you directly that the red objects signify that the main character is seeing a clue to solving the mystery. In essence, anything colored red represents, or symbolizes, a clue.

88. B: The primary purpose of visual aids is to extend or enhance meaning. Visuals can sometimes distract from the meaning of the presentation if used too much, as in Choice "a". Choice "c" could also create distractions in that students may be more likely to look at photos directly in front of them than pay attention to the student presenting. The final choice simply encourages students to read the information on screen, and will likely cause the presenting student to read aloud rather than communicate in his own words. Choice "b", however, utilizes the students' thought processes in determining where a visual might help enhance understanding, and requires them to use oral communication as well.

89. C: In teaching about this subject, students must be able to understand the intended meaning of a particular media image. To do this, they have to consider the image-creator's background, point of view, and anything else they might be able to determine from analyzing the image. Students need to be taught tools to dissect the barrage of images that they see on a daily basis. Choice "a" encompasses photos of real-life people and events. While these photos are valuable for many teaching purposes, it cannot be guaranteed that students would be able to apply their tools to current-day media analysis. Choice "b" is the choice least related to media influence in that it refers to a Social Studies text, likely created for didactic purposes. Choice "d" most likely refers to a cartoon found in the Funnies, created to entertain, rather than influence. The political cartoon in Choice "c" is the image most explicitly created to affect and influence public opinion by exaggerating personal traits and personalizing lofty issues.

90. C: Many factors affect the final outcome of a research paper or project, including the selection of sources, interpretation of source information, organization of ideas, and writing skills. The final project described in answer "a" is not always indicative of how efficiently a student has researched a topic because it is the end-result of many language processes at work. The outline mentioned in answer "b" would provide insight about the organization of ideas, but answer "c" would allow the instructor to assess the actual process of gathering and synthesizing sources of information.

91. A: One of the most important aspects of completing a research project is topic selection. A student must choose a topic that is appropriately narrow to avoid being overwhelmed by too much information. If the topic is too broad, the student will not be able to adequately research; if it is too narrow, he or she will get stuck. The student should also think critically about whether or not the topic can be researched. For instance, if a student chooses to study a current event, there may not be enough reliable information published yet to support a real research project. The teacher should play an active role in helping the student select a topic, especially on the student's first try.

92. A: The students tend to do well when they know they will be tested; this probably means that they only sit down to study when they are required to do so, unless they want to risk a poor test score. However, it is important for students to retain information each day and week, rather than cramming and memorizing for a test. By devoting a few minutes each day to preview or prepare students for what they will learn, they will begin to learn how to pay attention to the main ideas and salient details of the readings. By reviewing and summarizing, students can compare what they thought would be important during the preview to what they actually learned. The repetition will help the students retain the information from one day to the next.

93. B: If only the first graph was drawn, it may appear that the students were working simply on character analysis or even inferential comprehension. This first set of boxes creates a framework for analyzing and recording information about two specific characters and their personalities. However, taken with the second chart, it becomes apparent that the purpose of the first chart is to organize information in order to complete the second chart. The second chart requires students to think critically about how the two characters are the same and how they are different. This exercise most closely corresponds with Choice "b", comparing and contrasting, in the context of character traits. Choices "c" and "d" are certainly involved in this process, but are simply tools that are used in order to teach students how to compare and contrast

94. B: The question prompt states that the students' primary problems lie in homework: they are concerned about the volume of reading and ho to know what information is most relevant. Although Choice "d" is important and will help students, it will not improve their ability to deal with independent reading and assignments. Choice "c" will help students score more highly on tests, but will likely not improve their study skills. Choice "a" will simply encourage students to "cram' a lot of information for tests. Choice "b", however, teaching SQ3R, is a method by which students can study, internalize and sort through large amounts of information on an independent basis.

95. B: Writing a research paper is a learned skill that begins with proper topic selection. Students must learn to pick topics with guidance from their teachers that can be researched easily. They must be careful not to pick topics that are too broad or too narrow. In this scenario, students also need to pick a topic that can be found as the subject in a variety of sources, including newspapers, magazines, books, etc. Therefore, the topic should be well-known to most readers. Choice "a" is not likely to be found in these sources unless the Velasquez family is nationally, or at least locally, well-known. Choice "c" is probably not appropriate for the same reason. Choice "d" could be considered for an essay topic or another type of writing assignment, but may not be the best choice with respect to the variety of sources. Choice "b" offers a broad subject about which much will have been written.

96. D: The purpose of this kind of note-taking is, on one level, to help students distinguish between major ideas or concepts and the details that support or relate to them. This kind of note-taking also helps students understand how certain events and ideas influence one another. The most important benefit of this practice is that it helps the note-taker start to build meaning out of the information which they receive in class. Students often complain that they don't know how to pick out what will be on a test, or what is important, as they cannot possibly retain every sentence uttered in class. Students do best when they can pick out main ideas and organize their thinking around these concepts, learning details and supporting ideas as they go.

97. C: As is true with students and adults alike, we remember more information when we review it consistently over time. If a student takes meaningful and accurate notes, reviewing them periodically and consistently will help them retain the information and cut down on time spent studying right before the test. This practice also helps the student identify any ideas or questions that need to be addressed before the test or paper is due. Choices "a" and "b" create the impression that a student will struggle if he does not record (in writing or via tape recorder) every word uttered in class. It is more important for students to learn how to create meaning and understand relationships between all of the facts, figures, and concepts introduced in class. Choice "d" would be very time-consuming and would not guarantee that students are choosing the most important ideas and information for use.

98. C: Allowing the students to practice these types of questions starts to open up their ability to show that which they know. Many students experience stress in the transition to various types of testing that do not provide answer choices in multiple choice form, or lack word banks. Choice "c" shows students how to approach these kinds of questions in a safe, un-graded way, and solidifies their thinking by discussing their attempts afterward. Choice "a" may assist with students' recall of information, but does not provide direct instruction on how to formulate answers. Choice "b" will give students time to approach the questions and revise their answers if necessary. For those students who experience more difficulty, however, it may not be as helpful as Choice "c". Choice "d" might also be helpful for any students who experience test anxiety or are taking a bit longer to understand the process, but will not scaffold their attempts as well as Choice "c".

99. C: In a piece of writing such as Sully's, there are two important things which he needs to do; namely, he must select the most important ideas and focus on those, rather than attempt to include every single idea he may have. Once he has done that, he additionally must include details or evidence to support those ideas. Choice "c" gives him a concrete way to identify the most important ideas and match them with appropriate and relevant evidence. Choices "a" and "b" require him to start over on a project, which is unnecessary. Choice "d" would cause him to create a very lengthy and too-detailed report without much focus.

100. B: Studying can be a mystifying experience for students as they begin to do it more frequently. Often, students do not know how to prepare properly for specific kinds of assignments, and direct instruction is helpful. In Choice "b", Mrs. Bray can identify why the students' preparation is not adequate for the examinations and help them understand alternative methods of preparation. In Choice "a", students may or may not improve their performance while taking more quizzes; in fact, their motivation and confidence may decrease if they continue to receive poor grades. Choice "c" contradicts the question prompt, as Mrs. Bray does not want to give the students too many ideas about what will be

covered in the quiz; rather, she wants to improve their study skills. Choice "d" is less accurate and direct as a method for achieving her goals than is Choice "b", because parents do not always have good study skills or knowledge of the classroom.

Social Studies Practice Test

Practice Questions

1. Some countries in the Americas still have large populations of indigenous or partly indigenous peoples. Of the following, which pair of countries does not have comparatively as large of an indigenous population as the other countries?
    a. Guatemala and Peru
    b. Ecuador and Bolivia
    c. Paraguay and Mexico
    d. Argentina and Uruguay

2. Which of the following statements is *not* true regarding English expansionism in the 16th century?
    a. England's defeat of the Spanish Armada in 1588 brought a decisive end to their war with Spain.
    b. King Henry VIII's desire to divorce Catherine of Aragon strengthened English expansionism.
    c. Queen Elizabeth's support for the Protestant Reformation strengthened English expansionism.
    d. Sir Francis Drake and other English sea captains plundered the Spaniards' plunders of Indians.

3. Which of the following is *not* correct regarding the Virginia Companies?
    a. One of these companies, the Virginia Company of Plymouth, made its base in North America.
    b. One of these companies, the Virginia Company of London, made its base in Massachusetts.
    c. One company had a charter to colonize America between the Hudson and Cape Fear rivers.
    d. One company had a charter to colonize America from the Potomac River to north Maine.

4. Which of the following conquistadores unwittingly gave smallpox to the Indians and destroyed the Aztec empire in Mexico?
    a. Balboa
    b. Ponce de Leon
    c. Cortes
    d. De Vaca

5. Which statement best describes the significance of the Peter Zenger trial in colonial America?
    a. It was the earliest American case on the right to bear arms.
    b. It established a precedent for freedom of the press.
    c. It was the earliest American case on right of peaceable assembly.
    d. It established a precedent for freedom of religion.

6. Which of these factors was *not* a direct contributor to the beginning of the American Revolution?

a. The attitudes of American colonists toward Great Britain following the French and Indian War

b. The attitudes of leaders in Great Britain toward the American colonies and imperialism

c. James Otis's court argument against Great Britain's Writs of Assistance as breaking natural law

d. Lord Grenville's Proclamation of 1763, Sugar Act, Currency Act, and especially Stamp Act

7. Which of the following statements is *not* true regarding the Tea Act of 1773?

a. The British East India Company was suffering financially because Americans were buying tea smuggled from Holland.

b. Parliament granted concessions to the British East India Company to ship tea straight to America, bypassing England.

c. Colonists found that even with added taxes, tea directly shipped by the British East India Company cost less, and they bought it.

d. American colonists refused to buy less expensive tea from the British East India Company on the principle of taxation.

8. Which of the following is true concerning the formation of new state governments in the new United States of America following freedom from British rule?

a. By the end of 1777, new constitutions had been created for twelve of the American states.

b. The states of Connecticut and Massachusetts retained their colonial charters, minus the British parts.

c. The state of Massachusetts required a special convention for its constitution, setting a good example.

d. The state of Massachusetts did not formally begin to use its new constitution until 1778.

9. Which of the following is *not* a true statement regarding the Louisiana Purchase?

a. Jefferson sent a delegation to Paris to endeavor to purchase only the city of New Orleans from Napoleon.

b. Napoleon, anticipating U.S. intrusions into Louisiana, offered to sell the U.S. the entire Louisiana territory.

c. The American delegation accepted Napoleon's offer, though they were only authorized to buy New Orleans.

d. The Louisiana Purchase, once it was completed, increased the territory of the U.S. by 50% overnight.

10. Which of these was *not* a factor that contributed to the duel in which Aaron Burr killed Alexander Hamilton?

a. Some Federalists who opposed U.S. Western expansion were attempting to organize a movement to secede from the Union.

b. Alexander Hamilton challenged Aaron Burr to a duel because he objected to U.S. expansion into the West, which Burr supported.

c. Secessionist Federalists tried to enlist Aaron Burr's support for their cause by backing him in his run for Governor of New York.

d. Alexander Hamilton was the leader of the group that opposed Aaron Burr's campaign to run for New York Governor.

11. Which of the following did *not* occur during the War of 1812?

a. Early in the war, the U.S. executed a three-pronged invasion of Canada and succeeded on two of three fronts.

b. Early in the war, Americans won naval battles against the British, but were soon beaten back by the British.

c. Admiral Oliver Hazard Perry's fleet defeated the British navy on Lake Erie in September, 1813.

d. William Henry Harrison invaded Canada and defeated the British and the Indians in the Battle of the Thames.

12. Which of the following was *not* an immediate effect of rapid urban growth in the 1800s?

a. Poor sanitation conditions in the cities

b. Epidemics of diseases in the cities

c. Inadequate police and fire protection

d. Widespread urban political corruption

13. Which of the following laws was instrumental in spurring westward migration to the Great Plains between 1860 and 1880?

a. The Homestead Act

b. The Timber Culture Act

c. The Desert Land Act

d. All of these laws were instrumental in spurring westward migration to the Great Plains during that period.

14. What did *not* contribute to ending America's neutrality in World War I?

a. Germany's declaration of a war zone surrounding the British Isles in February, 1913

b. Germany's declaration of a war on Russia after Archduke Ferdinand's assassination

c. Germany's sinking the British ship *Lusitania,* which killed 128 American passengers

d. Germany's declaration of unrestricted submarine warfare on all ships in the war zone

15. Of the following international diplomatic conferences, which one made US-Soviet differences apparent?

a. The Potsdam conference

b. The conference at Yalta

c. Dumbarton Oaks conference

d. The Tehran conference

16. Which statement about relations between the Middle East and the US and Europe in the 1950s is *not* correct?
    a. President Nasser of Egypt refused to align with the US in the Cold War.
    b. President Eisenhower removed US funding from the Aswan Dam in 1956.
    c. President Nasser nationalized the Suez Canal, which was owned by England.
    d. In 1956, Egypt attacked Israel, and England and France joined in the war.

17. Of the following, which person or group was *not* instrumental in postwar advancement of civil rights and desegregation during the 1940s and 1950s?
    a. The President
    b. The Supreme Court
    c. The Congress
    d. The NAACP

18. Of the programs enacted by President Lyndon B. Johnson's administration, which was most closely related to John F. Kennedy's legacy?
    a. The Economic Opportunity Act
    b. The Civil Rights Act
    c. The Great Society program
    d. All of these were equally related to JFK's legacy.

19. Which statement regarding US international trade policy in the 1990s is *not* correct?
    a. In 1994, the General Agreement on Tariffs and Trade (GATT) was approved by Congress.
    b. The GATT was between 57 countries who agreed they would remove or reduce many of their tariffs.
    c. The GATT created the World Trade Organization (WTO) to settle international trade differences.
    d. The NAFTA (North American Free Trade Agreement), ratified in 1994, had originally been set up by George H.W. Bush's administration.

20. Which statement about factors related to the growth of the US economy between 1945 and 1970 is *not* correct?
    a. The Baby Boom's greatly increased birth rates contributed to economic growth during this time.
    b. The reduction in military spending after World War II contributed to the stronger US economy.
    c. Government programs and growing affluence nearly quadrupled college enrollments in 20 years.
    d. Increased mobility and bigger families caused fast suburban expansion, especially in the Sunbelt.

21. Which of the following statements regarding immigration to America during the 1980s is *not* true?
    a. Twice as many immigrants came to America during the 1980s than during the 1970s.
    b. Latin Americans comprised the largest proportion of immigrants to America in the 1980s.
    c. Most immigrants to the US in the 1980s were Latin American, Asian, and Caribbean.
    d. The 1986 Immigration Reform and Control Act reduced illegal Mexican immigration.

22. Which is *not* correct regarding black activism during the 1960s?
    a. There was a riot in the Los Angeles ghetto of Watts in 1965.
    b. There was a riot involving black activists in Newark, New Jersey, after the Watts riot.
    c. The Mississippi Freedom Democrats unseated that state's delegation at the convention.
    d. There was a riot involving black activists in Detroit, Michigan, after the riot in Watts.

23. What was the earliest written language in Mesopotamia?
    a. Sumerian
    b. Elamite
    c. Akkadian
    d. Aramaic

24. During which of these periods were pyramids *not* built in Egypt?
    a. The Old Kingdom
    b. The Middle Kingdom
    c. The New Kingdom
    d. The Third Dynasty

25. Which of the following is *not* true about the Crusades?
    a. Their purpose was for European rulers to retake the Middle East from Muslims
    b. The Crusades succeeded at European kings' goal of reclaiming the "holy land"
    c. The Crusades accelerated the already incipient decline of the Byzantine Empire
    d. Egypt saw a return as a major Middle Eastern power as a result of the Crusades

26. Which of the following events did *not* contribute to the growth of the Italian Renaissance?
    a. The Black Death killed 1/3 of the population of Europe
    b. The lower classes benefited from the need for laborers
    c. The middle classes developed from a need for services
    d. All these events contributed to the Italian Renaissance

27. Which of the following is *not* correct regarding assumptions of mercantilism?
    a. The money and the wealth of a nation are identical properties
    b. In order to prosper, a nation should try to increase its imports
    c. In order to prosper, a nation should try to increase its exports
    d. Economic protectionism by national governments is advisable

28. Which of the following is *not* true about the English Civil Wars between 1641 and 1651?
    a. These wars all were waged between Royalists and Parliamentarians
    b. The outcome of this series of civil wars was victory for Parliament
    c. These wars legalized Parliament's consent as requisite to monarchy
    d. Two of the wars in this time involved supporters of King Charles I

29. Which of the following choices is/are *not* considered among causes of the French Revolution?
    a. Famines causing malnutrition and starvation
    b. War debt, Court spending, bad monetary system
    c. Resentment against the Catholic Church's rule
    d. Resentment against the Protestant Reformation

30. Which statement best describes the role played by the French economy in causing the 1789 French Revolution?
    a. France's very large national debt led to heavy tax burdens on the French peasantry.
    b. Nearly sixty percent of annual national expenditures financed luxuries for the French nobility.
    c. Reforms in the guild system allowed many peasants to rise to the middle class.
    d. The king's attempt to curtail free trade led skilled journeymen to rebel against the monarchy.

31. Which of the following statements is accurate regarding the end of the First World War?
    a. The Treaty of Versailles brought peace among all countries involved in the war
    b. The Treaty of Versailles contained a clause for establishing the United Nations
    c. President Woodrow Wilson had proposed forming a coalition of world nations
    d. President Wilson succeeded in getting the USA to ratify the League of Nations

32. How did Russia's participation in World War I influence the Russian Revolution?
    a. Civilian suffering and military setbacks served as a catalyst for revolutionary forces.
    b. Nicholas III capitalized on battlefield successes to temporarily silence critics.
    c. The government eased laws banning collective action by factory workers to appease social discontent about the war.
    d. Anti-government protesters temporarily ceased protesting to show patriotism in a difficult war.

33. During the decolonization of the Cold War years, which of the following events occurred chronologically latest?
    a. The Eastern Bloc and Satellite states became independent from the Soviet Union
    b. Canada became totally independent from British Parliament via the Canada Act
    c. The Bahamas, in the Caribbean, became independent from the United Kingdom
    d. The Algerian War ended, and Algeria became independent from France

34. Why was U.S. industrialization confined to the Northeast until after the Civil War?
    a. Because the Civil War delayed the development of water-powered manufacturing
    b. Because the Northeast had faster-running rivers than the rivers found in the South
    c. Because Slater's first cotton mill with horse-drawn production lost so much money
    d. Because the technical innovations for milling textiles had not as yet been invented

35. Which of the following statements is *not* an accurate statement about the Puritans in England?
    a. The Puritans unconditionally gave all their support to the English Reformation
    b. The Puritans saw the Church of England as too much like the Catholic Church
    c. The Puritans became a chief political power because of the English Civil War
    d. The Puritans' clergy mainly departed from the Church of England after 1662

36. Which of the following statements is *not* true about the Gilded Age in America?
    a. The Gilded Age was the era of the "robber barons" in the business world
    b. The Gilded Age got its name from the excesses of the wealthy upper class
    c. The Gilded Age had philanthropy Carnegie called the "Gospel of Wealth"
    d. The Gilded Age is a term whose origins have not been identified clearly

37. Which of the following is *not* true about Democracy and the formation of the United States?

    a. The founding fathers stated in the Constitution that the USA would be a democracy

    b. The Declaration of Independence did not dictate democracy but stated its principles

    c. The United States Constitution stipulated that government be elected by the people

    d. The United States Constitution had terms to protect some, but not all, of the people

38. Which of the following statements does *not* describe the average European diet BEFORE the expansion of trade routes?

    a. Europeans ate for survival, not enjoyment.

    b. They had an abundance of preservatives such as salt that could make food last longer.

    c. Grain-based foods such as porridge and bread were staple meals.

    d. Spices were unavailable.

39. Which of these is true concerning the French Revolution, America, and Europe?

    a. When France's revolution spread and they went to war with other European countries, George Washington allied with the French.

    b. During the time period around 1792, American merchants were conducting trading with countries on both sides of the war.

    c. American traders conducted business with various countries, profiting the most from the British West Indies.

    d. The Spanish navy retaliated against America for trading with the French by capturing American trading ships.

40. Which group overtook Rome in the mid-600s B.C. and established much of its infrastructure, including sewers, roads, and fortifications, only to be driven out of the city in 509 B.C.?

    a. Latins.

    b. Etruscans.

    c. Greeks.

    d. Persians.

41. The writers of The Federalist Papers published under the pen name "Publius." Who were the authors?

    a. James Madison, John Jay, and Alexander Hamilton

    b. George Washington, Thomas Jefferson, and James Madison

    c. Alexander Hamilton, Benjamin Franklin, and Thomas Jefferson

    d. Benjamin Franklin, John Jay, and Thomas Jefferson

42. Social studies education has many practical applications. Which of the following is the most direct application of teaching high school seniors the structure of the U.S. government?

    a. Knowledge of the fundamentals of federalism

    b. Informed participation in school elections

    c. Knowledge of a system of checks and balances

    d. Informed participation in U.S. political processes

43. The U.S. government is best understood as a federalist government because:
   a. the legislative branch consists of two representative bodies.
   b. it is a representative democracy rather than a direct democracy.
   c. political power is divided between the federal government and the states.
   d. a national Constitution shapes national legislation.

44. One reason the Articles of Confederation created a weak government was because it limited Congress's ability to do what?
   a. Declare war
   b. Conduct a census
   c. Vote
   d. Tax

45. The philosophy of the late 17th-18th centuries that influenced the Constitution was from the Age of:
   a. Enlightenment
   b. Empire
   c. Discovery
   d. Industry

46. The votes of how many states were needed to ratify the Constitution?
   a. Five
   b. Ten
   c. Nine
   d. Seven

47. Virginian _____ advocated a stronger central government and was influential at the Constitutional Convention.
   a. Benjamin Franklin
   b. James Madison
   c. George Mason
   d. Robert Yates

48. Power divided between local and central branches of government is a definition of what term?
   a. Bicameralism
   b. Checks and balances
   c. Legislative oversight
   d. Federalism

49. The Senate and the House of Representatives are an example of:
   a. Bicameralism
   b. Checks and balances
   c. Legislative oversight
   d. Federalism

50. The Vice President succeeds the President in case of death, illness or impeachment. What is the order of succession for the next three successors, according to the Presidential Succession Act of 1947?
    a. President Pro Tempore of the Senate, Secretary of State, and Secretary of Defense
    b. Speaker of the House, President Pro Tempore of the Senate, and Secretary of State
    c. President Pro Tempore of the Senate, Speaker of the House, and Secretary of State
    d. Secretary of State, Secretary of Defense, and Speaker of the House

51. The President has the power to veto legislation. How is this power limited?
    I.   Congress can override the veto
    II.   The President cannot line veto
    III.   The President cannot propose legislation
    a. I and III
    b. II only
    c. I and II
    d. I only

52. The civil rights act that outlawed segregation in schools and public places also:
    a. Gave minorities the right to vote
    b. Established women's right to vote
    c. Outlawed unequal voter registration
    d. Provided protection for children

53. Which of the following is a power held only by the federal government?
    a. The power to levy taxes, borrow money, and spend money
    b. The power to award copyrights and patents to people or groups
    c. The power to establish the criteria that qualify a person to vote
    d. The power to ratify proposed amendments to the Constitution

54. Of the following actions, which one requires a three-fourths majority?
    a. State approval of a proposed amendment to the Constitution
    b. Submitting a proposal for an amendment to the Constitution
    c. Ratification for appointments to the Presidency in the Senate
    d. The introduction of charges for an impeachment in the House

55. Which of the following statements is *not* correct about U.S. westward expansion and Manifest Destiny?
    a. The idea that U.S. freedom and values should be shared with, even forced upon, as many people as possible had existed for many years.
    b. The term "Manifest Destiny" and the idea it represented had been used for many years prior to the 1830s.
    c. Many Americans believed that America as a nation should ultimately be extended to include Canada and Mexico.
    d. Increased nationalism after the resolution of the War of 1812 and rapid population growth added to Manifest Destiny.

56. Presidential candidates are eligible for public funding if they raise $5,000 per state in how many states?
    a. Twenty
    b. Ten
    c. Twenty-five
    d. Seventeen

57. What judicial system did America borrow from England?
    a. Due process
    b. Federal law
    c. Commerce law
    d. Common law

58. Which of the following is a possible absolute location for New Orleans?
    a. 30° S, 90° E
    b. 30° N, 90° E
    c. 30° S, 90° W
    d. 30° N, 90° W

59. On which type of map are different countries represented in different colors, with no two adjacent countries sharing a color?
    a. Physical map
    b. Political map
    c. Climate map
    d. Contour map

60. Which of the following statements about the equator is true?
    a. It intersects four continents.
    b. It is to the north of both horse latitudes.
    c. It is located at 0° longitude.
    d. It is not very windy.

61. The apparent distance between Greenland and Norway is greatest on a(n)
    a. Mercator Map.
    b. Conic Projection Map.
    c. Contour Map.
    d. Equal-Area Projection Map.

62. Which of the following is *not* a method of representing relief on a physical map?
    a. Symbols
    b. Color
    c. Shading
    d. Contour Lines

63. Which map describes the movement of people, trends, or materials across a physical area?
    a. Political Map
    b. Cartogram
    c. Qualitative Map
    d. Flow-line Map

64. What is the most common type of volcano on earth?
    a. Lava dome
    b. Composite volcano
    c. Shield volcano
    d. Cinder cone

65. Water is continuously recycled in the hydrosphere. By which process does water return to the atmosphere after precipitation?
    a. Percolation
    b. Cohesion
    c. Evaporation
    d. Condensation

66. Which type of rock is formed by extreme heat and pressure?
    a. Limestone
    b. Metamorphic
    c. Sedimentary
    d. Igneous

67. Which part of a hurricane features the strongest winds and greatest rainfall?
    a. Eye wall
    b. Front
    c. Eye
    d. Outward spiral

68. Which of the following are not included in a geographical definition of Southeast Asia?
    a. Myanmar, Laos, Cambodia, and Thailand
    b. Vietnam, the Malay Peninsula, and Brunei
    c. East Malaysia, Indonesia, and the Philippines
    d. These are all geographical parts of Southeast Asia

69. Which of the following exemplifies the multiplier effect of large cities?
    a. The presence of specialized equipment for an industry attracts even more business.
    b. The large population lowers the price of goods.
    c. Public transportation means more people can commute to work.
    d. A local newspaper can afford to give away the Sunday edition.

70. For thousands of years, Africans have cultivated the grasslands south of the Sahara Desert, an area known as the
    a. Qattara Depression.
    b. Great Rift Valley.
    c. Congo Basin.
    d. Sahel.

71. Tracy needs to determine the shortest route between Lima and Lisbon. Which of the following maps should she use?
    a. Azimuthal projection with the North Pole at the center
    b. Azimuthal projection with Lisbon at the center
    c. Robinson projection of the Eastern Hemisphere
    d. Robinson projection of the Western Hemisphere

72. Which of the following countries are separated by a geometric border?
    a. Turkish Cyprus and Greek Cyprus
    b. North Korea and South Korea
    c. France and Spain
    d. England and Ireland

73. During one year in Grassley County, there are 750 births, 350 deaths, 80 immigrations, and 50 emigrations. What is the natural increase rate for this year?
    a. 400
    b. 830
    c. 430
    d. More information is required.

74. Which of the following is *not* one of the world's four major population agglomerations?
    a. North Africa
    b. Eastern North America
    c. South Asia
    d. Europe

75. Which of the following statements concerning choice theory are correct?
    I.   Scarcity forces people, including producers, to make choices
    II. Producers make choices and, as a result, face trade-offs
    III. Opportunity cost is one way to measure the cost of a choice
    a. I only
    b. I and II only
    c. II and III only
    d. I, II, and III

76. John Maynard Keynes advocated what?
    a. Supply-side economics
    b. Demand-side economics
    c. Laissez faire economics
    d. The Laffer Curve

77. If a society wants greater income equity, it will:
    a. impose a progressive income tax.
    b. impose high estate taxes.
    c. impose a gift tax.
    d. All of the above

78. Which of the following best defines American GDP?

    a. The value, in American dollars, of all goods and services produced within American borders during one calendar year

    b. The value, in American dollars, of all goods and services produced by American companies during one calendar year

    c. The total value, in American dollars, of all American household incomes during one calendar year

    d. The value, in American dollars, of a "market basket" of goods and services in one year divided by the value of the same market basket in a previous year multiplied by 100

79. Ivy loses her job because her skills as a seamstress are no longer required due to a new piece of machinery that does the work of a seamstress more quickly and for less money. Which type of unemployment is this?

    a. Frictional

    b. Structural

    c. Cyclical

    d. Careless

80. Which is considered part of the natural rate of unemployment?

    I.   Structural unemployment

    II.   Frictional unemployment

    III.   Cyclical unemployment

    a. I only

    b. II only

    c. III only

    d. I and II only

81. Which of the following is a supply shock likely to produce?

    I.   An increase in input prices

    II.   An increase in price levels

    III.   A decrease in employment

    IV.   A decrease in GDP

    a. I and III only

    b. II and IV only

    c. I, II, and III only

    d. I, II, III, and IV

82. Which of the following are true of the demand curve?

    I.   It is normally downward sloping

    II.   It is normally upward sloping

    III.   It is influenced by the law of diminishing marginal unity

    IV.   It is unaffected by the law of diminishing marginal unity

    a. I and III only

    b. I and IV only

    c. II and III only

    d. II and IV only

83. The price of fleece blankets goes up from $10 to $11. At the same time, demand goes down from 1,000 blankets to 800 blankets. Which of the following statements is true?
    a. Demand is elastic
    b. Demand is inelastic
    c. The price elasticity quotient, or E_d, is less than 1
    d. The price elasticity quotient, or E_d, is equal to 1

84. The price of oil drops dramatically, saving soda pop manufacturers great amounts of money spent on making soda pop and delivering their product to market. Prices for soda pop, however, stay the same. This is an example of what?
    a. Sticky prices
    b. Sticky wages
    c. The multiplier effect
    d. Aggregate expenditure

85. Which of the following will result if two nations use the theory of comparative advantage when making decisions of which goods to produce and trade?
    a. Each nation will make all of their own goods
    b. Both nations will specialize in the production of the same specific goods
    c. Each nation will specialize in the production of different specific goods
    d. Neither nation will trade with one another

86. Which of the following is most likely to benefit from inflation?
    a. A bond investor who owns fixed-rate bonds
    b. A retired widow with no income other than fixed Social Security payments
    c. A person who has taken out a fixed-rate loan
    d. A local bank who has loaned money out at fixed rate

Consider the following table to answer Question 87:

Inputs	1	2	3	4
Output	20	50	80	100

87. What does the data in this table most directly describe?
    a. The Law of Diminishing Marginal Returns
    b. Law of Increasing Opportunity Cost
    c. Law of Demand
    d. Consumer surplus

88. How do banks create money?
    a. By printing it
    b. By taking it out of the Federal Reserve
    c. By loaning it out
    d. By putting it into the Federal Reserve

89. Which of the following correctly states the equation of exchange?
    a. MV = PQ
    b. MP x VQ
    c. MP / VQ
    d. VP = MQ

90. Economics is best defined as the study of what?
    a. Scarcity
    b. Business
    c. Trade
    d. Supply and demand

Constructed Response

1. During the latter half of the 19th century, the United States changed into a more and more mobile society. We see this increased mobility in the settling of the West by people from the eastern part of the United States. For many people, this movement westward would bring new opportunities for economic growth; for others this movement meant conflict and the ending of a way of life.

Discuss two reasons why American settlers moved westward. Describe the effect of the railroads on life in the Western United States. Explain how this westward expansion impacted the lives of Native Americans.

2.

> ### Selected Articles From the Articles of Confederation
>
> Article I.   "The Style of this Confederacy shall be "The United States of America."
>
> Article II.   "Each state retains its sovereignty, freedom and independence, and every power, jurisdiction, and right, which is not by this Confederation expressly delegated to the United States, in Congress assembled."
>
> Article III.   "The said States hereby severally enter into a firm league of friendship with each other, for their common defense, the security of their liberties and their mutual and general welfare, binding themselves to assist each other, against all force offered to, or attacks made upon them, or any of them, on account of religion, sovereignty, trade, or any other pretense whatever..."

According to the passage above, what form of government in the United States was established by the Articles of Confederation? Identify two advantages states had under this form of government and describe two reasons this form of government was later replaced by the United States Constitution.

3. A decades-long civil war in China ended in 1949, when a group of communist revolutionaries led by Mao Zedong overthrew Chiang Kai-shek's nationalist government and established the People's Republic of China.

Using your knowledge of world history, write an essay in which you:
- describe two consequences of the Chinese Revolution of 1949
- analyze how each of the consequences you have identified influenced the development of world history

Answers and Explanations

1. D: Of those countries listed here, the two countries whose respective indigenous populations are not as large as the populations of the other countries are Argentina and Uruguay. Argentina's population is approximately 86.4% of European descent, roughly 8% of mestizo (of mixed European and Amerindian heritage), and an estimated 4% of Arab or East Asian ancestry. Uruguay's population is estimated to be 88% of European descent, 4% of African, and 2% of Asian, with 6% of mestizo ancestry in its rural northwest region. Guatemala and Peru (a) have larger indigenous populations. Guatemala, in Central America, has approximately over 40% of its population as indigenous peoples. Peru, in South America, is estimated to have 45% indigenous peoples and 37% partly indigenous peoples for a total of 82%. Ecuador and Bolivia (b) in South America still have indigenous peoples. The population of Ecuador has an estimated 25% indigenous and 65% partly indigenous peoples, for a total of 90%. Paraguay in South America and Mexico in North America (c) both have sizeable indigenous populations. Paraguay's population is estimated to include 95% partly indigenous peoples. Mexico is estimated to have 30% indigenous and 60% partly indigenous peoples in its population for a total of 90%.

2. A: It is not true that England's defeat of the Spanish Armada in 1588 ended their war with Spain. It did establish England's naval dominance and strengthened England's future colonization of the New World, but the actual war between England and Spain did not end until 1604. It is true that Henry VIII's desire to divorce Catherine of Aragon strengthened English expansionism (b). Catherine was Spanish, and Henry split from the Catholic Church because it prohibited divorce. Henry's rejection of his Spanish wife and his subsequent support of the Protestant movement angered King Philip II of Spain and destroyed the formerly close ties between the two countries. When Elizabeth became Queen of England, she supported the Reformation as a Protestant, which also contributed to English colonization (c). Sir Francis Drake, one of the best known English sea captains during this time period, would attack and plunder Spanish ships that had plundered American Indians (d), adding to the enmity between Spain and England. Queen Elizabeth invested in Drake's voyages and gave him her support in claiming territories for England.

3. B: The Virginia Company of London was based in London, not Massachusetts. It had a charter to colonize American land between the Hudson and Cape Fear rivers (c). The other Virginia Company was the Virginia Company of Plymouth, which was based in the American colony of Plymouth, Massachusetts (a). It had a charter to colonize North America between the Potomac River and the northern boundary of Maine (d).

4. C: Hernando Cortes conquered the Mexican Aztecs in 1519. He had several advantages over the Indians, including horses, armor for his soldiers, and guns. In addition, Cortes' troops unknowingly transmitted smallpox to the Aztecs, which devastated their population as they had no immunity to this foreign illness. Vasco Nunez de Balboa (a) was the first European explorer to view the Pacific Ocean when he crossed the Isthmus of Panama in 1513. Juan Ponce de Leon (b) also visited and claimed Florida in Spain's name in 1513. Cabeza de Vaca (d) was one of only four men out of 400 to return from an expedition led by Panfilio de Narvaez in 1528, and was responsible for spreading the story of the Seven Cities of Cibola (the "cities of gold").

5. B: Peter Zenger was an 18th century journalist in New York who was charged with seditious libel after he published articles critical of New York governor William Cosby. His subsequent acquittal in 1735 established a precedent for American freedom of the press. Options A, C, and D can all be rejected because they do not accurately describe the historical significance of Peter Zenger's trial. Although these options name other important freedoms or rights in American history, these rights or freedoms were not central to Peter Zenger's trial. In particular, note that while answers B, C, and D all list rights contained in the First Amendment to the United States Constitution, only B contains the particular right at issue in the Zenger case.

6. A: The attitudes of American colonists after the 1763 Treaty of Paris ended the French and Indian War were not a direct contributor to the American Revolution. American colonists had a supportive attitude toward Great Britain then, and were proud of the part they played in winning the war. Their good will was not returned by British leaders (b), who looked down on American colonials and sought to increase their imperial power over them. Even in 1761, a sign of Americans' objections to having their liberty curtailed by the British was seen when Boston attorney James Otis argued in court against the Writs of Assistance (c), search warrants to enforce England's mercantilist trade restrictions, as violating the kinds of natural laws espoused during the Enlightenment. Lord George Grenville's aggressive program to defend the North American frontier in the wake of Chief Pontiac's attacks included stricter enforcement of the Navigation Acts, the Proclamation of 1763, the Sugar Act (or Revenue Act), the Currency Act, and most of all the Stamp Act (d). Colonists objected to these as taxation without representation. Other events followed in this taxation dispute, which further eroded Americans' relationship with British government, including the Townshend Acts, the Massachusetts Circular Letter, the Boston Massacre, the Tea Act, and the resulting Boston Tea Party. Finally, with Britain's passage of the Intolerable Acts and the Americans' First Continental Congress, which was followed by Britain's military aggression against American resistance, actual warfare began in 1775. While not all of the colonies wanted war or independence by then, things changed by 1776, and Jefferson's Declaration of Independence was formalized.

7. C: Colonists did find that tea shipped directly by the British East India Company cost less than smuggled Dutch tea, even with tax. The colonists, however, did not buy it. They refused, despite its lower cost, on the principle that the British were taxing colonists without representation (d). It is true that the British East India Company lost money as a result of colonists buying tea smuggled from Holland (a). They sought to remedy this problem by getting concessions from Parliament to ship tea directly to the colonies instead of going through England (b) as the Navigation Acts normally required. Boston Governor Thomas Hutchinson, who sided with Britain, stopped tea ships from leaving the harbor, which after 20 days would cause the tea to be sold at auction. At that time, British taxes on the tea would be paid. On the 19th night after Hutchinson's action, American protestors held the Boston Tea Party, dressing as Indians and dumping all the tea into the harbor to destroy it so it could not be taxed and sold. Many American colonists disagreed with the Boston Tea Party because it involved destroying private property.

8. C: Massachusetts did set a valuable example for other states by stipulating that its constitution should be created via a special convention rather than via the legislature. This way, the constitution would take precedence over the legislature, which would be subject to the rules of the constitution. It is not true that twelve states had new constitutions by the

end of 1777 (a). By this time, ten of the states had new constitutions. It is not true that Connecticut and <u>Massachusetts</u> retained their colonial charters minus the British parts (b). Connecticut and <u>Rhode Island</u> were the states that preserved their colonial charters. They simply removed any parts referring to British rule. Massachusetts did not formalize its new constitution in <u>1778</u> (d). This state did not actually finish the process of adopting its new constitution until <u>1780</u>.

9. D: The Louisiana Purchase actually increased the U.S.'s territory by 100% overnight, not 50%. The Louisiana territory doubled the size of the nation. It is true that Jefferson initially sent a delegation to Paris to see if Napoleon would agree to sell only New Orleans to the United States (a). It is also true that Napoleon, who expected America to encroach on Louisiana, decided to avoid this by offering to sell the entire territory to the U.S. (b). It is likewise true that America only had authority to buy New Orleans. Nevertheless, the delegation accepted Napoleon's offer of all of Louisiana (c).

10. B: Hamilton did not object to U.S. western expansionism, and Burr did not support it. There were certain Federalists other than Hamilton who opposed expansion to the west as a threat to their position within the Union, and these opponents did attempt to organize a movement to secede (a). To get Aaron Burr to champion their cause, they offered to help him run for Governor of New York (c). Hamilton did lead the opposition against Burr's campaign (d).

11. A: The U.S. did carry out a three-pronged invasion of Canada early in the war, but they did not succeed on two fronts. Instead, they lost on all three. Americans did win sea battles against the British early in the war, but were soon beaten back to their homeports and then blockaded by powerful British warships (b). Admiral Perry did defeat the British on Lake Erie on September 10, 1813 (c). Perry's victory allowed William Henry Harrison to invade Canada (d) in October of 1813, where he defeated British and Indians in the Battle of the Thames.

12. D: Political corruption was not an immediate effect of the rapid urban growth during this time. The accelerated growth of cities in America did soon result in services being unable to keep up with that growth. The results of this included deficiencies in clean water delivery and garbage collection, causing poor sanitation (a). That poor sanitation led to outbreaks of cholera and typhus, as well as typhoid fever epidemics (b). Police and fire fighting services could not keep up with the population increases, and were often inadequate (c).

13. D: All the laws (d) named were instrumental in spurring westward migration to the Great Plains. The Homestead Act (a), passed in 1862, gave settlers 160 acres of land at no monetary cost in exchange for a commitment to cultivating the land for five years. The Timber Culture Act (b), passed in 1873, gave the settlers 160 acres more of land in exchange for planting trees on one quarter of the acreage. The Desert Land Act (c), passed in 1877, allowed buyers who would irrigate the land to buy 640 acres for only 25 cents an acre. Thus, (d), all of these laws were instrumental in spurring westward migration to the Great Plains during that period, is correct.

14. B: Germany's declaration of war on Russia in 1914, following the assassination of Archduke Ferdinand (b), did not contribute to ending American neutrality in World War I. Once Germany declared war, England, France, Italy, Russia, and Japan joined as the Allied

Powers against the Central Powers of Germany and Austria-Hungary, and US President Woodrow Wilson declared America's neutrality. When Germany designated the area surrounding the British Isles as a war zone in February 1913 (a), and warned all ships from neutral countries to stay out of the zone, an end to American neutrality was prompted. President Wilson's responded to Germany's declaration by proclaiming that America would hold Germany responsible for any American losses of life or property. When Germany sank the British passenger vessel *Lusitania*, 128 American passengers were killed (c). This further eroded Wilson's resolve to remain neutral. In February 1917, Germany declared unrestricted submarine warfare on any ship in the war zone (d); this signified that ships from any country would face German attack.

15. A: The postwar conference that brought US-Soviet differences to light was (a) the Potsdam conference in July of 1945. The conference at Yalta (b), in February of 1945, resulted in the division of Germany into Allied-controlled zones. The Dumbarton Oaks conference (c) (1944) established a Security Council, on which with the US, England, Soviet Union, France, and China served as the five permanent members. Each of the permanent members had veto power, and a General Assembly, with limited power, was also established. The Tehran conference (d) included FDR's proposal for a new international organization to take the place of the League of Nations. This idea would later be realized in the form of the United Nations.

16. D: In 1956, Egypt did not attack Israel. On October 29, 1956, Israel attacked Egypt. England and France did join this war within two days. It is true that Egyptian President Gamal Abdul Nasser refused to take America's side in the Cold War (a). In reaction to his refusal, President Eisenhower's administration pulled its funding from the Aswan Dam project in Egypt (b). Nasser then nationalized the British-owned Suez Canal (c).

17. C: The person or group not instrumental in advancing civil rights and desegregation immediately after WWII was (c), Congress. As African American soldiers came home from the war, racial discord increased. President Harry Truman (a) appointed a Presidential Committee on Civil Rights in 1946. This committee published a report recommending that segregation and lynching be outlawed by the federal government. However, Congress ignored this report and took no action. Truman then used his presidential powers to enforce desegregation of the military and policies of "fair employment" in federal civil service jobs. The National Association for the Advancement of Colored People (NAACP) (d) brought lawsuits against racist and discriminatory practices, and in resolving these suits, the Supreme Court (b) further eroded segregation. For example, the Supreme Court ruled that primaries allowing only whites would be illegal, and it ended the segregation of interstate bus lines. The landmark civil rights laws were not passed by Congress until the 1960s.

18. B: Of the programs enacted by Johnson, the one most closely related to JFK's legacy was (b), the Civil Rights Act, which Johnson pushed through Congress using allusions to Kennedy's and his goals. While Kennedy received congressional backing for a raise in minimum wage and public housing improvements, his efforts regarding civil rights were thwarted by conservative Republicans and Southern Democrats in Congress. However, as the Civil Rights movement progressed through the campaigns of the Freedom Riders, Kennedy developed a strong commitment to the cause.

The Economic Opportunity Act gave almost $1 billion to wage Johnson's War on Poverty. The Great Society (c) was Johnson's name for his comprehensive reform program which included a variety of legislation (see also question #102).

19. B: The GATT countries did agree to abolish or decrease many of their tariffs, but this agreement did not include only 57 countries. It was much larger, including a total of 117 countries. The GATT was approved by Congress in 1994 (a). In addition to having 117 countries agree to increase free trade, the GATT also set up the World Trade Organization (WTO) for the purpose of settling any differences among nations related to trade (c). Another instance of free trade policy established in the 1990s was the Senate's ratification of NAFTA. The negotiation of this agreement was originally made by the first Bush administration, with President Bush and the leaders of Canada and Mexico signing it in 1992 (d), but it still needed to be ratified.

20. B: There was not a reduction in military spending after the war. Although the manufacturing demand for war supplies and the size of the military decreased, the government had increased military spending from $10 billion in 1947 to more than $50 billion by 1953—a more than fivefold increase. This increase strengthened the American economy. Other factors contributing to the strengthened economy included the significantly higher birth rates during the Baby Boom (a) from 1946 to 1957, which stimulated the growth of the building and automotive industries by increased demand. Government programs, such as the GI Bill (the Servicemen's Readjustment Act of 1944), other veterans' benefits, and the National Defense Education Act all encouraged college enrollments, which increased by nearly four times (c). Additionally, larger families, increased mobility and low-interest loans offered to veterans led to suburban development and growth (d) as well as an increased home construction.

21. D: The statement that the 1986 Immigration Reform and Control Act reduced illegal Mexican immigration is not true. This legislation punished employers with sanctions for hiring undocumented employees, but despite this the illegal immigration of Mexicans to America was largely unaffected by the law. It is true that twice as many people immigrated to America in the 1980s than in the 1970s (a): the number reached over nine million in the 80s. It is true that the majority of immigrants were Latin American (b). In addition to Latin Americans, other large groups of immigrants in the 1980s were Asians and Caribbean inhabitants (c).

22. C: The Mississippi Freedom Democratic Party did attend the 1964 Democratic convention; however, they were unable garner Johnson's support to unseat the regular delegation from Mississippi. A riot did break out in Watts in 1965 (a), and in the following three years, more riots occurred in Newark, N.J. (b) and in Detroit, Michigan (d). These riots were manifestations of the frustrations experienced by blacks regarding racial inequities in American society.

23. A: The earliest written language in Mesopotamia was Sumerian. Ancient Sumerians began writing this language around 3500 B.C.E. Elamite (b), from Iran, was the language spoken by the ancient Elamites and was the official language of the Persian Empire from the 6th to 4th centuries B.C.E. Written Linear Elamite was used for a very short time in the late 3rd century B.C.E. The written Elamite cuneiform, used from about 2500 to 331 B.C.E., was an adaptation of the Akkadian (c) cuneiform. Akkadian is the earliest found Semitic language. Written Akkadian cuneiform first appeared in texts by circa 2800 B.C.E., and full

Akkadian texts appeared by circa 2500 B.C.E. The Akkadian cuneiform writing system is ultimately a derivative of the ancient Sumerian cuneiform writing system, although these two spoken languages were not related linguistically. Aramaic (d) is another Semitic language, but unlike Akkadian, Aramaic is not now extinct. Old Aramaic, the written language of the Old Testament and the spoken language used by Jesus Christ, was current from c. 1100-200 C.E. Middle Aramaic, used from 200-1200 C.E., included literary Syriac (Christian groups developed the writing system of Syriac in order to be able to write spoken Aramaic) and was the written language of the Jewish books of Biblical commentary (Namely, the Talmud, the Targum, and the Midrash). Modern Aramaic has been used from 1200 to the present.

24. C: The New Kingdom was the period during which no more pyramids were built in Egypt. The Pyramids were built between the years of 2630 and 1814 B.C.E., and the New Kingdom spanned from circa 1550-1070 B.C. As a result, the last pyramid was built approximately 264 years before the New Kingdom began. 2630 B.C.E. marked the beginning of the reign of the first Pharaoh, Djoser, who had the first pyramid built at Saqqara. 1814 B.C.E. marked the end of the reign of the last Pharaoh, Amenemhat III, who had the last pyramid built at Hawara. In between these years, a succession of pharaohs built many pyramids. The Old Kingdom (a) encompasses both the Third (d) and Fourth (e) Dynasties; therefore, all three of these choices encompass pyramid-building periods. Djoser's had his first pyramid built during the Third Dynasty (d). The Pharaohs Kufu, Khafre, and Menkaure, respectively, build the famous Pyramids of Giza during the Fourth Dynasty during their reigns at different times between circa 2575 and 2467 B.C.E., the period of the Fourth Dynasty. The Middle Kingdom (b) encompassed the 11th through 14th Dynasties, from circa 2080 to 1640 B.C.E.—also within the time period (2630-1814 B.C.E.) when pyramids were built by the Pharaohs.

25. B: It is not true that the Crusades succeeded at Christians' reclaiming the "holy land" (the Middle East) from Muslims. Despite their number (nine not counting the Northern Crusades) and longevity (1095-1291 not counting later similar campaigns), the Crusades never accomplished this purpose (a). While they did not take back the Middle East, the Crusades did succeed in exacerbating the decline of the Byzantine Empire (c), which lost more and more territory to the Ottoman Turks during this period. In addition, the Crusades resulted in Egypt's rise once again to become a major power (d) of the Middle East as it had been in the past.

26. D: All these events contributed to the Italian Renaissance. After the Black Death killed a third of Europe's population (a), the survivors were mainly upper classes with more money to spend on art, architecture, and other luxuries. The plague deaths also resulted in a labor shortage, thereby creating more work opportunities for the surviving people in lower classes (b). As a result, these survivors' positions in society appreciated. Once plague deaths subsided and population growth in Europe began to reassert itself, a greater demand existed for products and services. At the same time, the number of people available to provide these products and services was still smaller than in the past. Consequently, more merchants, artisans, and bankers emerged in order to provide the services and products people wanted, thereby creating a class of citizens between the lower class laborers and the upper class elite (c).

27. B: In order to prosper, a nation should not try to increase its imports. Mercantilism is an economic theory including the idea that prosperity comes from a positive balance of

international trade. For any one nation to prosper, that nation should increase its exports (c) but decrease its imports. Exporting more to other countries while importing less from them will give a country a positive trade balance. This theory assumes that money and wealth are identical (a) assets of a nation. Mercantilism dictates that a nation's government should apply a policy of economic protectionism (d) by stimulating more exports and suppressing imports. Some ways to do accomplish this task have included granting subsidies for exports and imposing tariffs on imports. Mercantilism can be regarded as essentially the opposite of the free trade policies that have been encouraged in more recent years.

28. C: It is not true that the English Civil Wars between 1641 and 1651 legalized Parliament's consent as a requirement for a monarch to rule England. These wars did establish this idea as a precedent, but the later Glorious Revolution of 1688 actually made it legal that a monarch could not rule without Parliamentary consent. The wars from 1641-1651 were all fought between Royalists who supported an absolute monarchy and Parliamentarians who supported the joint government of a parliamentary monarchy (a). Parliament was the victor (b) in 1651 at the Battle of Worcester. As a result of this battle, King Charles I was executed, and King Charles II was exiled. In the first of these civil wars, from 1642-1646, and the second, from 1648-1649, supporters of King Charles I (d) fought against supporters of the Long Parliament.

29. D: Resentment against the Protestant Reformation was not a cause given for the French Revolution. Choices (a), (b), and (c) are just a few among many causes cited for the war. Famines caused malnutrition and even starvation among the poorest people (a). Escalating bread prices contributed greatly to the hunger. Louis XV had amassed a great amount of debt from spending money on many wars in addition to the American Revolution. Military failures as well as a lack of social services for veterans exacerbated these debts. In addition, the Court of Louis XVI and Marie Antoinette spent excessively and obviously on luxuries even while people in the country were starving, and France's monetary system was outdated, inefficient, and thus unable to manage the national debt (b). Much of the populace greatly resented the Catholic Church's control of the country (c). However, there was not great resentment against the Protestant Reformation (d); there were large minorities of Protestants in France, who not only exerted their influence on government institutions, but undoubtedly also contributed to the resentment of the Catholic Church.

30. A: In the 1780s, the French national debt was very high. The French nobility adamantly resisted attempts by King Louis XVI to reform tax laws, which led to a high tax burden on the French peasantry. The French government spent almost 50% of its national expenditures on debt-related payments during the 1780s; thus it could not and did not spend almost 60% to finance luxuries for the French nobility. This eliminates choice B. King Louis XVI temporarily banned the guild system to bolster, rather than stifle, free trade. Because this system gave skilled craftsmen economic advantages, journeymen opposed ending the system. This eliminates choice D. Regardless of the status of guilds before the French Revolution, French society did not offer many opportunities for upward social mobility. Few peasants were able to advance. This eliminates choice C.

31. C: The only accurate statement about the end of WWI is that President Wilson had proposed that the nations of the world form a coalition to prevent future world wars. While he did not give the coalition a name, he clearly expressed his proposal that such a group form in the fourteenth of his Fourteen Points. The Treaty of Versailles (1919) did not bring

peace among all countries involved in the war (a); Germany and the United States arrived at a separate peace in 1921. Furthermore, the Treaty of Versailles did not contain a clause for establishing the United Nations (b); it contained a clause for establishing the League of Nations. The League of Nations was created as dictated by the treaty, but when the Second World War proved that this group had failed to prevent future world wars, it was replaced by the United Nations after World War II. President Wilson did not succeed in getting the USA to ratify the League of Nations (d).

32. A: Russian's involvement in World War I brought social tension in Russia to a head. Contributing factors included military defeats and civilian suffering. Prior to Russia entering the war, Russian factory workers could legally strike, but during the war, it was illegal for them to act collectively. This eliminates answer C. Protests continued during World War I, and the Russian government was overthrown in 1917. This eliminates answer D. Answer B can be rejected because World War I did not go well for the Russian Army; Nicholas III, therefore, had no successes upon which to capitalize.

33. A: The latest occurring decolonization event was the Eastern Bloc and Soviet Satellite states of Armenia, Azerbaijan, Estonia, Georgia, Kazakhstan, Kyrgyzstan, Latvia, Lithuania, Moldova, Russia, Tajikistan, Turkmenistan, Ukraine, and Uzbekistan all became independent from the Soviet Union in 1991. (Note: This was the last decolonization of the Cold War years, as the end of the Soviet Union marked the end of the Cold War.) Canada completed its independence from British Parliament via the Canada Act (b) in 1982. In the Caribbean, the Bahamas gained independence from the United Kingdom (c) in 1973. Algeria won its independence from France when the Algerian War of Independence, begun in 1954, ended in 1962 (d).

34. B: U.S. industrialization was confined to the Northeast until after the Civil War because the Northeast had faster-running rivers than the South. The earliest American factories used horse-drawn machines. When waterpower was developed and proved superior, the Northeast's faster rivers were more suited to water-powered mills than the South's slower rivers. The war did not delay the development of water power (a). Waterpower was developed before the Civil War in the late 1790s. Steam power, a more efficient alternative to water power, was developed after the Civil War and eventually replaced waterpower. With steam-powered engines, industry could spread to the South, since steam engines did not depend on rapidly running water like water-powered engines. While British emigré Samuel Slater's first cotton mill using horse-drawn production did lose a lot of money (c), this was not a reason for industrial delay. In fact, Slater's Beverly Cotton Manufactory in Massachusetts, the first American cotton mill, in spite of its financial problems, was successful in both its volume of cotton production and in developing the water-powered technology that ultimately would succeed the horse-drawn method. Slater's second cotton mill in Pawtucket, Rhode Island, was water-powered. Industrial delay was not because milling technology had not yet been invented (d). Slater learned of new textile manufacturing techniques as a youth in England, and he brought this knowledge to America in 1789. Resistance of Southern owners of plantations and slaves did not slow the spread of industrialism. Rather, as seen in (b) above, the South did not have the geographic capability to sustain waterpower. Once steam power was developed, the South joined in industrialization.

35. A: The inaccurate statement is the Puritans unconditionally supported the English Reformation. While they agreed with the Reformation in principle, they felt that it had not

pursued those principles far enough and should make greater reforms. Similarly, they felt that the Church of England (or Anglican Church), though it had separated from the Catholic Church in the Protestant Reformation, still allowed many practices they found too much like Catholicism (b). The Puritans did become a chief political power in England because of the first English Civil War (c) between Royalists and Parliamentarians. The Royalists had a profound suspicion of the radical Puritans. Among the Parliament's elements of resistance, the strongest was that of the Puritans. They joined in the battle initially for ostensibly political reasons as others had, but soon they brought more attention to religious issues. Following the Restoration in 1660 and the Uniformity Act of 1662, thereby restoring the Church of England to its pre-English Civil War status, the great majority of Puritan clergy defected from the Church of England (d).

36. D: It is not true that the Gilded Age is a term whose origins have not been identified clearly. In 1873, Mark Twain and Charles Dudley Warner co-authored a book entitled The Gilded Age: A Tale of Today. Twain and Warner first coined this term to describe the extravagance and excesses of America's wealthy upper class (b), who became richer than ever due to industrialization. Furthermore, the Gilded Age was the era of the "robber barons" (a) such as John D. Rockefeller, Cornelius Vanderbilt, J.P. Morgan, and others. Because they accumulated enormous wealth through extremely aggressive and occasionally unethical monetary manipulations, critics dubbed them "robber barons" because they seemed to be elite lords of robbery. While these business tycoons grasped huge fortunes, some of them—such as Andrew Carnegie and Andrew Mellon—were also philanthropists, using their wealth to support and further worthy causes such as literacy, education, health care, charities, and the arts. They donated millions of dollars to fund social improvements. Carnegie himself dubbed this large philanthropic movement the "Gospel of Wealth" (c).

37. A: It is not true that the founding fathers specifically stated in the Constitution that the USA would be a democracy. The founding fathers wanted the new United States to be founded on principles of liberty and equality, but they did not specifically describe these principles with the term "Democracy." Thus, the Declaration of Independence, like the Constitution after it, did not stipulate a democracy, although both did state the principles of equality and freedom (b). The Constitution also provided for the election of the new government (c), and for protection of the rights of some, but not all, of the people (d). Notable exceptions at the time were black people and women. Only later were laws passed to protect their rights over the years.

38. B: Preservatives such as salt were only introduced to the European diet after trade routes opened and these goods could be brought to Europe.

39. B: In 1792, when the French Revolution turned into European war, American traders conducted business with both sides. It is not true that Washington allied with the French (a) at this time. Washington issued a Proclamation of Neutrality in 1792 when the French went to war with European countries. While they did trade with both sides, American merchants profited the most from the French West Indies, not the British West Indies (c). The Spanish navy did not retaliate against America for trading with the French (d). Though Spain was an ally of Britain, it was the British who most often seized American ships and forced their crews to serve the British navy.

40. B: The Etruscans were from a kingdom to the north that seized control of Rome from the Latins in the mid-600s B.C. They began urbanizing the settlement, improving roads,

adding drainage systems, etc. They were driven out of the region in 509 B.C. during an uprising of the Latins.

41. A: James Madison, John Jay, and Alexander Hamilton published The Federalist in the Independent Journal in New York. It was a response to the Anti-Federalists in New York, who were slow to ratify the Constitution because they feared it gave the central government too much authority.

42. D: A practical application of content learned involves action, not merely knowledge. Options A and C, although they describe content that students would reasonably learn in a class or unit on the structure of the U.S. government, do not describe applications of content, or applications of a social studies education. Therefore options A and C can both be rejected. Option B does involve action and not merely the acquisition of knowledge. However, it is not as directly tied to learning the structure of the U.S. government as option D, informed participation in U.S. political processes. This is because informed participation in school elections is quite possible without knowing the structure of the U.S. government. Informed participation in U.S. political processes requires knowledge of the structure of the U.S. government (i.e., voting on an issue requires an understanding of where a given candidate stands on that issue).

43. C: A federalist system of government is a government under which power is shared by a central authority and sub-components of the federation. In the United States in particular, power is shared by the federal government and the individual states. Option A, that the legislative branch consists of two representative bodies (the House of Representatives and the Senate) is true, of course, but does not describe a uniquely federalist structure. Rather, it describes the concept of bicameralism. Option A may thus be eliminated. Option B, likewise, describes different types of democracy but not federalism. B can thus be eliminated. Regarding option D, this statement is also true (the U.S. Constitution shapes national legislation) but it is not a descriptive statement of the federalist system because the statement makes no mention that power is shared by the states.

44. D: Congress did not have the authority to levy taxes under the Articles of Confederation. Without the ability to levy taxes, there was no way to finance programs, which weakened the government.

45. A: The Age of Enlightenment was a time of scientific and philosophical achievement. Also called the Age of Reason, human thought and reason were prized.

46. C: The Constitution was not ratified immediately. Only five states accepted it in early 1788; Massachusetts, New York, Rhode Island, and Virginia were originally opposed to the Constitution. Rhode Island reluctantly accepted it in 1790.

47. B: James Madison was a close friend of Thomas Jefferson and supported a stronger central government. George Mason and Robert Yates were both against expanding federal authority over the states. Benjamin Franklin was a proponent of a strong federal government, but he was from Massachusetts.

48. D: Some of the men who helped frame the Constitution believed the central government needed to be stronger than what was established under the Articles of Confederation. Others were against this and feared a strong federal government. A system of checks and

balances was established to prevent the central government from taking too much power. This arrangement is known as federalism.

49. A: The Senate and House of Representatives make up a bicameral legislature. The Great Compromise awarded seats in the Senate equally to each state, while the seats in the House of Representatives were based on population.

50. B: The Presidential Succession Act lists the Speaker of the House, President Pro Tempore of the Senate, and Secretary of State next in succession after the Vice President. However, anyone who succeeds as President must meet all of the legal qualifications.

51. C: The President has the power to veto legislation directly or use a pocket veto by not signing a bill within ten days after receiving it. Congress adjourns during this time period. A veto can be overridden if two-thirds of the House and the two-thirds of the Senate both agree. The President must veto a complete bill and does not have the authority to veto sections or lines.

52. C: The Civil Rights Act of 1964 affected the Jim Crow laws in the Southern states. Many minorities suffered under unfair voting laws and segregation. President Lyndon Johnson signed the Civil Rights Act of 1964 into law after the 1963 assassination of President Kennedy, who championed the reform.

53. B: Only the federal government has the power to give copyrights and patents to individuals or companies. The power to levy taxes, borrow money, and spend money (a) is a power shared by federal and state governments. The power to set the criteria that qualify individuals to vote (c) is a power given to state governments only. The power to ratify amendments proposed to the Constitution (d) is a power of only the state governments.

54. A: The action that needs a three-fourths majority vote is state approval of a proposed constitutional amendment. Proposing a constitutional amendment (b) requires a two-thirds majority vote. Ratifying presidential appointments in the Senate (c) also requires a two-thirds majority vote. Introducing charges for impeachment in the House of Representatives (d) requires a simple majority vote.

55. B: The term "Manifest Destiny" had not been used for many years before the 1830s. This term was coined in 1844. However, it is true that the idea this term expressed had been around for many years before that (a). It is also true that many Americans believed Manifest Destiny would mean America would ultimately encompass Canada and Mexico (c). Factors contributing to Manifest Destiny included the rise in nationalism that followed the War of 1812 and the population growth that increased that nationalism (d).

56. A: Presidential candidates are eligible for a match from the federal government (with a $250 per contribution limit) if they can privately raise $5,000 per state in twenty states. Candidates who accept public money agree to limit spending. Candidates who do not accept matching funds are free to use the money they raise privately.

57. D: America is a common law country because English common law was adopted in all states except Louisiana. Common law is based on precedent, and changes over time. Each state develops its own common laws.

58. D: The only answer choice that represents a possible absolute location for New Orleans is 30° N, 90° W. When a location is described in terms of its placement on the global grid, it is customary to put the latitude before the longitude. New Orleans is north of the equator, so it has to be in the Northern Hemisphere. In addition, it is west of the prime meridian, which runs through Greenwich, England, among other places. So, New Orleans must be in the Western Hemisphere. It is possible, then, to deduce that 30° N, 90° W is the only possible absolute location for New Orleans.

59. B: On a political map, countries are represented in different colors, and countries that share a border are not given the same color. This is so that the borders between countries will be distinct. Political maps are used to illustrate those aspects of a country that have been determined by people: the capital, the provincial and national borders, and the large cities. Political maps sometimes include major physical features like rivers and mountains, but they are not intended to display all such information. On a physical, climate, or contour map, however, the borders between nations are more incidental. Colors are used on these maps to represent physical features, areas with similar climate, etc. It is possible that colors will overrun the borders and be shared by adjacent countries.

60. D: Around the world, the area around the equator is known for a relative lack of wind. Indeed, the equatorial belt is sometimes called the doldrums because the constant warm water encourages the air to rise gently. To the north and south, however, there are trade winds that can become quite violent. The equator only intersects three continents: Asia, Africa, and South America. It is in between the north and south horse latitudes, which are belts known for calm winds. Finally, the equator is located at 0° latitude, not longitude, though the 0° line of longitude does intersect the equator.

61. A: The apparent distance between Greenland and Norway will be greatest on a Mercator map. The Mercator map is a type of cylindrical projection map in which lines of latitude and longitude are transferred onto a cylindrical shape, which is then cut vertically and laid flat. For this reason, distances around the poles will appear increasingly great. The Mercator map is excellent for navigation because a straight line drawn on it represents a single compass reading. In a conic projection map, on the other hand, a hemisphere of the globe is transposed onto a cone, which is then cut vertically (that is, from rim to tip) and laid flat. The apparent distances on a conic projection will be smallest at the 45th parallel. A contour map uses lines to illustrate the features of a geographic area. For example, the lines on an elevation contour map connect areas that have the same altitude. An equal-area projection map represents landmasses in their actual sizes. To make this possible, the shapes of the landmasses are manipulated slightly, and the map is interrupted (divided into more than one part).

62. A: Symbols are not used to represent relief on a physical map. A physical map is dedicated to illustrating the landmasses and bodies of water in a specific region, so symbols do not provide enough detail. Color, shading, and contour lines, on the other hand, are able to create a much more complicated picture of changes in elevation, precipitation, etc. Changes in elevation are known in geography as relief.

63. D: A flow-line map describes the movement of people, trends, or materials across a physical area. The movements depicted on a flow-line map are typically represented by arrows. In more advanced flow-line maps, the width of the arrow corresponds to the quantity of the motion. Flow-line maps usually declare the span of time that is being

represented. A political map depicts the man-made aspects of geography, such as borders and cities. A cartogram adjusts the size of the areas represented according to some variable. For instance, a cartogram of wheat production would depict Iowa as being much larger than Alaska. A qualitative map uses lines, dots, and other symbols to illustrate a particular point. For example, a qualitative map might be used to demonstrate the greatest expansion of the Persian Empire.

64. B: The composite volcano, sometimes called the stratovolcano, is the most common type of volcano on earth. A composite volcano has steep sides, so the explosions of ash, pumice, and silica are often accompanied by treacherous mudslides. Indeed, it is these mudslides that cause most of the damage associated with composite volcano eruptions. Krakatoa and Mount Saint Helens are examples of composite volcanoes. A lava dome is a round volcano that emits thick lava very slowly. A shield volcano, one example of which is Mt. Kilauea in Hawaii, emits a small amount of lava over an extended period of time. Shield volcanoes are not known for violent eruptions. A cinder cone has steep sides made of fallen cinders, which themselves are made of the lava that intermittently shoots into the air.

65. C: After precipitation, the heat of the sun causes evaporation, a process by which water molecules change from a liquid to a gas, ultimately returning to the atmosphere. The other options describe processes that pertain to properties of water, but not to water's return to the atmosphere. Percolation is the process by which water moves down through soil. Cohesion (specifically, structural cohesion) is the property of matter by which the molecules in a single substance stay together. Condensation is the process by which matter changes from a gas to a liquid; after evaporation, molecules of water form rain droplets through condensation.

66. B: Metamorphic rock is formed by extreme heat and pressure. This type of rock is created when other rocks are somehow buried within the earth, where they are subject to a dramatic rise in pressure and temperature. Slate and marble are both metamorphic rocks. Metamorphic rocks are created by the other two main types of rock: sedimentary and igneous. Sedimentary rock is formed when dirt and other sediment is washed into a bed, covered over by subsequent sediment, and compacted into rock. Depending on how they are formed, sedimentary rocks are classified as organic, clastic, or chemical. Igneous rocks are composed of cooled magma, the molten rock that emerges from volcanoes. Basalt and granite are two common varieties of igneous rock.

67. A: The eye wall of a hurricane has the strongest winds and the greatest rainfall. The eye wall is the tower-like rim of the eye. It is from this wall that clouds extend out, which are seen from above as the classic outward spiral pattern. A hurricane front is the outermost edge of its influence; although there will be heavy winds and rain in this area, the intensity will be relatively small. The eye of a hurricane is actually a place of surprising peace. In this area, dry and cool air rushes down to the ground or sea. Once there, the air is caught up in the winds of the eye wall and is driven outward at a furious pace.

68. D: These are all geographically parts of Southeast Asia. The countries of Myanmar (Burma), Laos, Cambodia, and Thailand (a) are considered Mainland Southeast Asia, as are Vietnam and the Malay Peninsula (b). Brunei (b), East Malaysia, Indonesia, and the Philippines (c) are considered Maritime Southeast Asia, as are Singapore and Timor-Leste. The Seven Sister States of India are also considered to be part of Southeast Asia, geographically and culturally. (The Seven Sister States of India are Arunachal Pradesh,

Assam, Nagaland, Meghalaya, Manipur, Tripura, and Mizoram, which all have contiguous borders in northeastern India.)

69. A: One example of the multiplier effect of large cities would be if the presence of specialized equipment for an industry attracted even more business. Large cities tend to grow even larger for a number of reasons: they have more skilled workers, they have greater concentrations of specialized equipment, and they have already-functioning markets. These factors all make it easier for a business to begin operations in a large city than elsewhere. Thus, the populations and economic productivity of large cities tend to grow quickly. Some governments have sought to mitigate this trend by clustering groups of similar industries in smaller cities.

70. D: The Sahel, a belt of grasslands just south of the Sahara Desert, has long been a focus of agricultural efforts in Africa. This semiarid region has provided sustenance to people and animals for thousands of years. In the last thousand years, stores of salt and gold were found there, giving rise to empires in Ghana and Mali. Changes in climate have expanded the Sahara, however, and pushed the Sahel farther south. The Qattara Depression is a low-lying desert in Egypt. The Great Rift Valley is a region of faults and rocky hills that extends along the southeastern coast of Africa. The Congo Basin is a repository of sediment from the Ubangi and Congo rivers. It is in the northern half of what is now called the Democratic Republic of the Congo.

71. B: To determine the shortest route between Lima and Lisbon, Tracy should use an azimuthal projection with Lisbon at the center. An azimuthal projection depicts one hemisphere of the globe as a circle. A straight line drawn from the center of the map to any point represents the shortest possible distance between those two points. Tracy could obtain her objective, then, with an azimuthal projection in which either Lisbon or Lima were at the center. If the North Pole were at the center, the map would not include Lima because this city is in the Southern Hemisphere. A Robinson projection approximates the sizes and shapes of landmasses but does distort in some ways, particularly near the poles.

72. B: North Korea and South Korea are separated by a geometric border, meaning that the boundary between the two nations is a straight line drawn on a map, without respect to landforms. Specifically, the boundary between the Koreas is the 38th parallel. Another example of a geometric border lies between the continental United States and Canada. The Turkish Cyprus–Greek Cyprus border is anthropogeographic, or drawn according to cultural reasons. The border between France and Spain is physiographic-political, a combination of the Pyrenees Mountains and European history. The Irish Sea separates England from Ireland.

73. D: More information is required to calculate the natural increase rate for Grassley County during this year. Natural increase rate is the growth in population measured as the surplus of live births over deaths for every thousand people. The calculation of natural increase rate does not take account of immigration or emigration. The natural increase rate for Grassley County cannot be calculated because the original population of the county is not given. As an example, if the beginning population of the county had been 10,000, the natural increase rate would be 40; 400 * 1,000/10,000 = 40.

74. A: North Africa is not one of the world's four major population agglomerations. These are eastern North America, South Asia, East Asia, and Europe. The largest of these is East

Copyright © Mometrix Media. You have been licensed one copy of this document for personal use only. Any other reproduction or redistribution is strictly prohibited. All rights reserved.

Asia, which encompasses Korea, Japan, and the major cities of China. The second-largest population agglomeration is South Asia, which includes India and Pakistan. Most of the population in this area is near the coasts. The European agglomeration is spread across the largest piece of land, while the much smaller agglomeration in eastern North America is primarily focused on the string of cities from Boston to Washington, DC.

75. D: It is true that scarcity causes producers (and other people) to make choices. Producers must choose what to produce with limited resources. It is also true that the choices a producer makes when faced with scarcity come with trade-offs. There are advantages and disadvantages to different production decisions. And, finally, calculating the opportunity cost of a choice provides a manner with which to measure the consequence of a choice and compare that against the consequence of other choices.

76. B: John Maynard Keynes argued that government could help revitalize a recessionary economy by increasing government spending and therefore increasing aggregate demand. This is known as demand-side economics.

77. D: If a society wants greater income equity, it will impose a progressive income tax, which taxes the wealthy at a higher rate; an inheritance tax, which prevents the wealthy from passing all their wealth on to the next generation; and a gift tax, which prevents the wealthy from simply giving their wealth away.

78. A: Answer B is a definition of gross national product, and answers C and D define other economic measures.

79. B: Structural unemployment is unemployment that results from a mismatch of job skills or location. In this case, Ivy's job skill—her ability to work as a seamstress—is no longer desired by employers. Frictional and cyclical are other forms of unemployment; economists do not use the term careless unemployment.

80. D: It is believed that some level of frictional and structural unemployment will always exist, and that the best economists (and politicians) can hope for is to reduce cyclical unemployment to zero. Therefore, frictional and structural unemployment are sometimes referred to as natural unemployment, meaning unemployment that naturally exists within an economy.

81. D: A supply shock is caused when there is a dramatic increase in input prices. This causes an increase in price levels and decreases in employment and GDP. A supply shock causes the AS curve to move to the left (in).

82. A: As people have more and more of something, they value it less and less. This is the law of diminishing marginal utility, and it is what causes the downward slope of the demand curve.

83. A: The change in demand is 20% (1,000 – 800 = 200), and the change in price is 10% ($11 - $10 = $1). Because the change in demand is greater than the change in price, the demand is considered elastic. In this case, the price elasticity quotient is greater than 1.

84. A: The phenomenon of "sticky prices" refers to prices that stay the same even though it seems they should change (either increasing or decreasing).

85. C: When a nation follows the theory of comparative advantage, it specializes in producing the goods and services it can make at a lower opportunity cost and then engages in trade to obtain other goods.

86. C: A person who has taken out a fixed-rate loan can benefit from inflation by paying back the loan with dollars that are less valuable than they were when the loan was taken out. In the other examples, inflation harms the individual or entity.

87. A: The input and output data illustrates the Law of Diminishing Marginal Returns, which states that as inputs are added during production, there eventually comes a time when increased inputs coincide with a decrease in marginal return.

88. C: Banks create money by giving out loans. For example, assume a person puts $100 into a bank. The bank will keep a percentage of that money in reserves because of the reserve requirement. If the reserve requirement is 10% then the bank will put $10 in reserves and then loan out $90 of it to a second person. The money total, which started at $100, now includes the original $100 plus the $90, or a total of $190. The bank creates $90 by loaning it.

89. A: The equation of exchange is MV = PQ. This means that M1 (a measure of the supply of money) multiplied by the velocity of money (the average number of times a typical dollar is spent on final goods and services a year) = the average price level of final goods and services in GDP x real output, or the quantity of goods and services in GDP.

90. A: Economics is defined as the study of scarcity, the situation in which resources are limited and wants are unlimited.

Secret Key #1 - Time is Your Greatest Enemy

Pace Yourself

Wear a watch. At the beginning of the test, check the time (or start a chronometer on your watch to count the minutes), and check the time after every few questions to make sure you are "on schedule."

If you are forced to speed up, do it efficiently. Usually one or more answer choices can be eliminated without too much difficulty. Above all, don't panic. Don't speed up and just begin guessing at random choices. By pacing yourself, and continually monitoring your progress against your watch, you will always know exactly how far ahead or behind you are with your available time. If you find that you are one minute behind on the test, don't skip one question without spending any time on it, just to catch back up. Take 15 fewer seconds on the next four questions, and after four questions you'll have caught back up. Once you catch back up, you can continue working each problem at your normal pace.

Furthermore, don't dwell on the problems that you were rushed on. If a problem was taking up too much time and you made a hurried guess, it must be difficult. The difficult questions are the ones you are most likely to miss anyway, so it isn't a big loss. It is better to end with more time than you need than to run out of time.

Lastly, sometimes it is beneficial to slow down if you are constantly getting ahead of time. You are always more likely to catch a careless mistake by working more slowly than quickly, and among very high-scoring test takers (those who are likely to have lots of time left over), careless errors affect the score more than mastery of material.

Secret Key #2 - Guessing is not Guesswork

You probably know that guessing is a good idea. Unlike other standardized tests, there is no penalty for getting a wrong answer. Even if you have no idea about a question, you still have a 20-25% chance of getting it right.

Most test takers do not understand the impact that proper guessing can have on their score. Unless you score extremely high, guessing will significantly contribute to your final score.

Monkeys Take the Test

What most test takers don't realize is that to insure that 20-25% chance, you have to guess randomly. If you put 20 monkeys in a room to take this test, assuming they answered once per question and behaved themselves, on average they would get 20-25% of the questions correct. Put 20 test takers in the room, and the average will be much lower among guessed questions. Why?

    1. The test writers intentionally write deceptive answer choices that "look" right. A test taker has no idea about a question, so he picks the "best looking" answer, which is

often wrong. The monkey has no idea what looks good and what doesn't, so it will consistently be right about 20-25% of the time.

2. Test takers will eliminate answer choices from the guessing pool based on a hunch or intuition. Simple but correct answers often get excluded, leaving a 0% chance of being correct. The monkey has no clue, and often gets lucky with the best choice.

This is why the process of elimination endorsed by most test courses is flawed and detrimental to your performance. Test takers don't guess; they make an ignorant stab in the dark that is usually worse than random.

$5 Challenge

Let me introduce one of the most valuable ideas of this course—the $5 challenge:

- *You only mark your "best guess" if you are willing to bet $5 on it.*
- *You only eliminate choices from guessing if you are willing to bet $5 on it.*

Why $5? Five dollars is an amount of money that is small yet not insignificant, and can really add up fast (20 questions could cost you $100). Likewise, each answer choice on one question of the test will have a small impact on your overall score, but it can really add up to a lot of points in the end.

The process of elimination IS valuable. The following shows your chance of guessing it right:

If you eliminate wrong answer choices until only this many remain:	Chance of getting it correct:
1	100%
2	50%
3	33%

However, if you accidentally eliminate the right answer or go on a hunch for an incorrect answer, your chances drop dramatically—to 0%. By guessing among all the answer choices, you are GUARANTEED to have a shot at the right answer.

That's why the $5 test is so valuable. If you give up the advantage and safety of a pure guess, it had better be worth the risk.

What we still haven't covered is how to be sure that whatever guess you make is truly random. Here's the easiest way:

- *Always pick the first answer choice among those remaining.*

Such a technique means that you have decided, **before you see a single test question**, exactly how you are going to guess, and since the order of choices tells you nothing about which one is correct, this guessing technique is perfectly random.

This section is not meant to scare you away from making educated guesses or eliminating choices; you just need to define when a choice is worth eliminating. The $5 test, along with a pre-defined random guessing strategy, is the best way to make sure you reap all of the benefits of guessing.

Secret Key #3 - Practice Smarter, Not Harder

Many test takers delay the test preparation process because they dread the awful amounts of practice time they think necessary to succeed on the test. We have refined an effective method that will take you only a fraction of the time.

There are a number of "obstacles" in the path to success. Among these are answering questions, finishing in time, and mastering test-taking strategies. All must be executed on the day of the test at peak performance, or your score will suffer. The test is a mental marathon that has a large impact on your future.

Just like a marathon runner, it is important to work your way up to the full challenge. So first you just worry about questions, and then time, and finally strategy:

Success Strategy

1. Find a good source for practice tests.
2. If you are willing to make a larger time investment, consider using more than one study guide. Often the different approaches of multiple authors will help you "get" difficult concepts.
3. Take a practice test with no time constraints, with all study helps, "open book." Take your time with questions and focus on applying strategies.
4. Take a practice test with time constraints, with all guides, "open book."
5. Take a final practice test without open material and with time limits.

If you have time to take more practice tests, just repeat step 5. By gradually exposing yourself to the full rigors of the test environment, you will condition your mind to the stress of test day and maximize your success.

Secret Key #4 - Prepare, Don't Procrastinate

Let me state an obvious fact: if you take the test three times, you will probably get three different scores. This is due to the way you feel on test day, the level of preparedness you have, and the version of the test you see. Despite the test writers' claims to the contrary, some versions of the test WILL be easier for you than others.

Since your future depends so much on your score, you should maximize your chances of success. In order to maximize the likelihood of success, you've got to prepare in advance. This means taking practice tests and spending time learning the information and test taking strategies you will need to succeed.

Never go take the actual test as a "practice" test, expecting that you can just take it again if you need to. Take all the practice tests you can on your own, but when you go to take the official test, be prepared, be focused, and do your best the first time!

Secret Key #5 - Test Yourself

Everyone knows that time is money. There is no need to spend too much of your time or too little of your time preparing for the test. You should only spend as much of your precious time preparing as is necessary for you to get the score you need.

Once you have taken a practice test under real conditions of time constraints, then you will know if you are ready for the test or not.

If you have scored extremely high the first time that you take the practice test, then there is not much point in spending countless hours studying. You are already there.

Benchmark your abilities by retaking practice tests and seeing how much you have improved. Once you consistently score high enough to guarantee success, then you are ready.

If you have scored well below where you need, then knuckle down and begin studying in earnest. Check your improvement regularly through the use of practice tests under real conditions. Above all, don't worry, panic, or give up. The key is perseverance!

Then, when you go to take the test, remain confident and remember how well you did on the practice tests. If you can score high enough on a practice test, then you can do the same on the real thing.

General Strategies

The most important thing you can do is to ignore your fears and jump into the test immediately. Do not be overwhelmed by any strange-sounding terms. You have to jump into the test like jumping into a pool—all at once is the easiest way.

Make Predictions

As you read and understand the question, try to guess what the answer will be. Remember that several of the answer choices are wrong, and once you begin reading them, your mind will immediately become cluttered with answer choices designed to throw you off. Your mind is typically the most focused immediately after you have read the question and digested its contents. If you can, try to predict what the correct answer will be. You may be surprised at what you can predict.

Quickly scan the choices and see if your prediction is in the listed answer choices. If it is, then you can be quite confident that you have the right answer. It still won't hurt to check the other answer choices, but most of the time, you've got it!

Answer the Question

It may seem obvious to only pick answer choices that answer the question, but the test writers can create some excellent answer choices that are wrong. Don't pick an answer just because it sounds right, or you believe it to be true. It MUST answer the question. Once you've made your selection, always go back and check it against the question and make sure that you didn't misread the question and that the answer choice does answer the question posed.

Benchmark

After you read the first answer choice, decide if you think it sounds correct or not. If it doesn't, move on to the next answer choice. If it does, mentally mark that answer choice. This doesn't mean that you've definitely selected it as your answer choice, it just means that it's the best you've seen thus far. Go ahead and read the next choice. If the next choice is worse than the one you've already selected, keep going to the next answer choice. If the next choice is better than the choice you've already selected, mentally mark the new answer choice as your best guess.

The first answer choice that you select becomes your standard. Every other answer choice must be benchmarked against that standard. That choice is correct until proven otherwise by another answer choice beating it out. Once you've decided that no other answer choice seems as good, do one final check to ensure that your answer choice answers the question posed.

Valid Information

Don't discount any of the information provided in the question. Every piece of information may be necessary to determine the correct answer. None of the information in the question is there to throw you off (while the answer choices will certainly have information to throw you off). If two seemingly unrelated topics are discussed, don't ignore either. You can be confident there is a relationship, or it wouldn't be included in the question, and you are probably going to have to determine what is that relationship to find the answer.

Avoid "Fact Traps"

Don't get distracted by a choice that is factually true. Your search is for the answer that answers the question. Stay focused and don't fall for an answer that is true but irrelevant. Always go back to the question and make sure you're choosing an answer that actually answers the question and is not just a true statement. An answer can be factually correct, but it MUST answer the question asked. Additionally, two answers can both be seemingly correct, so be sure to read all of the answer choices, and make sure that you get the one that BEST answers the question.

Milk the Question

Some of the questions may throw you completely off. They might deal with a subject you have not been exposed to, or one that you haven't reviewed in years. While your lack of knowledge about the subject will be a hindrance, the question itself can give you many clues that will help you find the correct answer. Read the question carefully and look for clues. Watch particularly for adjectives and nouns describing difficult terms or words that you don't recognize. Regardless of whether you completely understand a word or not, replacing it with a synonym, either provided or one you more familiar with, may help you to understand what the questions are asking. Rather than wracking your mind about specific

- 167 -

detailed information concerning a difficult term or word, try to use mental substitutes that are easier to understand.

The Trap of Familiarity

Don't just choose a word because you recognize it. On difficult questions, you may not recognize a number of words in the answer choices. The test writers don't put "make-believe" words on the test, so don't think that just because you only recognize all the words in one answer choice that that answer choice must be correct. If you only recognize words in one answer choice, then focus on that one. Is it correct? Try your best to determine if it is correct. If it is, that's great. If not, eliminate it. Each word and answer choice you eliminate increases your chances of getting the question correct, even if you then have to guess among the unfamiliar choices.

Eliminate Answers

Eliminate choices as soon as you realize they are wrong. But be careful! Make sure you consider all of the possible answer choices. Just because one appears right, doesn't mean that the next one won't be even better! The test writers will usually put more than one good answer choice for every question, so read all of them. Don't worry if you are stuck between two that seem right. By getting down to just two remaining possible choices, your odds are now 50/50. Rather than wasting too much time, play the odds. You are guessing, but guessing wisely because you've been able to knock out some of the answer choices that you know are wrong. If you are eliminating choices and realize that the last answer choice you are left with is also obviously wrong, don't panic. Start over and consider each choice again. There may easily be something that you missed the first time and will realize on the second pass.

Tough Questions

If you are stumped on a problem or it appears too hard or too difficult, don't waste time. Move on! Remember though, if you can quickly check for obviously incorrect answer choices, your chances of guessing correctly are greatly improved. Before you completely give up, at least try to knock out a couple of possible answers. Eliminate what you can and then guess at the remaining answer choices before moving on.

Brainstorm

If you get stuck on a difficult question, spend a few seconds quickly brainstorming. Run through the complete list of possible answer choices. Look at each choice and ask yourself, "Could this answer the question satisfactorily?" Go through each answer choice and consider it independently of the others. By systematically going through all possibilities, you may find something that you would otherwise overlook. Remember though that when you get stuck, it's important to try to keep moving.

Read Carefully

Understand the problem. Read the question and answer choices carefully. Don't miss the question because you misread the terms. You have plenty of time to read each question thoroughly and make sure you understand what is being asked. Yet a happy medium must be attained, so don't waste too much time. You must read carefully, but efficiently.

Face Value

When in doubt, use common sense. Always accept the situation in the problem at face value. Don't read too much into it. These problems will not require you to make huge leaps of logic. The test writers aren't trying to throw you off with a cheap trick. If you have to go beyond creativity and make a leap of logic in order to have an answer choice answer the question, then you should look at the other answer choices. Don't overcomplicate the problem by creating theoretical relationships or explanations that will warp time or space. These are normal problems rooted in reality. It's just that the applicable relationship or explanation may not be readily apparent and you have to figure things out. Use your common sense to interpret anything that isn't clear.

Prefixes

If you're having trouble with a word in the question or answer choices, try dissecting it. Take advantage of every clue that the word might include. Prefixes and suffixes can be a huge help. Usually they allow you to determine a basic meaning. Pre- means before, post- means after, pro - is positive, de- is negative. From these prefixes and suffixes, you can get an idea of the general meaning of the word and try to put it into context. Beware though of any traps. Just because con- is the opposite of pro-, doesn't necessarily mean congress is the opposite of progress!

Hedge Phrases

Watch out for critical hedge phrases, led off with words such as "likely," "may," "can," "sometimes," "often," "almost," "mostly," "usually," "generally," "rarely," and "sometimes." Question writers insert these hedge phrases to cover every possibility. Often an answer choice will be wrong simply because it leaves no room for exception. Unless the situation calls for them, avoid answer choices that have definitive words like "exactly," and "always."

Switchback Words

Stay alert for "switchbacks." These are the words and phrases frequently used to alert you to shifts in thought. The most common switchback word is "but." Others include "although," "however," "nevertheless," "on the other hand," "even though," "while," "in spite of," "despite," and "regardless of."

New Information

Correct answer choices will rarely have completely new information included. Answer choices typically are straightforward reflections of the material asked about and will directly relate to the question. If a new piece of information is included in an answer choice that doesn't even seem to relate to the topic being asked about, then that answer choice is likely incorrect. All of the information needed to answer the question is usually provided for you in the question. You should not have to make guesses that are unsupported or choose answer choices that require unknown information that cannot be reasoned from what is given.

Time Management

On technical questions, don't get lost on the technical terms. Don't spend too much time on any one question. If you don't know what a term means, then odds are you aren't going to get much further since you don't have a dictionary. You should be able to immediately recognize whether or not you know a term. If you don't, work with the other clues that you have—the other answer choices and terms provided—but don't waste too much time trying to figure out a difficult term that you don't know.

Contextual Clues

Look for contextual clues. An answer can be right but not the correct answer. The contextual clues will help you find the answer that is most right and is correct. Understand the context in which a phrase or statement is made. This will help you make important distinctions.

Don't Panic

Panicking will not answer any questions for you; therefore, it isn't helpful. When you first see the question, if your mind goes blank, take a deep breath. Force yourself to mechanically go through the steps of solving the problem using the strategies you've learned.

Pace Yourself

Don't get clock fever. It's easy to be overwhelmed when you're looking at a page full of questions, your mind is full of random thoughts and feeling confused, and the clock is ticking down faster than you would like. Calm down and maintain the pace that you have set for yourself. As long as you are on track by monitoring your pace, you are guaranteed to have enough time for yourself. When you get to the last few minutes of the test, it may seem like you won't have enough time left, but if you only have as many questions as you should have left at that point, then you're right on track!

Answer Selection

The best way to pick an answer choice is to eliminate all of those that are wrong, until only one is left and confirm that is the correct answer. Sometimes though, an answer choice may immediately look right. Be careful! Take a second to make sure that the other choices are not equally obvious. Don't make a hasty mistake. There are only two times that you should stop before checking other answers. First is when you are positive that the answer choice you have selected is correct. Second is when time is almost out and you have to make a quick guess!

Check Your Work

Since you will probably not know every term listed and the answer to every question, it is important that you get credit for the ones that you do know. Don't miss any questions through careless mistakes. If at all possible, try to take a second to look back over your answer selection and make sure you've selected the correct answer choice and haven't made a costly careless mistake (such as marking an answer choice that you didn't mean to mark). The time it takes for this quick double check should more than pay for itself in caught mistakes.

Beware of Directly Quoted Answers

Sometimes an answer choice will repeat word for word a portion of the question or reference section. However, beware of such exact duplication. It may be a trap! More than likely, the correct choice will paraphrase or summarize a point, rather than being exactly the same wording.

Slang

Scientific sounding answers are better than slang ones. An answer choice that begins "To compare the outcomes..." is much more likely to be correct than one that begins "Because some people insisted..."

Extreme Statements

Avoid wild answers that throw out highly controversial ideas that are proclaimed as established fact. An answer choice that states the "process should used in certain situations, if..." is much more likely to be correct than one that states the "process should be discontinued completely." The first is a calm rational statement and doesn't even make a definitive, uncompromising stance, using a hedge word "if" to provide wiggle room, whereas the second choice is a radical idea and far more extreme.

Answer Choice Families

When you have two or more answer choices that are direct opposites or parallels, one of them is usually the correct answer. For instance, if one answer choice states "x increases" and another answer choice states "x decreases" or "y increases," then those two or three answer choices are very similar in construction and fall into the same family of answer choices. A family of answer choices consists of two or three answer choices, very similar in construction, but often with directly opposite meanings. Usually the correct answer choice will be in that family of answer choices. The "odd man out" or answer choice that doesn't seem to fit the parallel construction of the other answer choices is more likely to be incorrect.

Special Report: How to Overcome Test Anxiety

The very nature of tests caters to some level of anxiety, nervousness, or tension, just as we feel for any important event that occurs in our lives. A little bit of anxiety or nervousness can be a good thing. It helps us with motivation, and makes achievement just that much sweeter. However, too much anxiety can be a problem, especially if it hinders our ability to function and perform.

"Test anxiety," is the term that refers to the emotional reactions that some test-takers experience when faced with a test or exam. Having a fear of testing and exams is based upon a rational fear, since the test-taker's performance can shape the course of an academic career. Nevertheless, experiencing excessive fear of examinations will only interfere with the test-taker's ability to perform and chance to be successful.

There are a large variety of causes that can contribute to the development and sensation of test anxiety. These include, but are not limited to, lack of preparation and worrying about issues surrounding the test.

Lack of Preparation

Lack of preparation can be identified by the following behaviors or situations:
- Not scheduling enough time to study, and therefore cramming the night before the test or exam
- Managing time poorly, to create the sensation that there is not enough time to do everything
- Failing to organize the text information in advance, so that the study material consists of the entire text and not simply the pertinent information
- Poor overall studying habits

Worrying, on the other hand, can be related to both the test taker, or many other factors around him/her that will be affected by the results of the test. These include worrying about:
- Previous performances on similar exams, or exams in general
- How friends and other students are achieving
- The negative consequences that will result from a poor grade or failure

There are three primary elements to test anxiety. Physical components, which involve the same typical bodily reactions as those to acute anxiety (to be discussed below). Emotional factors have to do with fear or panic. Mental or cognitive issues concerning attention spans and memory abilities.

Physical Signals

There are many different symptoms of test anxiety, and these are not limited to mental and emotional strain. Frequently there are a range of physical signals that will let a test taker know that he/she is suffering from test anxiety. These bodily changes can include the following:
- Perspiring
- Sweaty palms
- Wet, trembling hands
- Nausea
- Dry mouth
- A knot in the stomach
- Headache
- Faintness
- Muscle tension
- Aching shoulders, back and neck
- Rapid heart beat
- Feeling too hot/cold

To recognize the sensation of test anxiety, a test-taker should monitor him/herself for the following sensations:
- The physical distress symptoms as listed above
- Emotional sensitivity, expressing emotional feelings such as the need to cry or laugh too much, or a sensation of anger or helplessness
- A decreased ability to think, causing the test-taker to blank out or have racing thoughts that are hard to organize or control.

Though most students will feel some level of anxiety when faced with a test or exam, the majority can cope with that anxiety and maintain it at a manageable level. However, those who cannot are faced with a very real and very serious condition, which can and should be controlled for the immeasurable benefit of this sufferer.

Naturally, these sensations lead to negative results for the testing experience. The most common effects of test anxiety have to do with nervousness and mental blocking.

Nervousness

Nervousness can appear in several different levels:
- The test-taker's difficulty, or even inability to read and understand the questions on the test
- The difficulty or inability to organize thoughts to a coherent form
- The difficulty or inability to recall key words and concepts relating to the testing questions (especially essays)
- The receipt of poor grades on a test, though the test material was well known by the test taker

Conversely, a person may also experience mental blocking, which involves:
- Blanking out on test questions

- Only remembering the correct answers to the questions when the test has already finished.

Fortunately for test anxiety sufferers, beating these feelings, to a large degree, has to do with proper preparation. When a test taker has a feeling of preparedness, then anxiety will be dramatically lessened.

The first step to resolving anxiety issues is to distinguish which of the two types of anxiety are being suffered. If the anxiety is a direct result of a lack of preparation, this should be considered a normal reaction, and the anxiety level (as opposed to the test results) shouldn't be anything to worry about. However, if, when adequately prepared, the test-taker still panics, blanks out, or seems to overreact, this is not a fully rational reaction. While this can be considered normal too, there are many ways to combat and overcome these effects.

Remember that anxiety cannot be entirely eliminated, however, there are ways to minimize it, to make the anxiety easier to manage. Preparation is one of the best ways to minimize test anxiety. Therefore the following techniques are wise in order to best fight off any anxiety that may want to build.

To begin with, try to avoid cramming before a test, whenever it is possible. By trying to memorize an entire term's worth of information in one day, you'll be shocking your system, and not giving yourself a very good chance to absorb the information. This is an easy path to anxiety, so for those who suffer from test anxiety, cramming should not even be considered an option.

Instead of cramming, work throughout the semester to combine all of the material which is presented throughout the semester, and work on it gradually as the course goes by, making sure to master the main concepts first, leaving minor details for a week or so before the test.

To study for the upcoming exam, be sure to pose questions that may be on the examination, to gauge the ability to answer them by integrating the ideas from your texts, notes and lectures, as well as any supplementary readings.

If it is truly impossible to cover all of the information that was covered in that particular term, concentrate on the most important portions, that can be covered very well. Learn these concepts as best as possible, so that when the test comes, a goal can be made to use these concepts as presentations of your knowledge.

In addition to study habits, changes in attitude are critical to beating a struggle with test anxiety. In fact, an improvement of the perspective over the entire test-taking experience can actually help a test taker to enjoy studying and therefore improve the overall experience. Be certain not to overemphasize the significance of the grade - know that the result of the test is neither a reflection of self worth, nor is it a measure of intelligence; one grade will not predict a person's future success.

To improve an overall testing outlook, the following steps should be tried:

- Keeping in mind that the most reasonable expectation for taking a test is to expect to try to demonstrate as much of what you know as you possibly can.
- Reminding ourselves that a test is only one test; this is not the only one, and there will be others.
- The thought of thinking of oneself in an irrational, all-or-nothing term should be avoided at all costs.
- A reward should be designated for after the test, so there's something to look forward to. Whether it be going to a movie, going out to eat, or simply visiting friends, schedule it in advance, and do it no matter what result is expected on the exam.

Test-takers should also keep in mind that the basics are some of the most important things, even beyond anti-anxiety techniques and studying. Never neglect the basic social, emotional and biological needs, in order to try to absorb information. In order to best achieve, these three factors must be held as just as important as the studying itself.

Study Steps

Remember the following important steps for studying:

- Maintain healthy nutrition and exercise habits. Continue both your recreational activities and social pass times. These both contribute to your physical and emotional well being.
- Be certain to get a good amount of sleep, especially the night before the test, because when you're overtired you are not able to perform to the best of your best ability.
- Keep the studying pace to a moderate level by taking breaks when they are needed, and varying the work whenever possible, to keep the mind fresh instead of getting bored.
- When enough studying has been done that all the material that can be learned has been learned, and the test taker is prepared for the test, stop studying and do something relaxing such as listening to music, watching a movie, or taking a warm bubble bath.

There are also many other techniques to minimize the uneasiness or apprehension that is experienced along with test anxiety before, during, or even after the examination. In fact, there are a great deal of things that can be done to stop anxiety from interfering with lifestyle and performance. Again, remember that anxiety will not be eliminated entirely, and it shouldn't be. Otherwise that "up" feeling for exams would not exist, and most of us depend on that sensation to perform better than usual. However, this anxiety has to be at a level that is manageable.

Of course, as we have just discussed, being prepared for the exam is half the battle right away. Attending all classes, finding out what knowledge will be expected on the exam, and knowing the exam schedules are easy steps to lowering anxiety. Keeping up with work will remove the need to cram, and efficient study habits will eliminate wasted time. Studying should be done in an ideal location for concentration, so that it is simple to become interested in the material and give it complete attention. A method such as

SQ3R (Survey, Question, Read, Recite, Review) is a wonderful key to follow to make sure that the study habits are as effective as possible, especially in the case of learning from a textbook. Flashcards are great techniques for memorization. Learning to take good notes will mean that notes will be full of useful information, so that less sifting will need to be done to seek out what is pertinent for studying. Reviewing notes after class and then again on occasion will keep the information fresh in the mind. From notes that have been taken summary sheets and outlines can be made for simpler reviewing.

A study group can also be a very motivational and helpful place to study, as there will be a sharing of ideas, all of the minds can work together, to make sure that everyone understands, and the studying will be made more interesting because it will be a social occasion.

Basically, though, as long as the test-taker remains organized and self confident, with efficient study habits, less time will need to be spent studying, and higher grades will be achieved.

To become self confident, there are many useful steps. The first of these is "self talk." It has been shown through extensive research, that self-talk for students who suffer from test anxiety, should be well monitored, in order to make sure that it contributes to self confidence as opposed to sinking the student. Frequently the self talk of test-anxious students is negative or self-defeating, thinking that everyone else is smarter and faster, that they always mess up, and that if they don't do well, they'll fail the entire course. It is important to decreasing anxiety that awareness is made of self talk. Try writing any negative self thoughts and then disputing them with a positive statement instead. Begin self-encouragement as though it was a friend speaking. Repeat positive statements to help reprogram the mind to believing in successes instead of failures.

Helpful Techniques

Other extremely helpful techniques include:
- Self-visualization of doing well and reaching goals
- While aiming for an "A" level of understanding, don't try to "overprotect" by setting your expectations lower. This will only convince the mind to stop studying in order to meet the lower expectations.
- Don't make comparisons with the results or habits of other students. These are individual factors, and different things work for different people, causing different results.
- Strive to become an expert in learning what works well, and what can be done in order to improve. Consider collecting this data in a journal.
- Create rewards for after studying instead of doing things before studying that will only turn into avoidance behaviors.
- Make a practice of relaxing - by using methods such as progressive relaxation, self-hypnosis, guided imagery, etc - in order to make relaxation an automatic sensation.
- Work on creating a state of relaxed concentration so that concentrating will take on the focus of the mind, so that none will be wasted on worrying.
- Take good care of the physical self by eating well and getting enough sleep.

- Plan in time for exercise and stick to this plan.

Beyond these techniques, there are other methods to be used before, during and after the test that will help the test-taker perform well in addition to overcoming anxiety.

Before the exam comes the academic preparation. This involves establishing a study schedule and beginning at least one week before the actual date of the test. By doing this, the anxiety of not having enough time to study for the test will be automatically eliminated. Moreover, this will make the studying a much more effective experience, ensuring that the learning will be an easier process. This relieves much undue pressure on the test-taker.

Summary sheets, note cards, and flash cards with the main concepts and examples of these main concepts should be prepared in advance of the actual studying time. A topic should never be eliminated from this process. By omitting a topic because it isn't expected to be on the test is only setting up the test-taker for anxiety should it actually appear on the exam. Utilize the course syllabus for laying out the topics that should be studied. Carefully go over the notes that were made in class, paying special attention to any of the issues that the professor took special care to emphasize while lecturing in class. In the textbooks, use the chapter review, or if possible, the chapter tests, to begin your review.

It may even be possible to ask the instructor what information will be covered on the exam, or what the format of the exam will be (for example, multiple choice, essay, free form, true-false). Additionally, see if it is possible to find out how many questions will be on the test. If a review sheet or sample test has been offered by the professor, make good use of it, above anything else, for the preparation for the test. Another great resource for getting to know the examination is reviewing tests from previous semesters. Use these tests to review, and aim to achieve a 100% score on each of the possible topics. With a few exceptions, the goal that you set for yourself is the highest one that you will reach.

Take all of the questions that were assigned as homework, and rework them to any other possible course material. The more problems reworked, the more skill and confidence will form as a result. When forming the solution to a problem, write out each of the steps. Don't simply do head work. By doing as many steps on paper as possible, much clarification and therefore confidence will be formed. Do this with as many homework problems as possible, before checking the answers. By checking the answer after each problem, a reinforcement will exist, that will not be on the exam. Study situations should be as exam-like as possible, to prime the test-taker's system for the experience. By waiting to check the answers at the end, a psychological advantage will be formed, to decrease the stress factor.

Another fantastic reason for not cramming is the avoidance of confusion in concepts, especially when it comes to mathematics. 8-10 hours of study will become one hundred percent more effective if it is spread out over a week or at least several days, instead of doing it all in one sitting. Recognize that the human brain requires time in order to assimilate new material, so frequent breaks and a span of study time over several days will be much more beneficial.

Additionally, don't study right up until the point of the exam. Studying should stop a minimum of one hour before the exam begins. This allows the brain to rest and put things in their proper order. This will also provide the time to become as relaxed as possible when going into the examination room. The test-taker will also have time to eat well and eat sensibly. Know that the brain needs food as much as the rest of the body. With enough food and enough sleep, as well as a relaxed attitude, the body and the mind are primed for success.

Avoid any anxious classmates who are talking about the exam. These students only spread anxiety, and are not worth sharing the anxious sentimentalities.

Before the test also involves creating a positive attitude, so mental preparation should also be a point of concentration. There are many keys to creating a positive attitude. Should fears become rushing in, make a visualization of taking the exam, doing well, and seeing an A written on the paper. Write out a list of affirmations that will bring a feeling of confidence, such as "I am doing well in my English class," "I studied well and know my material," "I enjoy this class." Even if the affirmations aren't believed at first, it sends a positive message to the subconscious which will result in an alteration of the overall belief system, which is the system that creates reality.

If a sensation of panic begins, work with the fear and imagine the very worst! Work through the entire scenario of not passing the test, failing the entire course, and dropping out of school, followed by not getting a job, and pushing a shopping cart through the dark alley where you'll live. This will place things into perspective! Then, practice deep breathing and create a visualization of the opposite situation - achieving an "A" on the exam, passing the entire course, receiving the degree at a graduation ceremony.

On the day of the test, there are many things to be done to ensure the best results, as well as the most calm outlook. The following stages are suggested in order to maximize test-taking potential:
- Begin the examination day with a moderate breakfast, and avoid any coffee or beverages with caffeine if the test taker is prone to jitters. Even people who are used to managing caffeine can feel jittery or light-headed when it is taken on a test day.
- Attempt to do something that is relaxing before the examination begins. As last minute cramming clouds the mastering of overall concepts, it is better to use this time to create a calming outlook.
- Be certain to arrive at the test location well in advance, in order to provide time to select a location that is away from doors, windows and other distractions, as well as giving enough time to relax before the test begins.
- Keep away from anxiety generating classmates who will upset the sensation of stability and relaxation that is being attempted before the exam.
- Should the waiting period before the exam begins cause anxiety, create a self-distraction by reading a light magazine or something else that is relaxing and simple.

During the exam itself, read the entire exam from beginning to end, and find out how much time should be allotted to each individual problem. Once writing the exam, should more time be taken for a problem, it should be abandoned, in order to begin another problem. If there is time at the end, the unfinished problem can always be returned to and completed.

Read the instructions very carefully - twice - so that unpleasant surprises won't follow during or after the exam has ended.

When writing the exam, pretend that the situation is actually simply the completion of homework within a library, or at home. This will assist in forming a relaxed atmosphere, and will allow the brain extra focus for the complex thinking function.

Begin the exam with all of the questions with which the most confidence is felt. This will build the confidence level regarding the entire exam and will begin a quality momentum. This will also create encouragement for trying the problems where uncertainty resides.

Going with the "gut instinct" is always the way to go when solving a problem. Second guessing should be avoided at all costs. Have confidence in the ability to do well.

For essay questions, create an outline in advance that will keep the mind organized and make certain that all of the points are remembered. For multiple choice, read every answer, even if the correct one has been spotted - a better one may exist.

Continue at a pace that is reasonable and not rushed, in order to be able to work carefully. Provide enough time to go over the answers at the end, to check for small errors that can be corrected.

Should a feeling of panic begin, breathe deeply, and think of the feeling of the body releasing sand through its pores. Visualize a calm, peaceful place, and include all of the sights, sounds and sensations of this image. Continue the deep breathing, and take a few minutes to continue this with closed eyes. When all is well again, return to the test.

If a "blanking" occurs for a certain question, skip it and move on to the next question. There will be time to return to the other question later. Get everything done that can be done, first, to guarantee all the grades that can be compiled, and to build all of the confidence possible. Then return to the weaker questions to build the marks from there.

Remember, one's own reality can be created, so as long as the belief is there, success will follow. And remember: anxiety can happen later, right now, there's an exam to be written!

After the examination is complete, whether there is a feeling for a good grade or a bad grade, don't dwell on the exam, and be certain to follow through on the reward that was promised...and enjoy it! Don't dwell on any mistakes that have been made, as there is nothing that can be done at this point anyway.

Additionally, don't begin to study for the next test right away. Do something relaxing for a while, and let the mind relax and prepare itself to begin absorbing information again.

From the results of the exam - both the grade and the entire experience, be certain to learn from what has gone on. Perfect studying habits and work some more on confidence in order to make the next examination experience even better than the last one.

Learn to avoid places where openings occurred for laziness, procrastination and day dreaming.

Use the time between this exam and the next one to better learn to relax, even learning to relax on cue, so that any anxiety can be controlled during the next exam. Learn how to relax the body. Slouch in your chair if that helps. Tighten and then relax all of the different muscle groups, one group at a time, beginning with the feet and then working all the way up to the neck and face. This will ultimately relax the muscles more than they were to begin with. Learn how to breathe deeply and comfortably, and focus on this breathing going in and out as a relaxing thought. With every exhale, repeat the word "relax."

As common as test anxiety is, it is very possible to overcome it. Make yourself one of the test-takers who overcome this frustrating hindrance.

Additional Bonus Material

Due to our efforts to try to keep this book to a manageable length, we've created a link that will give you access to all of your additional bonus material.

Please visit http://www.mometrix.com/bonus948/priipacaes4-8 to access the information.